Bayard Rustin

Bayard Rustin and the Civil Rights Movement

Daniel Levine

Rutgers University Press

New Brunswick, New Jersey, and London

Library of Congress Cataloging-in-Publication Data

Levine, Daniel, 1934–
    Bayard Rustin and the civil rights movement / Daniel Levine.
        p.   cm.
    Includes bibliographical references and index.
    ISBN 0-8135-2718-X (cloth : alk. paper)
    1. Rustin, Bayard, 1912–1987. 2. Afro-Americans Biography. 3. Civil rights
workers—United States Biography. 4. Afro-American pacifists—United
States Biography. 5. Afro-Americans—Civil rights—History—20th century.
6. Civil rights movements—United States—History—20th century.
7. Nonviolence—United States—History—20th century. I. Title.
E185.97.R93L49   1999
323'.092—dc21
[B]   99-34245
                                                                                    CIP

British Cataloging-in-Publication data for this book is available from the British
Library

Coyright © 2000 by Daniel Levine

Manufactured in the United States of America

For Rebekah, Brendan, and Kelsey

Contents

Acknowledgments

I am grateful to all the people who spoke with me. They are mentioned in the notes. The following people have read all or part of the manuscript and have helped enormously: William Chafe, Rachelle Horowitz, William Leuchtenburg, August Meier, Walter Naegle, Patrick Rael, Peter Riesenberg, Trudy Riesenberg, Randolph Stakeman, Robert Weisbrot, and Allen Wells.

My first readers are always my wife, Susan, and son, Timothy, always to my benefit.

Errors of omission and commission are my own.

Abbreviations

ADL	Anti-Defamation League
AFL-CIO	American Federation of Labor–Congress of Industrial Organizations
AFSC	American Friends Service Committee
AME	African Methodist Episcopal
APRI	A. Philip Randolph Institute
ASU	American Student Union
BASIC	Black Americans to Support Israel Committee
BLS	Bureau of Labor Statistics
CCNY	City College of New York
CND	Campaign for Nuclear Disarmament
COME	Committee on the Move to Equality
COPE	Committee on Public Education (of AFL-CIO)
CORE	Congress of Racial Equality
COs	Conscientious Objectors
CPS	Civilian Public Service
FEPC	Fair Employment Practices Commission
FOR	Fellowship of Reconciliation
GAO	Government Accounting Office
ILGWU	International Ladies' Garment Workers Union
IRC	International Rescue Committee
JAP	Joint Apprenticeship Program
JLC	Jewish Labor Committee
LID	League for Industrial Democracy
MFDP	Mississippi Freedom Democratic Party
MIA	Montgomery Improvement Association
MOW	March on Washington

NAACP	National Association for the Advancement of Colored People
NCNW	National Council of Negro Women
NVDA	nonviolent direct action
OEO	Office of Economic Opportunity
PAFMECA	Pan African Freedom Movement East Central Africa
PLO	Palestine Liberation Organization
RTP	Recruitment and Training Program
SANE	Committee for a Sane Nuclear Policy
SCLC	Southern Christian Leadership Conference
SDS	Students for a Democratic Society
SNCC	Student Nonviolent Coordinating Committee
UAW	United Auto Workers
UFT	United Federation of Teachers
UNHCR	United Nations High Commission for Refugees
WDL	Workers Defense League
WPA	Works Progress Administration
WRL	War Resisters League
YCL	Young Communist League
YPSL	Young People's Socialist League

Bayard Rustin

Introduction

Bayard Rustin was an inmate at the Ashland, Kentucky, Federal Correctional Institution from March 9, 1944, to July 1945. Ashland was one among a handful of prisons where the federal government, during World War II, housed conscientious objectors (COs). These were men who, out of religious or firmly held moral principles, were opposed to war or who would not cooperate with the draft. The prison was segregated, as were all federal prisons. "Negroes," the term then used, were downstairs, whites upstairs. An inmate committee worked with the warden on prisoner complaints and prison conditions, including segregation. When Bayard Rustin, as a black draft refuser, arrived in the spring of 1944, the other COs (there were only a half dozen or so at Ashland) pressed the issue, because they were separated from one of their companions. The prison administration did not explicitly agree to end segregation in the cell blocks, but on Sundays, during recreation time when the inmates could move around the prison, the door to the stairs was left open. Bayard Rustin was the only black inmate to go upstairs to the white cells. On Sundays he would join his white friends—other COs—to listen to the symphony on the radio. A white prisoner on the floor named Huddleston told Bayard that he'd better stop coming or he, Huddleston, would beat him up. Bayard skipped one Sunday, hoping that things would cool off, but when he next went upstairs, Huddleston got a mop handle from the utility room. He rushed at Bayard and hit him a mighty blow over the head. The other COs rushed between the two, wrestling for the mop handle with Huddleston. Bayard told them to stop, and Huddleston continued to beat Rustin until the mop handle broke. Bayard did not resist;

he simply endured the beating. Huddleston was completely unnerved by Rustin's nonresistance and, shaking all over, sat down. A guard heard the fracas, rushed over, and ordered Rustin downstairs. When the guard learned who was at fault, Huddleston was sentenced to "the hole"—solitary confinement—but the COs intervened and asked that Huddleston not be punished. One result of the beating was that a bone in Bayard's wrist, the left wrist, was fractured, leading a friend to write him that "perhaps this will force you to join the majority for a change, and be a right handed man."

In talking about it later, the COs agreed that the incident was a perfect example of what Richard Gregg described in *The Power of Non-Violence*, a sort of "moral jiu-jitsu" in which the unexpected nonviolent response to violence clearly unnerves the aggressor.

The COs pressed further in their challenges to segregation, this time in the recreation room. One Sunday in May, they entered as a group, with Rustin among them. They were greeted with blows, and as Rustin wrote, "To the man, blow after blow, all stood 'without violence in word or deed' to quote my dear and often thought of friend, J. Holmes Smith. And the power of it? The maintenance of non-violence did several things (1) served as an example to all of the power of non-violence, (2) placed us in a position where we could ask the administration to maintain a firm and progressive position, (3) raised the CO in the minds of the inmates, guards etc., particularly that 'we took it' but refused to allow punishment to the user of violence, (4) revealed to the Negroes involved that progress is possible only if non-violence is used (for certainly in this case, one violent word or act on our part would have meant defeat in ever so many ways.)."[1]

This took place eleven years before the Montgomery bus boycott, sixteen years before the sit-ins in Greensboro, North Carolina. These demonstrations against segregation were inside a segregated federal prison, in a segregated state. They were led by a pacifist group in the midst of a very popular war being fought by a segregated military. The leaders of the action were members of something called the Fellowship of Reconciliation (FOR), a collection of words almost no American would have found familiar. The method used was "nonviolent direct action" (NVDA), another phrase that most Americans had never heard and would not have understood if they had. A more unlikely circumstance for social action would be hard to imagine.

Yet for about a dozen years, NVDA would drive the most significant social change in the United States since World War II.

Throughout the civil rights movement, Bayard Rustin was always there. He was there in the 1940s, when the struggle for equality for black people seemed discouragingly small. He was there as the movement accelerated during the 1950s. He was at the center when Martin Luther King and others began to create a broader movement. He was a presence, actual and intellectual, when the students revitalized "the movement" in 1960. Bayard Rustin's moment in the sun came when he organized the massive March on Washington in the summer of 1963. He was not actually in Mississippi for the Mississippi summer of 1964, but he was in constant contact through friends and associates. He was in the heat of battle during the 1964 Democratic convention in Atlantic City. He was in New York during the demonstrations in Selma and the march to Montgomery, but King was constantly on the telephone with him.

Then he was there, trying to hold things together when the civil rights movement seemed intent upon self-immolation, aided by defection of supporters and increasing strength of opponents. He went to Watts when that Los Angeles neighborhood exploded in the summer of 1965, and the young people scorned both him and Martin Luther King. As "We Shall Overcome" began to be shouted down by cries of "Black Power!" and integration seemed to be blotted out by various forms of nationalism and separatism, he insisted on integration as the aim and coalition politics as the method. Against increasingly loud anti-Jewish shouts, he tried to hold Jewish support in the civil rights coalition. He tried to maintain and strengthen ties between organized labor and blacks. As liberal supporters of the civil rights movement came to excoriate Lyndon Johnson, Rustin insisted on the need for Democratic Party support of the movement. As legalized segregation ended, he insisted on the need for a massive governmental attack on the poverty that was in part a consequence of segregation.

An aide to Lyndon Johnson once described Rustin as one of the five smartest men in America. One does not have to endorse the statistical accuracy of that conclusion to realize that Rustin's analysis of the movement through action, speaking, and writing teaches us much about the shape of the civil rights movement: its coalescing, its near falling apart, its continued survival. Looking back at the years up to the middle sixties, one marvels at the pace of change. Looking back at the years after the middle sixties, one thinks of the alternatives Bayard Rustin presented, and is tempted to repeat over and over again "if only."

By the time Bayard Rustin died in 1987, he was much criticized but also much praised and much honored. He had honorary degrees from many institutions, including Harvard and Yale. In February 1988 the High School for the Humanities on West Eighteenth Street in Manhattan was renamed the Bayard Rustin High School for the Humanities in response to requests from the parent-teacher association. The local school board determined that "given Rustin's stature as an outstanding educator, civil rights leader and humanitarian, the request had merit."[2] A few years later I had a conversation at Bowdoin College, where I teach, with a student of that school. "Do they tell you anything about the person the school was named after?" I asked. "Is there any orientation, any introduction to the school or Bayard Rustin?" "Yeah," the student answered a little vaguely, "some civil rights guy." This book is an answer to that student's vagueness. Bayard Rustin was, indeed, "some civil rights guy," and I want to tell what sort of a civil rights guy he was.

Part I

Everything that rises must converge.

—Flannery O'Connor

1

Preparation,

Personal and

Political

When Bayard Rustin wanted to empathize with troubled youth, he would sometimes claim he came from a fatherless home. In a literal sense, this was true. His father had a brief encounter with his mother when she was fifteen or sixteen, in 1911. Bayard was born March 17 of the next year. His father, a man named Archie Hopkins, did not stay around and in fact was never around. He did not want anything to do with his son, and Bayard did not want anything to do with him. For Bayard's early years, he was told that "Cissy," his mother, whose real name was Florence, was an older sister. When he was about eleven years old, he was told that she was his mother. She did not have much to do with him either. She had children by several men and was never a mother to Bayard.[1] Eventually she married a Jamaican named William John and started another family.

Bayard was raised by his grandparents, Julia and Janifer Rustin, along with eight brothers and sisters who were actually aunts and uncles. He later said that the revelation about his parents turned his world upside down, but it did not really. For all psychological purposes, his caregivers were his grandparents, and he had a relatively stable, warm, and supportive family. He continued to think of his grandparents as "mama" and "papa" all their lives.[2]

Rustin was born near Philadelphia in West Chester, Pennsylvania, a town that, although by no means free of racism, was more benign than many places.[3] The family was there because in the days of slavery, his grandmother's mother had been bought by an antislavery Quaker family named Butler and Julia was reared in their household as a Friend. Bayard's grandmother was born in 1873, so she was already middle aged when Bayard arrived. She was the dominant intellectual influence in his growing up, frequently referred to, often quoted. His grandfather, Janifer, a caterer, was less of an influence, though he was always there, always supportive, a reliable and stable presence. Janifer Rustin's business meant that at times the whole large family would be involved in catering a large party. One of Bayard's earliest memories was of making mayonnaise and then helping lay out the flatware for some major occasion.

Because he was a caterer, Janifer Rustin had contact with what Bayard called "the country club set." A wealthy family named Ricci had a large house in West Chester, but they wanted a bigger one. So they rented their too small house, which was in fact a large three-story structure with all modern conveniences, to the Rustins.[4] "That house became a sort of center of activity in the town," Rustin recalled. "All the young people came because they were made to feel comfortable, and by the time I was, I guess a freshman in [the integrated] high school, everybody referred to my grandmother as Ma Rustin and my grandfather as Pa Rustin. It was a hubbub."

The hubbub came not only from the family and the neighborhood kids but also from blacks migrating from the South to "the promised land." In a sense, the Rustin household became a stop on another underground railroad, as the "Great Migration" swept through a part of the country most active in the original underground railroad. "Very often we would be hustled out of our beds late at night to make room for a family which didn't have anywhere to go and was passing through town."

One night when Bayard was sleeping in the room next to a family of migrants, he woke up hearing moaning and groaning from the next room. He ran down the hall to his grandfather. "My God," exclaimed Janifer, "there's gas. Get everybody out of here." He went upstairs and found the migrant family overcome. These poor people from the South had never seen gas lights before. As with an oil lamp, they simply took off the shade, blew out the flame, and went to bed, leaving the gas flowing. No one died, but some of them had to go to the hospital for a couple of days.[5]

The family attended the African Methodist Episcopal (AME) Church, which was Janifer's church, and every summer Julia organized an outdoor Bible school on an empty lot. Here they studied, learned, memorized passages from the first five books of the Bible "because my grandmother was thoroughly convinced that when it came to matters of the liberation of black people, that we had much more to learn from the Jewish experience than we had to learn out of Matthew, Mark, Luke or John." Bayard, at least a little, resented it at the time, but the Bible school gave him a good source for quotations in his later speeches.

He recalled the family as large, embracing, and warm, a family "which gave me the feeling of being totally accepted." Memory gave his mind's eye somewhat rose-colored spectacles, for there was conflict. "Cissy" led a wild, irresponsible life. Only his grandmother always supported Bayard, even if she disagreed with some particular stance or action. In later years, Rustin resented his siblings' (really aunts and uncles) leaving the care of their aging mother to him, and in fact he did not have much to do with the family—except his grandparents and two aunts—once he left home. But conflict does not mean coldness, and Bayard throughout his growing-up years felt neither neglected nor rootless.

Bayard's recollections of his childhood were made after decades of activism and writing about the civil rights movement. He naturally recalled those parts of the past relating to his later life. If he had become a musician, he might have recalled singing in church or the choir at Cheyney State College and his time with Josh White's "Charioteers." Had he become a teacher, another possibility, he might have recalled his courses at Cheyney State, his teaching new immigrants in the Works Progress Administration (WPA), or his classes in the 1940s for fellow prisoners who had little or no education. But as it was, he recalled early roots for his later career.

West Chester was segregated in 1912—indeed, the entire country was segregated—but there was at least communication rather than antagonisms between the parts. "Negroes" could not swim at the YMCA, could not eat at the local five-and-ten, could not try on clothes at the local store, had to sit in special sections of the movie theaters. On the other hand, the annual Christmas service was more a community get-together than a religious service. Black and white, Protestant and Catholic, and even some Jewish community members turned out. At one such service, when Bayard was about eight, he nudged his grandmother. "Did you see who just came in?" he asked. She said, "Quiet, now. Who was it?" Bayard replied that it was the town drunk. "I'm really quite shocked to see him here," said the self-satisfied little Bayard. "When we get home, we'll talk about it," she said. And when they got home, she counseled him against judging others, adding, "If, as you say, he is the town drunk and no good, then it must have taken much more energy for him to have come than it took for us."[6]

In this community, Julia Davis Rustin was active and highly respected. She was the first black graduate from the local Quaker high school and was active in race relations. She was an early member of the NAACP,[7] formed an integrated garden club, and helped found a day nursery for black children, a visiting nurses' association, and a community center.

The boy learned about the brutality of racism early on, but only indirectly. "I remember the great exciting evening," recalled Rustin in a 1973 interview, "when we were all washed and cleaned up because W.E.B. Du Bois was coming to speak and we were all going to hear him, and he missed the last train because of the length of the question period and he was put up at our house." Other black notables, like James Weldon Johnson and Mary McLeod Bethune, came to the house, so that words like "Ku Klux Klan" and "lynching" were in the air. When Bayard first heard the latter, he asked his grandmother, "Do people really do that sort of thing?" She answered, "Yes, I'm afraid they do." So he knew about racial murder, but it was all rather abstract. There was no Ku Klux Klan evident. No one in West Chester was lynched.

One of his teachers was a Negro and a member of the Bahai faith, who wanted black history included in American history. Bayard early on learned about Sojourner Truth, Booker T. Washington, abolitionists, slave revolts, the underground railroad. Since there were many Quaker homes in the area where runaway slaves had been hidden, the class went and saw the secret trap doors, the hollowed-out cellars that hid the fugitives from slave catchers. In later years, Bayard Rustin became known as an opponent of "Black Studies," but it was only the exclusive, black nationalist, "black is beautiful" studies he opposed—what he called "feel good" courses. He vigorously favored blacks and whites learning about black history. He told one correspondent years later that when he was growing up "we knew that West Chester was a stop on the underground railroad, we read Negro poetry and were steeped in the folk tales of our grandparents."[8]

The elementary schools in West Chester were segregated, but there were white and black teachers in the black schools and so much interracial activity that Bayard was unaware that he was attending a segregated school. Children in the younger grades would go the public library for integrated storytelling. The local college, Cheyney State, which was founded by Quakers, had always been integrated. Concerts and lectures given there were attended by an integrated audience, including Bayard and his family.

The Rustins lived at the edge of the white Catholic section of town, and though Bayard's classmates were all black, his chums on the street were not. An Italian family lived across the street, and Rustin remembered that he was great friends with the son, Pascele Dubondo. There was a temporary crisis in the relationship when Pascele accused Bayard of "acting like a nigger," but they soon made friends again. The Rustins and Dubondos were very friendly, and when the mother in one family was sick, the other would often bring over food for the family.

Once, when he was in about the fifth grade, Bayard and a group of his white cronies went to a laundry owned by the one Chinese family in town. "Chink chink chinaman, eats dead rats, hit 'em on the head with a baseball bat," they shouted in at the door. Bayard, the only black boy in the group, was easily identified. The owner came to Janifer Rustin and complained. For the next two weeks, his grandparents decreed, Bayard had to work without pay at the laundry. So he learned about racism from the vantage point of the prejudiced.

The high school was integrated. Bayard's extraordinary intelligence was quickly recognized, and he was put into a special class for the bright students, many of them Jewish.[9] At a time when most black students were pushed toward menial jobs, he arranged speeches by black doctors, dentists, and skilled technicians. Contrast his treatment with that, a dozen years later, of another very bright, ambitious young black man in Michigan. When Malcolm Little told his teacher that he wanted to be a lawyer, the teacher answered, "A lawyer—that's no realistic goal for a nigger." He should be realistic and settle for a good steady job like a carpenter, said the teacher.[10] Bayard Rustin was supported and inspired in his intellectual striving. White people were not some irrational menacing threat, as they were for Richard Wright. So, though in a segregated town, though knowing about racial brutality, the child grew up within an at least partly integrated world, in which black children could be encouraged and racism was actively resisted.

And Bayard as a high school student did actively resist. Bayard was a champion athlete, particularly in track. At the state track meet one year Rustin and Charles Porter, the other black team member, were told that they could not stay in the same hotel as their white teammates. They said that if they could not stay there, they would not run. Since they were top runners, they won their point. Rustin was also a varsity football player.

Nor was it only the black students who resisted. One of Bayard's pals in high school, who was in the special class for bright children as well as on the track team, was a boy of French background named Jean Cessna. When, during the winter, the Y would not let Bayard in to practice, Jean actually sat in at the office of the director. Jean's aunt, with whom he lived, would not let him bring his black friend home with him, and Jean said she would find out if Jean went to Bayard's house. The two boys discussed it quite openly and decided to meet in the library after supper to study together the Greek, Latin, and literature for their special classes for gifted students.

Rustin learned, too, about prejudice against other groups: Catholics from the Dubondos, and also when, in 1928, he and a Jewish friend were campaigning for Al Smith in a rather tony part of town. The passersby did not abuse Rustin—whom they thought of as simply a tool of the white boy—but they said awful things to the Jewish boy and even spat at him.

In Rustin's adult years, new acquaintances often noticed and commented on his accent, a clipped British or West Indian pronunciation. The source of the accent is uncertain. One of his teachers had that sort of accent and was probably from "the islands." Rustin may have acquired his accent from that teacher. Alternatively, he may have hoped to be taken into the family of his mother's husband, the Jamaican William John. Many people with a slight stutter, which Bayard had, used a broad accent as a way of covering it. In an interview in 1964 he said that he deliberately chose the speaking style during a period when he was trying to deny that he was American.[11] It was acquired, "put on," rather than naturally inherited. To many people it sounded phony. In later years the accent became less pronounced and more simply a precision in diction, except that sometimes, when he wanted to sound imperious, he could deliberately use it.

Bayard also had a clear and powerful speaking voice and, with his precise diction, was frequently asked to give Bible readings in both black and white churches. He also was known for his fine tenor voice. Since he often sang a cappella, he may have had perfect pitch. He sang spirituals with moving intensity, but he considered them to be too simple musically in relation to baroque composers. However, he had no compunctions then or later about singing what might have been stereotyped as Negro music.

He was, he recalled a few months before he died, not aware of his homosexuality in high school. As he told it at the age of seventy-five, the process of increasing awareness was without trauma and in fact implicitly accepted by his family. In high school he was an outstanding athlete and student. His social contacts were with the other students in the special class and in the locker room, as "one of the boys." He spent a great deal of time in gyms and playing fields. He was also good friends with two of the girls in his honors class. He was somewhat attracted to a couple of his teammates but also to some of the girls. He recalled, from that later standpoint, that he first became an active homosexual in college. But from earlier accounts nearer to the events, a somewhat different story emerges. When he was in prison as a conscientious objector during World War II, he told the prison doctor that both awareness and activity began around the age of fourteen. He went to visit his mother, and because quarters were so cramped, he spent the night in the same bed as a man who was living there. He had his first homosexual experience that night and continued thereafter. In addition, it was clear from events in prison as well as in the early 1950s that he was ambivalent and conflicted about his own homosexuality. His attitudes, those of people around him, and those of the wider society meant that his homosexuality was a continuing issue in his life.[12]

He was valedictorian of the class of 1932, sang a solo, and was voted the most important member of the graduating class. He had done superbly in high school; was a member of the French Club, the History Club, the Science Club, the Dramatics Club, and the chorus; had won awards and prizes. The epigram beside his picture in the year book said "Yes, Bayard, 'thou wert a hero on many a field,' rising to the sublime in all because of determination to be the best and to give the best. Here's to your success at college and in later life." These words were carefully chosen to fit their subject, not an echo of words about all other of his classmates. One was characterized as "unassuming modest and shy," another as "peppy and carefree." Bayard clearly was an extraordinary young person in a number of ways, a person who should continue his education.[13]

His grandparents knew that, but there was no money. However, the bishop of the local African Methodist Episcopal church was from a wealthy family and helped arrange a music scholarship at Wilberforce University. Wilberforce had been founded by Methodists after the Civil War but, by 1932, was a Negro college of the Ohio state system. So in the fall of 1932 Bayard took the train for Xenia, Ohio. He lasted a little over a year. After that first year, the college authorities reported, "his attendance became irregular," and he did not complete his work, which he later recalled was not intellectually challenging. He returned to West Chester and to Cheyney Training School for Teachers, where he lived in a dormitory rather than at home.[14] This was not necessarily an academic step downward. Cheyney was in the ambience of the Society of Friends and was in many ways a lively intellectual institution. He stayed at Cheyney for two and a half years, by far a more satisfying experience than Wilberforce, but not so much for the courses.[15]

One might have expected Bayard, known in the area as a champion on the athletic fields, to continue for Cheyney State. At Cheyney, however, he became a major musical force. He was often soloist with the chorus, which led to being invited to do a solo concert with organ accompaniment not simply at a concert but on the radio. He organized a sixteen-member men's chorus and sang in the "Cheyney Quartet." Mostly they sang what was expected of a Negro chorus, spirituals, but occasionally they would do Handel, Bach, or Palestrina. Music, therefore, was one possible future career.[16]

Bayard had formally joined the Society of Friends in 1936. In the summer of 1937, with war already a probability, he became a peace activist. He was one of 160 college students from colleges in New England, the Middle West, and as far south as Florida who were "Peace Volunteers" as part of an American Friends Service Committee summer program. They trained for two weeks at Cheyney and then went to small towns in what the *New York Times* described as "the grain and corn belts." They worked with the farmers during the day and spent evenings speaking to any group who would listen on the absolute necessity of avoiding war and, if it should come to Europe, of keeping the United States out. On weekends they taught Sunday school, wrote sermons, or actually preached in the churches.[17]

For Bayard Rustin religion could be said to be instrumental. For him in these years, God was the source for moral values, but these values were to be translated into actions in this world. So for Bayard, social activism with a religious basis, maybe in race relations, maybe in antiwar work, was always a possibility.

Social activism? Musician and performer? College student? In fact, he went to New York and continued all tracks at once, though higher education took a decreasing portion of his energies. Bayard Rustin's move to New York in the fall of 1937, ostensibly to study at the City College of New York (CCNY), was decisive. He never voluntarily lived anywhere else. He roomed with his aunt, Bessie LeBon, a retired public school teacher, on St. Nicholas Avenue in Harlem. It was a section called "Sugar Hill," where the black elite lived.[18] He only lived in Harlem while he needed room and board from his aunt.

After his release from prison in 1946, when he established his own apartment in Little Italy, he never lived there again. In New York, he entered a world of social activism, flavored by the world of artists, actors, writers, and musicians. The world of social activism was mostly, but not entirely, white; that of performers and writers was mostly, not entirely, black.

So the boy from small-town Pennsylvania did quite a bit in the big city besides go to college. He took a WPA job teaching English to recent immigrants.[19] So being a teacher was still a possibility, though decreasingly probable. He was spending more and more time with artists and musicians. He sang in a group backing up Josh White, the well-known pioneer of the "folk song" revival. White sang standard "folk" but also songs with a strong social message and with a strange lilt and twist of his own. For example, there was the song introduced by Billie Holiday in 1939:

Southern trees bear a strange fruit,
Blood on the leaves and blood at the root.
Black bodies hanging in the Southern trees.
Strange fruit hanging from the poplar trees.

Rustin knew Leadbelly, Marylou Williams, Art Tatum at Cafe Society Downtown (on Sheridan Square in the West Village) or Cafe Society Uptown (on Fifty-eighth Street). He claimed to be friends with Alain Locke. He had a small part in *John Henry*, a play with Paul Robeson in the title role. Rustin admired Robeson's artistry, but before the end of the decade Rustin, by then strongly anti-Communist, would join A. Philip Randolph and other black spokespeople in denouncing Robeson's pro-Soviet politics.[20] The performers and intellectuals all accepted him as a bright young man working his way through City College. He went to parties with them and remembered an easy acceptance into that world. It was, he recalled years later, a world in which some people were gay, some straight, some were white, some black, and all got along as artists, performers, literary people.[21] So being a performer was still a possibility.

In fact, Bayard Rustin was something of a performer all his life. He frequently used music, especially his own singing, to lighten a conference that was inherently serious, to engender a sense of companionship, to inspire commitment. He might start with a moment of silence, perhaps close his eyes and put his fingertips to the bridge of his nose, then launch into a haunting a cappella "Sometimes, I feel like a motherless child." People who heard him, especially in those early years, recall a reaction of hushed awe. He was always a striking figure, six feet one inch, and slender, so he appeared even taller. In later years his hair was white and was cut so as to add another inch or two to his height. His speaking was dramatic but not histrionic: always supremely well organized. He never needed to say "umm" or backtrack to some previous point. Sentences would arrange themselves into paragraphs and paragraphs into a logical construct. The delivery would be intense and affecting. "We have to remember three profound points," he might say. Then holding up a long forefinger, he would lean over the lectern, seeming to look every individual directly in the eye, "First, the fundamental nature . . . ," and he would go firmly on. He would sometimes overstate things for effect, but mostly he would make his point with seamless logic. His more casual conversation would have the same logical imperatives, but he might lounge in a chair with his long legs stretched out in front of him. His British or island accent waxed and waned, depending on the circumstances. As it evolved into merely a precision in diction, it was taken as simply a part of his persona. He could imitate other accents including black street talk. He was frequently described by the word "flamboyant" in dress, manner, way of talking. This flamboyance, his joshing or reaction to others, was at least partly a conscious performance. He was always aware of the figure he cut.

By the late thirties, the days when "Harlem Was in Vogue" had passed, but Duke Ellington and other great jazz musicians were still packing them in at the Apollo Theater. Marcus Garvey had long since been deported, but his spirit lived on, as well as that of Father Devine and others. Bayard and his friends enjoyed the Harlem scene, but often Rustin took the subway downtown. In fact, he was as much a member of Greenwich Village society as that of Harlem. He had a homosexual partner in a sort of cooperative house on Bank Street. It was a bachelor house, though not particularly homosexual, where a dozen young men shared housekeeping and cooking facilities. Bayard lived in Harlem but would frequently be at the house, where discussions would last long into the night. There was hardly any need to discuss politics, since everyone was a pacifist and more or less left. Of course, different factions of the Left could always dispute, but Charles Bloomstein, who later became a fast friend and associate of Rustin's, remembers that the discussions were mostly of literature, often Shakespeare. Rustin had a vast knowledge of Shakespeare's plays.[22]

He was presumably a student at City College, but the only record the registrar's office can turn up, after considerable searching, is that he took some evening courses during the 1940–1941 academic years. Outside of a B in one English course, he withdrew from other courses without credit. His self-education, however, continued. Quite apart from courses, "City" was a whirl of social activism; in fact, more talk about social activism than actual activity. This was the period of the famous alcoves in the dining room: one for the Stalinists, one for the Trotskyites, one for the socialists, and so forth. It was also the period of the "Popular Front," when the Communist Party emphasized its Americanness, its desire to work with other reform groups for justice at home, including racial justice and international peace. The student branch of the party, the Young Communist League (YCL), required that its members be American citizens, because "the Communist Party of the United States is an American party. It is carrying on the struggle for Socialism under American conditions."[23]

The Communist Party had taken up the cause of the "Scottsboro Boys," nine black young men condemned to death in 1936 on trumped-up charges of raping two white girls. The Young Communist League had a black vice president, it favored such changes as black ball players in the big leagues, and it worked assiduously for international peace. Rustin might logically have joined Norman Thomas's Socialist Party, but he later recalled that Thomas considered the race problem essentially a class problem. That left Rustin cold. "While people were being lynched and beaten up, I said, this son-of-a-bitch wants us to stand around and get lynched until there is a workers' state!" In later years, Rustin and the son-of-a-bitch became friends and allies, but not yet. Besides, said Rustin, "at Socialist parties, the girls would talk with blacks, but never would they dance. At Communist affairs, the white women danced and dated black men. The Communists were not only recruiting blacks, but they were deeply involved in civil rights questions."[24] It seemed natural for Bayard Rustin, then, to join the YCL. He said in an interview late in life that he was an organizer for the state of New York, traveling all over in the service of the YCL. He was certainly rank-and-file, rather than leadership. His name does not appear in any of the YCL files at CCNY or in any YCL publications. He also recalled being a "foot soldier," ringing doorbells and knocking on doors, for Adam Clayton Powell's campaign to open up jobs in Harlem in stores that hired only white clerks. "Don't buy where you can't work!" was the slogan on the picket lines. A. Philip Randolph thought that Powell's group was too dominated by the Communists, and he formed a rival pressure group. Randolph would soon become the mentor, father figure, and close associate of Bayard Rustin.[25]

While the Communist Party nationally may have been concerned with race relations, the branch at City College was primarily a peace organization. It would have been difficult to organize a black group among the students because there were hardly any black students in those years. Peace was the issue. There were rallies to get students to sign the "Oxford Oath," which declared that they would not fight if war came, and a strike against war was sponsored by a coalition of peace groups, including two of Bayard Rustin's future employers, the Fellowship of Reconciliation and the War Resisters League.[26] Since the YCL was not listed as a sponsor of that strike, it may have been a rally rejecting Communist participation. Factionalism was rife among student groups, with each calling its rivals "fascist."

Factionalism for a while was played out in a student coalition organization called the American Student Union. The ASU had been briefly captured by the Young Communist League, but on October 1, 1937, a flyer announced triumphantly that, in spite of YCL attempts to disrupt the meeting, an independent candidate for president, Donald Slaiman, had been elected. Slaiman was a regularly enrolled degree candidate. Rustin was part-time in the evening division. They never met in those years, and their organizations were rivals, but in the mid-sixties they would become firm allies when "Donny" Slaiman became civil rights director for the AFL-CIO and Bayard Rustin became executive secretary of the A. Philip Randolph Institute, which was almost a branch of organized labor.[27]

One faction of the anti-Stalinist Left was the "Trotskyites," supposing that Leon Trotsky, because he opposed Stalin, was a social democrat. In 1938, a panel of speakers defended Trotsky against Stalin and condemned the purge trials in the Soviet Union at which Stalin crushed his opposition. Max Shachtman, who would later turn strongly anti-Communist but at the time was a Trotskyite, was one of the speakers. There is no record of whether Bayard was in the audience, but in later years, Bayard was good friends with and strongly influenced by Shachtman. He spent many Sunday afternoons at Shachtman's house on Long Island.[28]

Rustin later said that the problem with the Communist Party was that it demanded total loyalty, total identification. In 1938 and 1939 he was a loyal "cadre," using his extraordinary intelligence and gift of gab to persuade others. When the Nazi-Soviet pact was signed, the word came down, and the YCL justified it. When the Soviet Union invaded Finland, the word came down, and the YCL justified it. Bayard was a little troubled by the Nazi-Soviet pact, but he was working on an assignment the party had given him, a Committee Against Discrimination in the Armed Forces. That was a program he could feel enthusiastic about, and an issue he and A. Philip Randolph came back to in the late forties. The party had given him the assignment in 1939, but after the German invasion of the Soviet Union in June 1941, the leaders asked him to come up with a plan to dissolve the committee. Now the war, which had been a capitalist war, became a people's war, and defending the Soviet Union against Hitler was more important than either peace or racial justice. Bayard was given three days to formulate the plan for dissolving the committee he had built. At the end of the three days, he told the leadership he refused to do so. The leaders tried to cajole him, saying that he had a great future as a black leader. When that did not work, the leaders threatened him with expulsion. He simply refused and walked out.

Communism for Bayard Rustin could not be the God that failed, for he had never worshiped it. It was an instrument, not a religion. But it had failed him, and within a few years he was harshly critical of the Communist Party. At the same time, he incorporated a basic economic analysis of society into his religious ethical philosophy.

Nonrevolutionary Marxism without Marxist atheism was absorbed into a religious ethic, eventually without the theism.

As communism was fading in his mind as a method of social change, two other movements became possible vehicles: the Fellowship of Reconciliation, lead by A. J. Muste, and the March on Washington movement, whose leader was A. Philip Randolph. Bayard Rustin is best known as the person who organized the 1963 March on Washington (MOW). He was actually the "deputy director" of that march. Its director was A. Philip Randolph, founder and head of the Brotherhood of Sleeping Car Porters and, in 1941, of the March on Washington movement. A. Philip Randolph had come through the fire. He had not been a Communist—he was in fact anti-Communist—but was a strong socialist, and he, too, retained a basic economic analysis of American society. He angrily rejected W.E.B. Du Bois's emphasis on "the talented tenth," arguing that it was the black working people, the masses, not a small segment, who would bring changes in race relations. Porters in Pullman sleeping cars were invariably Negroes before World War II. Randolph saw the opportunity and in 1925 overcame great odds to create an all-black labor union, the Brotherhood of Sleeping Car Porters. As the creator and president of the only black labor union, he became in his own eyes, and perhaps in others' as well, the spokesman for the Negro working class. It was not that he was more persuasive than all the others—though he was persuasive. It was not that he was a better organizer than all the others—though he was an effective organizer. It was simply that there were no others.

Any active black person knew of "Mr. Randolph" and revered him as a great man. When, in early 1941, Rustin and his college friend Milton Kramer, white and Jewish, wanted to get involved with youth work in Harlem, Kramer suggested, "Why don't we go over and talk to A. Philip Randolph?"

"Are you crazy?" said Rustin. "We can't just go talk to A. Philip Randolph."

"Let's just call his secretary," suggested Kramer.

So on Milton Kramer's urging, they called Randolph's secretary and got to see the great man the next day. Randolph greeted them courteously and talked with them for some time. As they left, he said to Rustin in his deep voice and careful, almost British articulation, "I'm sorry to know that you are associated with the Communists because I think you're going to discover that they are not really interested in civil rights. They are interested in utilizing civil rights for their own purposes."

In the course of the next several months, as Rustin became increasingly skeptical about the Communists, he had a number of conversations with Randolph. The older man was a great follower of Gandhi and encouraged Rustin to read him. Rustin found the philosophy attractive but was not sure the ideas were very useful in the United States. "India was over there and I was over here," recalled Rustin.[29] Randolph and Rustin each impressed the other, so that when Randolph moved into a new phase of activism, he called on Bayard Rustin.

Randolph knew that wartime production created great opportunities for labor of all sorts, including Negro workers. The national demand for labor seemed infinite. With great fractions of the American economy under the control of the federal government, Randolph saw and seized the opportunity to combat discrimination in employment. Perhaps the federal government did not have the constitutional power to tell private employers whom they could or could not hire. But in the defense industry dependent on government contracts, there was more leverage. An executive order from the president, requiring that all government contracts contain language against racial discrimination, could have an enormous effect on the lives of hundreds of thousands of black Americans. Randolph went around the country in 1941 talking up the idea, urging action on the president, warning about what might happen. If Franklin Roosevelt did not issue such an order, threatened Randolph, there would be a great March on Washington of Negro Americans—one thousand, ten thousand, a hundred thousand? No one, certainly not Randolph, knew what was possible. To some extent, his threat was a bluff, or might turn out to be a bluff. But in the hope that reality might follow claims, Randolph began to organize.

Bayard Rustin, at that time still a sometime student at City College, was appointed "youth director" of the MOW. He traveled around the country, that is, the North, east of the Mississippi, sometimes by train but more usually hitchhiking, organizing young people to support the march—and incidentally gathering experience that he would later use in organizing other marches. In some cities he had to take up a collection so he could make it to the next city. He learned to "piggyback" on other meetings, like the NAACP or the Urban League, and the importance of ministers in organizing the black community.

A whole list of high administration officials, as well as Eleanor Roosevelt, tried to get Randolph to call off the march, but he insisted that on July 1, 1941, it would happen. Finally he was called into the Oval Office, and Roosevelt tried to work his will in person. Randolph, in a highly respectful but firm tone, made it clear that he would not be moved. The president of the United States then agreed to issue what became Executive Order 8802. This executive order forthrightly ordered that "there shall be no discrimination in the employment of workers in defense industries of government because of race, creed, color or national origin" and created a Fair Employment Practices Commission (FEPC) in the executive branch of the government to enforce the order. To most of the Negro press, this was taken as triumphant victory. True, segregation in the armed forces had not been touched, which had been one of Randolph's original demands. True, creating a committee can be a bureaucratic way of avoiding an issue. But one individual, and of a race widely despised by white Americans, had forced action from the president of the United States. The white press did not notice the whole process, but the black press did. The *New York Times* did not even list the March on Washington or Randolph's efforts in its index. The *Baltimore Afro-American*, however, reported each stage in the story, including Eleanor Roosevelt's long letter asking Randolph to call off the march. The *Amsterdam Star News* termed the president's order "epochal." Roy Wilkins in the *Crisis* judged that the FEPC was composed of fair-minded men and urged Negroes to make use of it. The thought of thousands of Negroes coming to Washington had terrified Franklin Roosevelt into action. Randolph interpreted 8802 as achieving his goals, or near enough, and canceled the march. However, he would continue the "MOW movement" as an independent organization. Rustin and the "Youth Division," as they called themselves, of the MOW angrily argued that the victory was only partial, that the march should have continued, that Negroes needed it to emphasize to themselves and others their strength and unity.

Randolph, however, was wiser. He had had a goal, and that goal had been achieved. "The specific and main objectives of the march had been won," he argued in a reply to the Youth Division. Randolph went on to accuse the Youth Division of being full of romantic talk and no action. "It is a grave question in my mind whether the Youth Division would have actually mobilized 25 youths to go to Washington." The march was like a labor strike, Randolph went on. It did not achieve its maximum demands but did achieve its major demands. To insist on more would have meant betraying the president and throwing away what was attained. And of course, carrying out the threat bore the risk of revealing it as hollow. Bayard Rustin in future years was an expert in the strategy of protest marches, an expert on accepting practical steps rather than grand and empty slogans, but he had not yet learned precepts he would later consistently apply. In a whole list of marches and demonstrations during the fifties and sixties, Bayard Rustin became the acknowledged master strategist of mass demonstrations.[30] In 1941, he was not yet that master.

A. Philip Randolph was one longtime pole star in guiding Bayard Rustin's course, but almost as important was A. J. Muste, the head of a Christian, pacifist, nonviolent protest group called the Fellowship of Reconciliation. It was actually Randolph who introduced Rustin to Muste. Both were followers of Gandhi. Rustin, after breaking with the Communists, felt a vacuum in his life. Randolph was a disappointment—albeit a temporary one. In the Fellowship of Reconciliation Rustin felt he had found a philosophy and program, nonviolent direct action, compatible with his own ideas. In 1941, Bayard Rustin went to work for the Fellowship of Reconciliation.

2

Nonviolent

Direct Action

There was a small nonviolent tradition in the United States: Henry David Thoreau at the time of the Mexican War, some abolitionists, Quakers.[1] More significant, the history of the United States can be written as a series of wars, as the history of conquest, as a history of internal battles such as the 1892 Homestead Steel strike and the "Battle of the Overpass," a pitched battle in 1937 in Detroit between the United Auto Workers and policemen defending the Ford plant. Slavery was maintained by violence, and after slavery segregation and racial oppression were maintained by violence, threatened and actual. When nonviolent direct action (NVDA) was introduced into the United States during the 1950s, no reference was made to a tradition in the United States. Rather, the references were to India.

A few "historic peace churches," the Society of Friends (Quakers), Mennonites, Brethren, were traditionally opposed to violence of all kinds, including war, but World War I, and the reaction to it, pushed people who were not part of that tradition to the founding of new antiwar associations. The Women's International League for Peace and Freedom (WILPF) was one, founded in the United States in 1914, and the Fellowship of Reconciliation (FOR), first founded in England that same year, was another. Opposition to war was a minor sentiment during the war itself but grew in its aftermath. Supporters of the League of Nations hoped that the league would make war obsolete, and war was actually "outlawed" (though it wasn't clear what that meant) in 1928. Of course, this broad antiwar sentiment collapsed as soon as another war actually came.

For members of FOR, opposition to war, the hope for international reconciliation, was the organization's raison d'être. But the theory and hope was that nonviolent action would be used for all sorts of social change: freeing colonies from European empires, moving toward justice in race relations, and, later, ending atomic testing. All sorts of social progress, as the FOR people defined it, should be moved forward by nonviolent methods.

What nonviolent tradition there was in the United States was pacifist or "noncooperation." Nonviolent direct action was different in principle and practice. Pacifism was traditionally a refusal. Members of the Society of Friends would not participate in what they regarded as evil: war or slavery. The nonparticipant, however, did not find ways to confront the evil to try to end it. The originators of nonviolent direct action sought points of contact where the evil could be actively opposed and perhaps ended—all without violence and without destroying the opponent either physically or mentally, and without destroying the social fabric. The model was obviously Mohandas Gandhi and the Indian freedom movement against the British empire. Gandhian nonviolence however, was developed in relation to India and the British empire. As Bayard explained years later, the Indian freedom movement aimed at a vast majority taking power completely from a tiny minority at the top. The American movement was a minority taking only a portion of power, or even better, sharing the power of a large majority.[2] Could lessons from one situation be applied to the other?

During the years between 1941, when he first joined FOR, and the middle 1950s, Bayard Rustin rode twin horses. One was participating in international antiwar efforts, through nonviolent means, the other confronting racism, by nonviolent means. Looking back at the civil rights movement, at events like marches, sit-ins, voting campaigns, it now seems self-evident that nonviolent direct action was an applicable and effective methodology. But in the 1940s, that method and philosophy, constructed for quite other purposes in quite other circumstances, had to be adapted to suit this problem at this time in these circumstances. Tactics and strategy had to be tried and altered.

Bayard Rustin was one of those very few who was working, tentatively and by trial and error, to apply NVDA to racial injustice in the United States. He was not the only one—there were James Farmer, Glenn Smiley, George Houser, and a few others—but he was one of a small band. Increasingly race relations overshadowed international peace work for Rustin, and by the 1960s he was almost entirely in the civil rights movement. Nonviolent confrontation with evil was his constant method and his constant social philosophy, whatever the evil.

One can perhaps find some nonviolent tradition in the United States from the Boston Tea Party to strikes in the labor movement. Neither objecting to a tax on tea nor arguing for an increase in wages, however, is really in the spirit of the Gandhian social philosophy. That philosophy was brought to the United States by two books published during the 1930s: Richard Gregg's *The Power of Non-Violence* (1934) and Krishnalal Shridharani's *War without Violence* (1939). The first was meant to explain and extol the ideology, ultimate morality, and effects of NVDA. Practitioners of nonviolence knew that as they moved to confront an evil without violence, they would often be met with violence, and that violence was incorporated into the philosophy. Gregg talked about a moral jiu-jitsu that would so unnerve evildoers, the violent ones, that they would be stopped in their tracks and be forced to reconsider both their actions and their moral position. "Undoubtedly the sight of another person voluntarily undergoing suffering for a belief or ideal moves the assailant and beholders alike and tends to change their hearts and make them all feel kinship with the sufferer."

Gregg's book was essentially a moral and religious argument. Shridharani's book was that as well but also a recipe, a series of steps that a practitioner of nonviolence should follow. The first chapter is called simply "How It Is Done." Since the aim was to change the evil but not destroy the evildoer either physically or psychologically, Rustin later explained that the successful practitioner of NVDA must be able to see things through the eyes of his or her opponent, to understand that opponent and to some extent to sympathize with him or her.[3] As Martin Luther King was wont to say much later, we must learn to hate the sin but love the sinner. The first step was to negotiate, to try to find a ground for reconciliation—and still eliminate the evil. The second step was to make the issue a public one, perhaps through newspaper stories or handbills, or perhaps, as was done during the 1960s, to get the issue on national television. The third step was the inner preparation of the participants: to make sure they knew what to expect but also to ensure that their motives were not self-interested in any psychological sense—the thrill of action or rebellion against authority, for example. During the Mississippi summer in 1964, this inner preparation took place at Miami, Ohio, before the students went farther south. Only after such inner purification, said Shridharani, would one be justified to create a relevant form of non-violent social disruption. An important word was "relevant." The disruption should be related to the evil.[4] And, of course, the practitioners of NVDA must be fully prepared to take the consequences of the action without violent response, be that beating by segregationists or prison sentences for resisting the draft.

When Rustin joined FOR in 1941, the executive director was A. J. Muste, known to everyone, even his immediate family, as A. J. ("Ayjay"). A. J. was a man of firm convictions who would brook no compromise on principles. But that firmness and those principles had, by 1941, led him in a variety of directions—always in pursuit of his vision of social justice. He had started his career as a minister in the Dutch Reformed Church, the denomination into which he was born in Holland in 1885. No matter how far afield his ideas seemed to go, he would always return to a fundamental Christian vision. By the 1920s he was an organizer of radical unions among miners and steel workers, and "Musteism" became a word for a faction of the left labor movement. Musteite unions were industrial unions and insisted on including both black and white members. The Musteite movement faded as the CIO organized and the New Deal supported, to some degree, organized labor of both the industrial and craft sort. Muste was, for a while, a supporter of Leon Trotsky and thus part of the anti-Stalinist Left. He then became a pacifist and a vehement advocate of social change through NVDA. No matter how far from communism his ideas might seem to go, he never lost his basic economic approach in analyzing oppression and never lost his hope for "the revolution," in some form. Religious values and Marxist social analysis were, for Muste, part of the same social vision.[5] A. J. was thus in his mid-fifties, a seasoned campaigner in unpopular, even marginal causes, when Bayard Rustin first met him, perhaps through Randolph, in 1941.

Rustin, in 1941, was a bright, articulate, outgoing, and energetic young man, filled with idealism, but an idealism at loose ends. Even though he had been a member of the Young Communist League for three years, he still spoke of the moral imperatives of the world in religious terms, and FOR was, at its base, a religious expression. FOR could give his idealism a shape he had hoped for and found temporarily in the YCL. At the same time, he was just what FOR needed: bright, idealist, energetic. He was also black, and while FOR had racial justice as a theoretical goal, the organization had not been able to practice what it preached as long as it had only white members. He was a wonderful recruit to the FOR cause.

Compared with some other groups trying to apply Gandhian principles to American race relations, FOR, with under one thousand members, was a large, respectable organization. Jay Holmes Smith was an American minister who had supported Gandhi in India and been expelled by the British authorities. He returned to the United States and in 1941 established a Gandhian "ashram," or religious community, in Harlem. Rustin was a nonresident member (although exactly what this entailed is unclear), and his understanding of Gandhi was deepened by talks with Smith. There was also "Ahimsa" farm, near Cleveland, made up of seven former students from Antioch College, influenced by a couple of faculty members who knew about FOR and the Gandhian approach.[6] If one had to predict the future, it would have sounded slightly balmy to foresee that NVDA would be an important force for social change in the United States.

A few months after Rustin joined, another bright young black man joined FOR: James Farmer. Farmer was based in Chicago, Rustin in New York. The two first met at the National Council Meeting of FOR in 1942, and there was tension and disguised conflict between them from the very first. Here were two very bright, ambitious young black men—often the only black faces in the room. They could have been allies, and in a larger sense they were. Both became major figures in the civil rights movement. But personally and as they sought

A. J.'s favor, they were competitors. Farmer felt that Rustin was Muste's "fair haired boy" and would take any position on any issue to please the older man.[7] Farmer was called the "race relations secretary," and Rustin was "youth field worker," then by September 1942 the "youth secretary," but Rustin found himself also increasingly drawn to issues of race relations.

Farmer explicated "The Race Logic of Pacifism" in *Fellowship*, the magazine of FOR, early in 1942. "One of the most powerful forces fostering injustice and violence in America is that of racial discrimination." He contrasted the United States war propaganda about the American way of life with the realities of racism and also predicted that the Negroes would not in the future be willing to accept the customs of the past. But how was change to proceed? The government, "the creature of oppressive social practices," must be pressured by the development, as he rather wordily expressed it, "of instrumentalities among the people whereby opposition to those practices become so vivid and articulate that it can no longer safely be ignored." Our religious faith urges that "putting an end to racial discrimination should be one of our major goals." What is needed, he said, "is a cooperative endeavor recognizing no distinctions of race and mobilizing men of conscience" to a nonviolent campaign.[8] Thus right from the 1940s, the Fellowship of Reconciliation pursued the campaign to end racism as simply an obvious correlate to its active pacifism.

In those years, active pacifism meant relations with the war effort. The "Keep America out of War" movement had failed. The Selective Service and Training Act of 1940 was passed, and by the end of 1941, the United States was in the war, a war with more public support than any in which the country had been or would be engaged. What now? The situation for conscientious objectors (COs) during World War II was restrictive, but less so than during World War I. Essentially, no provision was made during the first conflict. The law reestablishing the draft for World War II systematized the exemptions for men who, on religious grounds, opposed war in all forms, but the provisions were quite specific. Members of "historic peace churches" could be exempt from military service. However, such exempted men had to be willing to live in "Civilian Public Service camps," usually old Civilian Conservation Corps camps, most of which were run by the churches, and work in public parks and preserves. Conscientious objectors might also be "paroled" to do other work "of national importance," usually either in hospitals or on farms. Ordained ministers as well as theology students could be completely exempted, without any requirement that they do alternative service.[9]

Some pacifists simply decided that the war had to be fought and won. They joined the common effort. Others were "conscientiously opposed to war" in all its forms. These COs refused, in various degrees, to participate.

Some COs refused to contribute in any way to the war effort, including Civilian Public Service, or refused to cooperate in any way with the Selective Service and Training Act. For them, there was no alternative but prison.[10] Bayard Rustin, as a Quaker, could have routinely been exempted from military service had he otherwise complied with the law. He started out doing that. Believing, as he said, that war was contrary to "the social teachings of Jesus" and having before him "Jesus' continued resistance to that which he considered evil," he registered as a conscientious objector in October 1940. However, in September 1941 he became convinced that his conscience would not permit him to comply in any way with the conscription law, and therefore he refused to show up for his physical, on November 16, 1943. "Conscription as well as war equally is inconsistent with the teachings of Jesus. I must resist conscription also." His reasons were partly religious, partly that he rejected privileges that his friends who were not members of historic peace churches could not claim, and partly also related to segregation in the armed forces. "Today I feel that God motivates me to use my whole being to combat by non-violent means the ever growing racial tension in the United States; at the same time the State directs that I shall do its will: which of those dictates can I follow—that of God or that of the State?" The whole military "separates black from white. . . . Such segregation is based on the moral error that racism can overcome racism."

He was supported, of course, by his friends in FOR, but perhaps as important, he received in April a warm letter of support from his other mentor, A. Philip Randolph. "I want to applaud you for your profound conviction as well as consecration to the principles on non-

violence and the brotherhood of man. . . . I hope I may have the pleasure of keeping in touch with you and getting a word from you now
and then."[11] Rustin later said on several occasions that if he had
known the full inhumanity of Nazi racism, the death camps, he might
not have been a noncooperator. He certainly would not have served
as a combat soldier, but he might have contributed to the effort in
some other way.[12]

Bayard knew that his refusal would eventually mean jail, but in
the meantime there was work to do. That first fall, he traveled, usually by hitchhiking, throughout New York, Pennsylvania, and Ohio.
Sometimes he would talk with and inspire—reactivate—peace groups.
"Reactivate" meant talking about the religious and philosophical basis
for pacifism and seeking new members for FOR. Sometimes he would
visit colleges or churches, but more often he would find an eager
audience in Civilian Public Service (CPS) camps. In his visits to these
camps, he would explain the nature of FOR, often producing new
members for the organization, and talk with individual COs about
their problems. He became an effective counselor. He was an FOR
delegate at the annual meetings of related groups: the War Resisters
League (his later employers), the Young Friends, the National Negro
Youth Congress.

His work in the camps led him to recommend a more active presence of pacifist leadership. Leaders, and he meant Muste, should make
more of an effort to see people and to provide a sense of common
purpose to the COs. Always the practical man, he also proposed that
FOR establish a "pacifist emergency fund" to provide help for the
families of men who had lost their jobs, who needed lawyers, or who
had other material needs.[13]

Almost immediately, however, he was drawn into race relations.
In April 1942, he tried to visit a CPS camp in Magnolia, Arkansas.
He could not because the colonel in charge had made it clear "in no
uncertain terms" that Negroes could not speak or even visit.[14] In the
course of his travels in the spring of that year, he was on his way
from Nashville to Louisville by bus. He boarded the bus in Nashville
and sat down in the front. The driver got up, came back to him, and
said,

"Hey you, you're supposed to sit in the back seat."

"Why?"

"Because that's the law. Niggers ride in back."

Rustin patiently explained, "I believe that is an unjust law. If I were to sit in back, I would be condoning injustice."

The driver got out and returned with four policemen, who ordered Rustin to move and, when he didn't, began to beat him. They dragged him out of the bus and continued to kick and beat him. In his words: "Knowing that if I tried to get up or protect myself in the first heat of their anger they would construe it as an attempt to resist and beat me down again, I forced myself to be still and wait for their kicks, one after another. Then I stood up, spreading out my arms parallel to the ground, and said, 'There is no need to beat me. I am not resisting you.'" He was taken to the station house, where the captain looked at him and said, "Come here, nigger," and then, when Bayard approached, "Nigger, you're supposed to be scared when you come in here."

Imagine the failure of communication when Rustin answered, "I am fortified by truth, justice and Christ. There is no need for me to fear." Eventually he was taken to the assistant district attorney, Benjamin West. West and Rustin discussed pacifism, FOR, and the *Christian Century*, which Rustin had in his luggage, for a good half hour. West then had the policemen come in and tell their versions of what had happened. The assistant district attorney then asked Rustin to wait in a side room. After an hour, West came in and said very kindly, "You may go, *Mister* Rustin."[15]

Mister Rustin went free, but the Nashville to Louisville buses remained segregated. Bayard later said that these individual efforts, though they did not change anything in society, were learning experiences for him.[16]

When, in 1960, Fisk University students started what became a massive nonviolent protest against segregation called the "Nashville Movement," the mayor of Nashville, who eventually arranged a peaceful end to Jim Crow in his city, was Benjamin West. If the methods Bayard Rustin was experimenting with could somehow become massive protests, with thousands of people—perhaps black and white—these tiny detached incidents might have a larger existence.

By the fall of 1942, Bayard Rustin began his report to FOR with a long discussion of racial tensions, the disillusionment of Negroes with the country, and their disgust with fighting for a country that denied them basic rights. Clearly here Rustin was looking for evidence to support his and FOR's views, because in fact most Negroes did join in the war and were anxious to prove themselves brave and loyal Americans. In this same report, however, Rustin prefigured his later career by reporting that the constant question from Negro young people was "How can I get a job?" He did not give the obvious, and for many Negroes, actual answer: get a job in a defense plant.

Rustin ended his 1942 report with a plea for nonviolent direct action. "In the last generation we did a superb job of causing men to fear, dislike and see the waste of war. We failed to show them that we have a creative, capable, workable means of dealing with force and injustice." Clearly he was thinking not just of the injustice of war but of other sorts as well.[17]

Rustin had no family responsibilities, and he was a very effective speaker, singer, and, it turned out, organizer. It was natural for him to spend much of his time traveling around the country, spreading the FOR message, running FOR weekend "workshops," and visiting conscientious objectors in the Civilian Public Service camps. Some of the workshops were devoted to international pacifism, some to race relations. Gradually the race relations "institutes" eclipsed those devoted to international peace. In his view, race relations were the perfect place to apply NVDA to the real world. He would not have put it in quite the same words twenty years later, but he wrote in 1942, "Certainly the Negro possesses qualities essential for nonviolent direct action. He has long since learned to endure suffering. He can admit his own share of guilt and he has to be pushed hard to become bitter. He has produced, and still sings, such songs as 'It's Me, Oh Lord, Standing in the Need of Prayer.' . . . He is creative and has learned to adjust himself to conditions easily. But above all he possesses a rich religious heritage and today finds the church the center of his life."[18] In later years, such simple stereotyping, such generalizing would have been unthinkable. He would put more emphasis on social and economic structures, but the actions stemming from these words were the same.

By 1943 he was holding race relations "institutes" or "workshops" in cities throughout the country, except for the South: Utica; Dayton; Kansas City, Kansas; St. Louis; Berkeley; Detroit; San Francisco; and New York. Sometimes the workshops would be simply FOR affairs, sometimes a local Congress of Racial Equality (CORE) chapter would be co-sponsor, often they would be under the aegis of the local American Friends Service Committee (AFSC). The three organizations, and often a local human relations committee, had overlapping membership, worked together, and were, for these purposes, almost one organization. Often, the locus of the institute would be a church, perhaps a black church, sometimes a college. The sessions were generally held over a weekend and followed a pattern. Friday evenings there would be a basic lecture on the question of what "race" was or was not. The point had to be made over and over again—perhaps it was the most important point in the institutes—that there was no scientific basis for the whole idea of "race." Usually the brochures on the workshops referred to recent publications, like Ruth Benedict's *Race, Science, and Politics*. On Saturdays there would be a discussion of the local situation and of particular forms of discrimination. Bayard Rustin would explain the ideals and techniques of nonviolent direct action. Then there might even be some probing demonstrations of protest methods in restaurants or movie theaters that discriminated against blacks.

Rustin was also sent out simply as a speaker, to churches, colleges, and local human relations groups. In these speeches his theme would often be the crisis in race relations in the United States and the need to combat racism, always by nonviolent means.

On April 2–4, 1943, a workshop with major figures, or people soon to be major figures, was held at the Grace Congregational Church in New York. The Friday night lead address, "What Science Has to Say about Race," was delivered by E. Franklin Frazier, head of the Department of Sociology at Howard, formerly head of the Atlanta University School of Social Work, the only school of social work specifically directed at problems of American Negroes. Already well known among black educators in 1943, Frazier in 1957 would become nationally famous, or notorious, as the author of *Black Bourgeoisie*. Ostensibly a sociological study, the book in effect mocked

the pretensions of its subject. Next, Lillian Smith gave a speech entitled "The Race Situation Today—in the United States and Abroad."
Strange Fruit, her novel of the southern dark secret, relations between white men and black women, would shock the country and
infuriate some when it appeared in 1944. She had taken the title from
the Billie Holiday song, lyrics by Abel Meeropol, who in 1953 would
adopt the sons of Julius and Ethel Rosenberg. At the 1943 workshop,
James Farmer delivered a speech titled "Non-Violent Techniques for
the United States." Farmer had just founded the Congress of Racial
Equality as a nonpacifist, nonreligious, though still nonviolent, offshoot of FOR, though a separate organization. The final day heard an
address by A. Philip Randolph titled "A Program for Today." The last
speech, by A. J. Muste, was "The Spiritual Basis for Non-
violence." Bayard Rustin conducted the symposium on workshops
and, as testimony of the continuing religious spring of his activism,
also led the final worship service on Sunday. His role appeared minor, but he was the link connecting many of these people together.
Much—not all, but much—of the civil rights movement of the 1960s
was represented at that workshop. Most conspicuously absent were
a civil rights lawyer and a black southerner, perhaps a minister.[19]

That workshop was all talk and inspiration—good talk, important inspiration—but not action. In the fall of 1943, there was actual
application of NVDA—cautious and tentative but still action—at a
workshop in San Francisco held during the weekends of October 9
through November 7. Rustin, by the fall of 1943, was already enormously respected in FOR and AFSC circles and was asked to come to
California because of "his skill in handling inter-racial situations,
aimed at reaching the cause of discrimination." This workshop was
devoted to training leaders in the techniques of NVDA. There would
be three weekends of training, with the same group of people, and
then the final weekend, the national convention of FOR. During these
weekends, as in New York and Washington, there was much talk,
discussion, and soul-searching, in preparation for very small actions.
The question was, was NVDA something that would blossom into a
new revolutionary method of social change, or would it be always
the belief of a few saints and fools?

Small beginnings, saints or fools, eleven of them, all white, registered for the workshop, and a few more showed up for the open discussions. Saturday, October 9, started with a lecture and then a discussion on the philosophy of nonviolence; later on came a description of the racial situation in the United States. The discussion afterward emphasized that the purpose of direct action was to change not only behavior but attitudes. The group heard how court action by the NAACP had recovered damages from a Detroit restaurant that discriminated, but direct action by the Detroit chapter of CORE in fact opened up the restaurant to Negroes and changed the owner's attitude. "If legal action is used," concluded the all-white (except for Bayard) San Francisco group, "personalities may be violated, while if non-violence is used, the exploited must be willing to suffer a little longer. Courts are to be used only as a last resort."

The next weekend there were gentle probes into San Francisco establishments. While only whites signed up for the leadership training, black and white participated in the probes. Edward Booker reported that he had not been allowed to try on a suit in Hastings clothing store, because he was "colored." At the end of October, Jean McKay, head of the San Francisco FOR, interviewed the manager of Hastings, who said the policy had been changed. Anyone was free to try on the clothing.

At the Ambassador Skating Rink "two couples, one Negro and one white, went to the rink. The Negro couple, who went in first, were told that a private party for servicemen was in progress. When the white couple then appeared, they were told the same thing, but as soon as the Negroes left, the cashier told the whites that they could go in. The reason given was that whenever Negroes skated, there was always trouble between them and the servicemen." In this case, FOR determined that before any further action "thorough investigation" was necessary. Clearly, a revolution would not be made by such probes, yet a technique might be developed, maybe.

Jean McKay, head of the San Francisco FOR, wrote to Rustin that she was bothered that the participants in the leadership training were much like one another. Only half in jest, she wrote that she would like to find "a few likely young boiler makers or ladies garment workers. . . . Perhaps a placard prominently displayed in the local union halls beside the United for Victory: Wanted, a Pacifist."[20] The middle of war was not the time for any sort of radicalism. Yet in a sense McKay was prescient. When nonviolent direct action became a major force in the 1950s, much support, much of the money, came from a segment of the labor movement, including the International Ladies' Garment Workers Union (ILGWU).

There had been other direct actions, actions in which Rustin was not involved. The one that later became most famous was in late 1942 in Chicago, where the largest CORE chapter, lead by James Farmer and George Houser, had integrated the only restaurant in the Loop that discriminated. The victory at Stoners was greeted with great enthusiasm by FOR and CORE members.[21]

If the revolution, any revolution, was going to come in the United States, it would not come through eleven like-minded San Franciscans forcing a department store to allow "colored people" to try on suits, or even in integrating a restaurant in a state with antidiscrimination laws already on the books. Somehow, mass action and political leverage would have to be added.

In later years, Bayard Rustin made the forging of alliances the touchstone of much of his work. He started in the 1940s. In February 1943, at an FOR institute in Syracuse, Rustin went out of his way to praise the CIO as "one of the greatest factors in doing away with racial discrimination in the south, where it is working to organize Negro and white workers into the same union." He would always regard organized labor as one of the major supports for the civil rights movement. Norman Thomas, the longtime leader of the American Socialist Party, was at that institute, and social democracy was always the bedrock of Rustin's political philosophy. Later that year Bayard wrote a memo saying that through the March on Washington movement and the CIO, FOR should try to get "more trade union leadership" and should reach out to Jewish, Nisei, and Puerto Rican groups. Randolph and Rustin may have disagreed about the 1941 March on Washington, but they agreed on much else. In the summer of 1943, Randolph appeared at an FOR race relations institute in Washington with Rustin, a symbol of alliances with labor and the March on Washington movement. In 1944, FOR; the Socialist Party, the Workers Defense League, a social democratic organization; and the March on Washington movement planned a joint demonstration at the capitol against a southern filibuster opposing the abolition of the poll tax. Tentative alliances were being formed, but still, mostly on the fringes of American society.[22]

Rustin and his friends knew that as a conscientious objector and noncooperator, he would soon have to go to jail. The first "conscientious objectors" to go to jail, the first to define themselves as "noncooperators," became known as the Union Eight. These were students, among them the young George Houser, at Union Theological Seminary. Houser would become a longtime associate of Rustin's, joining with him in demonstrations and in founding the American Committee on Africa. As theology students, they could have been completely exempted from the draft. In 1940, they decided not to cooperate in any way with what at the time was a draft during peacetime. They were sentenced to a year and a day in prison and were sent to Danbury, Connecticut.[23] As they served out their sentences, others were jailed. The original eight had started a protest against segregation in the prison, but the largest protest was in the fall of 1943. By that time, Bayard Rustin was well known among COs, and the strikers kept in touch with him. They went on a work strike in October 1943, and the strike continued until December. For punishment, they were locked in their cells for all but a forty-five-minute exercise period once a day. The prison authorities remained firm. The director of the Bureau of Prisons stated that the prison "must follow the generally accepted practice of the community at large," and segregation was maintained.[24] But at other prisons, the COs kept up their protests or started new ones.

They would soon be joined by Bayard Rustin. On February 17, 1944, he was convicted of not complying with the Selective Service Act. Three weeks later he entered the Federal Correctional Institution at Ashland, Kentucky.

3

Prison

The federal prison at Ashland, Kentucky, was actually in the small town of Summit, about $2^1/2$ miles south of the Ashland city limits, in an area of low, rolling hills. It was a "federal correctional institution" of medium security. That is, its staff regarded it as working to rehabilitate inmates. No one was sent there for longer than five years, and it had all sorts of vocational and educational units: a farm with dairy and animals, which made the institution almost self-sufficient in food; a tobacco-processing plant; a furniture plant; classes in a wide variety of subjects. Cells were for single prisoners, and the "honors" cells were small but reasonably comfortable. People could keep photographs, books, and small items in their cells. Prisoners went freely to and from classes, to and from work, and otherwise were often free to move around the prison or to be alone in their cells, as they wished. The warden, Robert Hagerman, was a man open to ideas from the inmates (there was an inmate committee) and from their friends on the outside. But as a prison warden must, he ultimately valued order rather than any socially defined justice.[1]

Rustin was one of a number of COs in the prison, mostly Brethren but also others. He was there as an idealist, as a noncooperator, as a practitioner of NVDA in the cause of racial equality. A highly articulate spokesman for his ideas, he also had what an FBI informant called his "exaggerated limey accent," and he was a flagrant, almost defiant homosexual.[2] It is not at all clear that his idealism would have been understood anyway by the prison authorities or anyone else, but his blatant homosexuality allowed the authorities, as well as some of the inmates, to see him as simply a troublemaker, as a "psychopath," as "depraved."

He was constantly pushing against the system of racial segregation, as other COs did in other prisons. It may be that in those years, the federal prisons were actually on the cutting edge of the civil rights movement.[3] There was the incident described in the introduction to this book, in which Bayard Rustin did a very simple thing: walked upstairs to hear the symphony with his friends. As a result, he received a beating from a white prisoner. A few days later, Dr. Hagerman "called in Bayard and literally apologized for the way the administration had been treating him," saying, "We acted as though you had done something wrong." Hagerman said he appreciated the nonviolent response, that he and many of the staff were impressed with the COs, and that he would again open the gate so that there could be mingling between the white and Negro prisoners.

Bayard Rustin also challenged segregation in the dining hall. There were designated white and "colored" tables at mealtimes. One day, Bayard had come in a little late, after all the "colored" tables were full, so he was eating by himself at a vacant table. There was also an empty table and one at which a lone white prisoner was eating. Four Negroes were ushered in from quarantine by a guard. There were three possibilities for the guard. He could seat the four at the one remaining empty table. But that would violate a principle of keeping prisoners in compact groups rather than spreading them out. He could seat them at the table where Rustin was sitting, but that would violate their quarantine. He could seat them at the table where the white prisoner was sitting, but that would violate the principle of strict segregation. He ordered Rustin to move to one of the already occupied "colored" tables. Rustin refused to aid the policy of segregation. A supervisor ordered Rustin to leave and threatened him with "the hole" if he disobeyed. Rustin refused, and a group of guards began dragging him—with Rustin not resisting. They got him as far as the door to the dining room, where they were surrounded by a group of white COs, Rustin's friends, who convinced the guards that manhandling Rustin would not cause him to change his ideas. The guards let Rustin go, and the next day the COs and the warden held a long discussion. The decision was not to punish Rustin and not, in the future, to use force against a man whose conscience might lead him to disobey an order.[4]

Was that a victory? At least a partial one. Segregation rules had been defied, and no punishment resulted. The warden talked to the COs and seemed to understand their positions.

Once, in November 1944, Rustin emerged from his cell, and a guard noticed that he had a letter in his hand. "What is that, Rustin?" asked the guard. "A letter," replied Rustin. "Show it to me!" commanded the guard. Rustin refused, and angry words were spoken. Another guard came over and asked what was going on. "It's about this nigger," said the first guard. At that, of course, Bayard became furious, refusing all future commands. The guard wrote, "He is quite tall, and standing over me, he sputtered and fumed and attempted to assume as threatening an attitude as possible, evidently believing he could frighten me." In a letter to the associate warden explaining the incident, the guard said that the word "nigger" was a normal word used to describe black people. Probably for him it was. Rustin was punished by being put in isolation, without any reading material.[5]

Bayard had larger aims than desegregating the dining room or recreation room or church. He and the other COs consulted with the white prisoners to find out how they felt about segregation in the cell blocks. He concluded that not more than one or two of the white prisoners in E block, where he and the other COs were housed, would object to a desegregated system of cells—that is, one-man cells. The idea was proposed to the warden but never put into effect.[6]

He also had a long-term strategy for after the war. In a letter to Kessel Johnson, a friend who had decided to serve in the army, he wrote, "I am still here in prison, having recently refused to sign a paper which might have meant parole. . . . I want to be during this war . . . in that place where I can gain the best political experiences for the task we shall have at the end of the war. Negroes especially will have to struggle for economic and political freedom. . . . I am learning the many factors involved in organizing the underprivileged and the fearful." Talking of the years after the war, he wrote and underlined, *"Things don't happen, they are brought about."* The letter remained in the Bureau of Prison files, since prisoners were not permitted to write about anything political; Rustin clearly intended to be one of those people who "brought about" change.[7]

The problems of the underprivileged and fearful were already clear at Ashland. Bayard may have detected an increased respect for the COs who had "taken it," but the black prisoners were more interested in a very immediate form of freedom—getting out of prison as soon as possible—than in the more abstract freedom of a less racist society. The social revolutionaries got no help from the group in whose behalf they were supposedly acting—prefiguring some of the frustrations of the Mississippi summers of 1963 and 1964.

So social activism continued in prison as it had since high school. So did self-education. Prisons leave a lot of time for the inmates to be alone in their cells. Rustin was practiced at self-education, and he used the time for reading—he was constantly taking books out of the library. He also learned the mandolin and lute, which he would later often use to accompany his singing, and he studied harmony, so he could figure out chords to accompany his songs. His reading was constant: newspapers like the *New York Times* and *Philadelphia Bulletin*, magazines like *Newsweek* and more "radical" journals like *Christian Century*. There were books, always more books. When *Strange Fruit* came out in 1944, he devoured it. The COs read it as a group, and after a few weeks, he reported that he had loaned it out some thirty times. Richard Wrights's *Black Boy* got the same reception. Bayard made sure that the assistant warden saw them both. His letters to a younger friend on the outside were full of references to current books like Henry Seidel Canby's biography of Walt Whitman, Petirim Sorokin's *The Crisis of Our Age*, and the poetry of García Lorca, as well as references to the Gitas, to William James, Josiah Royce. He particularly recommended George Santayana. Bayard Rustin had limited use for formal higher education, but he was a prodigious reader and a highly cultivated person.[8]

He was also a teacher and musician. He ran literacy classes for the men who could not read, and he reported in a letter that his white students had some difficulty getting used to having a Negro teacher. He organized a chorus that made a big hit singing spirituals. He hoped to broaden their musical taste to include Palestrina and De Lassus.

For many months he had no visitors. A. J. visited him in July and discussed Rustin's overall plan for integrating the cell block. No one in his family visited him at Ashland. Only two members of his family, his mother and grandmother, visited him at all, and this after he was transferred to Lewisburg, closer to home. Only his grandmother, with her Quaker upbringing, really understood his pacifism. Other members of the family supported the war, and they were proud of a nephew who was serving in India. When his mother and grandmother arrived, he greeted them with a handshake and kiss, in violation of the rule against physical contact. The women were concerned, but Bayard answered, "Oh, never mind about that. I don't pay any attention to the rules of these people around here. I'm just not cooperating." The remark was certainly arrogant, but there was some truth in it. Warden Hagerman did say in a letter to James V. Bennett, director of the Bureau of Prisons, that Rustin had been given more leeway than other prisoners.[9]

Janifer Rustin did not visit him, but for medical, not political, reasons. He was seventy-nine when Bayard entered prison and fell seriously ill soon thereafter. Bayard was granted leave from prison and, accompanied by a guard, visited the bedside of his grandfather in November 1944. On April 20 of the next year, he received a telegram from his grandmother, "Pa passed peacefully 3:40 A.M. Friday. Services 2 P.M. Bethel Church Tuesday."[10]

The leeway granted Rustin had limits, and the limits were Rustin's indiscreet, almost defiant, homosexual activity. Rustin had a firm relationship, though it turned out to be temporary, on the outside, with Davis Platt, the visitor who had brought him the mandolin. He knew that his sentence was only three years, less with "good time." Yet he was constantly making passes at other prisoners, and having brief sexual encounters, almost under the eyes of the guards. This was not logically part of his noncooperation, which had a political and religious basis, but it may have had some psychological connection with an attitude of defiance. Homosexuality is a constant issue in prisons, yet Rustin's activity was extreme and almost open. In September 1944 two prisoners complained, possibly to gain favor with the system. A hearing was held, and Bayard was "convicted." In a letter to the director of the Bureau of Prisons, Warden Hagerman wrote that "a diagnosis of psychopathic personality, homosexuality" is unmistakable. As a result Bayard was put in administrative segregation. Partly this was punishment, but the Classification Committee of the prison said it was also for his own protection, since there was "intense inmate feeling against" him.[11]

Bayard, far from being defiant, accepted and acknowledged his own "guilt." He, too, felt that his actions deserved condemnation and even self-denigration. Since he was still thinking very much in religious terms, he clearly regarded his own actions as sins. To the prison doctor, he said he wanted to control his aberrant sexual impulses and knew he could do so. In fact, he did. He wanted to start all over and to demonstrate "Christian humility" by performing menial duties such as mopping floors, as a way of purging his conscience. He wanted to be like other men, and from his letters one can read that he gave deep consideration as to whether he could make a life with a woman. At that point in his life there was at least one, and the letters seem to indicate that there may have been two, who were desperately in love with him. A. J., his revered and loving father figure, visited him in Ashland soon after the hearing. At first Rustin claimed the whole thing was a frame-up but then admitted his guilt. "You have been guilty of gross misconduct," wrote A. J., sternly, "specially [*sic*] reprehensible in a person making the claims to leadership and—in a sense—moral superiority. . . . You have engaged in practices for which there was no justification . . . [and] in prison they would be instantly exposed." A. J. concluded by hoping that in spite of these harsh words "my love for you and hope for you shines through." Soon after his visit, A. J. telegrammed, "You are in my thoughts and prayers. My admiration for your courage and estimate of your possibilities never greater. God is our refuge and strength." Thus the father reenforced Bayard's own guilt and need to seek God's pardon.

A month after A. J.'s visit, Rustin wrote a tortured letter to him. Bayard thanked him for the visit, saying, "I feared the truth. I feared facing the reality of the ugly facts. . . . I feared the humiliation and dishonor. . . . It was my own weakness and stupidity that defeated the immediate campaign and jeopardized immeasurably the causes for which I believe I would be willing to die. You have helped me to come closer to the truth, to see my own guilt clearly and to center upon clarifying the 'springs within.'"[12] He was defiant and arrogant in his actions but also humble and guilt-ridden. Such tensions and contradictions were to haunt him for years. And his homosexuality was to haunt his civil rights activities.

Whether contrite or not, reformed or not, Bayard Rustin presented unusual problems for the prison system. He was not merely a law breaker on the outside who had defied prison rules on the inside. He was imprisoned for his idealism, and his protests against segregation had received not widespread but some publicity in the outside world. Warden Hagerman recommended his transfer to another institution, possibly a classification as a homosexual, and that he be sent to Springfield, Missouri, a transfer endorsed by Director Bennett on November 15, 1944. Springfield was the Medical Facility for Federal Prisoners, for the prison system considered homosexuality to be a medical problem. By the next summer, the transfer had not been carried out. Hagerman wrote Bennett to explain why. "He has succeeded in getting the sympathy and backing of quite a number of organizations and 'name' preachers, as well as that of the more radical C.O.s who are still in prison, and inasmuch as his homosexuality is no longer the chief tangible problem relating to his case, his transfer to Springfield could occasion a tremendous wave of protest from sympathizers on the outside as well as hunger strikes in several of the institutions. . . . The case is hot." Hagerman suggested that he be transferred to Lewisburg, Pennsylvania, or Danbury, Connecticut, "his transfer to be made simultaneously with others so as to appear not too conspicuous or pointed toward the particular case of Rustin." Bennett came to the same conclusion, adding, "We might take one or two of the other boys out and move them to Lewisburg or Danbury and put them into the group of non-cooperators up there. They certainly can't do us any more harm or cause any greater difficulty than the group we already have in those two institutions."[13] As a result, Bayard was transferred not to another "federal correctional institution" but to the more strictly run "federal penitentiary" at Lewisburg.

In the new institution as in the old, Rustin continued to pursue his ideals—and to be a difficult prisoner. In August 1945, only a couple of weeks after his arrival, he renewed his protests against segregation. In the terse words of a discipline committee, "This inmate objects to institutional ruling in not allowing Whites and Negroes to intermingle in so far as eating and sleeping is concerned. He will not walk in a line segregated or be segregated in the dining hall. Today [August 4, 1945] at the noon meal he came out with the Quarantine group but refused to line up with the Negroes, but instead started to deliver an oration on his opinions of segregation, etc. He was told to line up as required by institutional rules, but this he refused to do and then had to be escorted back to his cell. Inmate placed in Administrative Segregation." Administrative Segregation in this case meant the prison library. Rustin was among a dozen prisoners confined there, with permission to read any book they wanted but separated from the other prisoners. In early March 1946, Rustin and Rodney Owen, a white CO, went on a hunger strike against racial discrimination, and they were force-fed for three weeks.[14]

Since Bayard had been sentenced to three years in February 1944, the end of the war did not mean the end of his time in prison. In late March 1946, A. J. visited again, and a new factor entered Rustin's thinking. A. J. and the other pacifists were stunned by the fact of the atomic bomb. The peace movement seemed ever more urgent and perhaps ever more hopeless. All possible resources, including Bayard Rustin, had to be mobilized against this increased threat. For Muste, and temporarily for Rustin, "the bomb" seemed to diminish the importance of racism. The next day, Bayard wrote Director Bennett that he "was in prison because I felt that conscription and racial segregation, embodied in the Selective Service Act were the greatest evils of our nation. . . . Today, I see that the Atomic Bomb, its use and disposition, to be the truly urgent problems of our time, for as A.J. said yesterday '*why speak of equality of men when there may be no men unless men of good will devote themselves to stop what may become world war III.*'"[15] He promised to abandon his fight against segregation, be a model prisoner, and try to get out as soon as possible to pursue what he now saw as a more urgent task. Lewisburg, like Ashland, had farms and factories. In May 1946 he was transferred to the Farm Colony as a teacher and clerk. He performed his duties in a satisfactory manner, and on June 11, he was released conditionally, that is, he was required to report his whereabouts to the Bureau of Prisons. To the last, he and the prison officials failed to communicate. On his release, he was, like all prisoners, given a suit of clothes. "What is your name and number, boy?" asked the guard in charge of distributing release clothing. Angrily, Rustin explained that he was not a boy but a man, and the guard reported that there was much "insolent talk," the details of which the guard couldn't recall and clearly did not understand.

On March 6, 1947, Rustin's sentence was fulfilled, and he was finally released.[16]

4

After Prison,

to Prison

In his exit interview from prison, Bayard Rustin
told the authorities that he would move into a one-room apartment
in New York. He might well have found something in Harlem, but
he did not. Instead he found a tiny apartment at 217 Mott Street in a
section known as Little Italy. He never lived in Harlem again. The
property at 217 Mott Street had an entrance, then a courtyard, and
then a back building. The back building was more or less taken over
by "the movement." That term encompassed artists, musicians, and
social activists of some version of the Left. Some people might have
been first of all pacifists, but that was the beginning of their social
analysis, not its end. They did not want the world to be just as it
was, but without war. They wanted to change society, by nonviolent means, toward a new moral order in the direction of social justice, as they defined it. Some people came at social change from a
Marxist point of view, some from an anti-Marxist socialism, some
from a view of Christian ethics that might or might not be combined with Marxism, some from simply a secular rejection of the
amount of human misery society was willing to put up with. But
the mood was not all high-minded social goals or puritanical. People
were young, full of fun and energy. Bill Sutherland, later with Rustin
in Africa, tells how in the great blizzard of December 1948 they
were snowed in for three days. The result was a three-day, three-
floor party. Bayard was known as a wonderful guy to have at a party—
full of jokes, songs, and good stories.[1]

Yet social action was the glue that held them all together. During the time that Bayard Rustin was in prison, George Houser codified how nonviolent direct action might be applied to race relations. In a memo dated June 19, 1944, probably to Farmer, he wrote, "There probably has never been a genuine non-violent campaign against the evil of race prejudice. This is due partly to the fact that the method is not well known. . . . It is impossible to know if the campaign would be successful. . . . However there are enough persons who have heard of the non-violent direct action procedure . . . that there is a good probability of the success of such an organized campaign." He recognized that three groups had done some experimenting with nonviolent direct action: the Congress of Racial Equality, the Fellowship of Reconciliation, and, slightly, the March on Washington movement. CORE in 1944 was small and with a local rather than national existence. A program like the one Houser was suggesting might make it into a "large scale movement." "It is important to note that in India," he continued, "where the NVDA strategy has been worked out and experimented with most perfectly, success has been dependent upon having a comparatively large group of persons over a sustained period." He proposed just that for the United States. A community would be chosen for the first experiment "where the race problem is neither too intensive nor too quiescent." He thought perhaps Chicago, Cincinnati, Dayton, Washington, or Baltimore. He hoped that thirty to fifty volunteers could devote from three months to as much as a year to what he continued to call the "experiment." First there would be intensive education and spiritual training, then test cases, negotiations, and finally direct action. The whole proposal, wrote Houser, needed a lot of discussion in CORE, FOR, and maybe the MOW.[2] The discussions went on, and his proposals were not put into effect until the summer of 1947.

Houser was right and he was prescient: a mass organization was needed. But it would be neither CORE nor FOR nor the MOW. They all would become follower organizations, after an entity not even imagined in 1946 when Bayard Rustin emerged from prison. At first Rustin resumed his travels in the cause of peace, as a loyal worker for A. J. Almost immediately after release he went to an AFSC conference in Cape May, New Jersey; then, for the first half of July, to a

Friends' conference on international relations in Reading, Pennsylvania; then, for the first ten days in August, to an AFSC meeting in upper New York State. But race relations was always on his mind, and from July 14 to 21, he was at a camp for high school students in Morris, New York, talking about integration.

Soon he and George Houser were talking about a new and, for the time, spectacular idea: the Journey of Reconciliation. The problem that both he and Rustin saw was that nonviolent direct action was a fringe phenomenon, known to only a few saints and fools. CORE and FOR could integrate one restaurant, one swimming pool at a time, and the sun would burn itself out before any major change came to American society. There was some momentum on the national level. In December 1946, President Truman created a Presidential Committee on Civil Rights, soon to issue *To Secure These Rights*, bold proposals, most of whose ideas would not be implemented for almost twenty years. The president's committee urged "the elimination of segregation based on race, color, creed or national origin, from American life," specifically in education, housing, employment, transportation, and public accommodations. Once in a long while a hopeful decision would come down from the Supreme Court: in 1944 that white primaries were unconstitutional; in June 1946 that state segregation laws could not apply to interstate travel. Could there be anything in either of those decisions? Both were widely evaded. Perhaps interstate travel offered possibilities, but for what?

Houser, who had just moved from Chicago to New York, was executive secretary of CORE. He and Rustin were co-secretaries of the newly established Racial-Industrial Department of FOR. Probably it was the thinking of the old labor organizer A. J. Muste to link race and class in one department. The two co-secretaries began considering whether an interracial bus journey through the South might have some use. On the one hand, it would certainly provoke resistance, perhaps even violence. Would it further divide the races? But, they reasoned, Jesus did not immediately reconcile the community but rather aroused some conflict.[3] Houser argued at the executive committee of CORE in Cleveland in September 1946 that the idea had some attractive aspects. Bus travel was something that affected great numbers of poor southern blacks, as mortgage rules did not. As a national phenomenon, a demonstration on interstate buses might attract national attention, in the way integrating a movie house in Chicago would not. Since the Supreme Court had already decided that interstate travel could not be segregated, a journey like this would be following, rather than challenging, a law. From a purely organizational point of view, a journey through several states might help CORE become more unified rather than a series of local semi-independent chapters and might help establish the organization in the South. In FOR, where the title "Journey of Reconciliation" was chosen, the journey was seen as a new application of NVDA. FOR decided that it should not be simply a journey to test Jim Crow but an interracial group traveling from place to place to lecture on NVDA.

Houser and Rustin tried to get support from other Negro leaders. Only A. Philip Randolph and Roy Wilkins, at that time assistant to NAACP president Walter White, were at all supportive. Thurgood Marshall, director of the NAACP Legal Defense Fund, said, "You know Rustin, you're insane to try anything like this. This is dumb. But, you know, if you want to try it, I'll have a lawyer in every bus station to look after you, but this is insane." The NAACP was officially against demonstrating. It thought litigation was the better way. But in fact, and without publicity, that organization backed the plans by providing safe houses, contacts, and the promise of legal support when necessary.[4]

The whole demonstration was meticulously planned. George Houser and Bayard Rustin got in touch with whomever they could in the various southern cities. They tried to get southern whites but had no luck, and even finding northern white liberals willing to go took quite a bit of searching.[5] They had originally planned to go from Washington, D.C., to New Orleans, the ultimate goal for the Freedom Rides of 1961. In 1946, however, their southern contacts advised them in no uncertain terms that they should avoid the Deep South—maybe another time, after they saw what happened on this first trip, but not now. Rustin and Houser also decided that the group should be all men. Having a mixed-sex group would enflame the issue more than they were prepared to cope with. The two traveled the whole route in preparation. If they were in a bus or train, they obeyed local segregation rules. This preparatory trip was simply planning, not a demonstration. Once, in North Carolina, they were in a plane, which was not segregated, and they could sit together. Neither had been in a plane before. After a good deal of calling and letter writing, sixteen men, eight white and eight black, were the chosen volunteers. Representatives of two black newspapers, the *Pittsburgh Courier* and *Baltimore Afro-American*, also went along for parts of the journey.

All subsequent demonstrations that Rustin organized were as carefully planned as this one. No longer would there be sudden reactions to an insult. If possible, courses of action and alternatives would be previously considered and available. In the great 1963 march, Bayard had instructions for the marchers from the moment they boarded the buses in their home communities until the buses rolled out of Washington on the way home.

The sixteen, including Bayard Rustin and George Houser, were experienced in nonviolent demonstrations. Some, like Jim Peck, who would also ride in 1961, had been in prison as conscientious objectors. Still, they met for two days in Washington before their departure for spiritual preparation, but also for realistic consideration of possibilities. They planned where they would sit in the buses—there were two teams, one for Greyhound, one for Trailways—and what they would say under certain circumstances. They enacted sociodramas as a way of preparing for their reception, including if it was a violent one. They had names and addresses of local contacts.

Still, they were nervous when they headed for the bus station on the morning of April 9, 1946. Traveling in Virginia, they had no particular trouble, although local laws required blacks to sit in the back of the bus. On the Greyhound, Jim Peck, white, was sitting in the back. But he was reading the *New York Times*, so he was obviously an outsider. A black woman said, with a chuckle, to her friend, "He wouldn't know what it was all about if he was asked to move."

At a rest stop on the way from Petersburg, Virginia, to Durham, North Carolina, the driver asked Rustin, who was sitting in the front of the bus, to move to the rear. He calmly refused. This situation had been anticipated. The driver said he "would deal with that in Blackstone," but he didn't, and there was no further incident until the group reached Oxford, North Carolina. There a middle-aged

Negro schoolteacher was brought aboard—presumably at the behest of white community leaders—to plead with Rustin. "Don't do this," he said. "You'll reach your destination either in front or in back." Rustin patiently explained his reasons for not moving and was supported by other Negro passengers. In Durham, "this skinny kid," as Bayard later described him, "came over and asked if he could join us." The others were worried, first of all that he did not have any training in NVDA, and second, because he seemed so young. They checked with his father and found he was actually twenty-five years old. They then allowed him to join for the rest of the trip. The young man's name was Floyd McKissick. He would become James Farmer's successor as national chairman of CORE and, in 1966, would turn it into an exclusively black organization and, in essence, drive it to irrelevancy.[6]

The journey went on. In fact, there was no real trouble until the Trailways bus station in the most liberal university town in the South, Chapel Hill, North Carolina.

Joseph Felmet, white, of the Workers Defense League, and Andrew Johnson, black, a student from Cincinnati, were seated in the front of the bus. As soon as the driver got on the bus—probably he knew what was going on—he asked the two to move. The police arrived quickly from the police station across the street and arrested the two. When Joseph Felmet did not react quickly enough, he was seized and thrust out of the bus. Igal Roodenko, white, Jewish, and also a resident of 217 Mott Street, and Rustin, sensing a supportive mood inside the bus, moved up to the seats vacated by Felmet and Johnson. They, too, were arrested. Meanwhile, the bus had not started, and a number of the passengers, including the participants in the journey, got out. A group of taxi drivers were standing around. "Coming down here to stir up the niggers!" said one, hitting Jim Peck on the head. Peck stood without reacting. Jim Peck would be horribly beaten on the Freedom Rides in 1961 and ended up at that time in the hospital, heavily bandaged and barely able to talk. The violence in 1947, however, was less severe. There was a wait of a couple of hours while the four arrested men posted a fifty-dollar bond each. The whole group was then whisked home by Reverend Charles Jones, a white Presbyterian minister who was on the board of FOR, chased by two cabs filled with men with sticks and rocks. There was no violence at Reverend Jones's house, although the man from the cabs milled around outside and an anonymous phone call said, "Get those damn niggers out of town or we'll burn your house down. We'll be around to see that they go." Rustin recalled that the Jones family, including the children, were terrified, as were the riders. They went— to Greensboro, where they had a speaking date.

The journey went on to Tennessee and Kentucky and then back to North Carolina and Virginia. Drivers several times asked the riders to move, which they refused to do. Sometimes on hearing about the Supreme Court decision, the drivers simply did not insist. In a couple of instances, the riders were arrested, but the incident in Chapel Hill was the only time there was violence or the possibility of violence.

In their final report, Bayard Rustin and George Houser wrote understandingly of the "Uncle Tom" reaction of Negroes like the schoolteacher who had tried to persuade Bayard to give up the journey. Bayard had experience dealing with the "underprivileged and fearful," and they both felt the strong necessity of having not just "outside" but also southern activists if they were to make any progress in the South.[7]

It was clear not only that the Supreme Court decision on interstate travel was not being enforced but also that no one was interested in enforcing it. If the interracial organizations hoped that their actions would ignite national attention to race relations in interstate travel, they were disappointed. The Negro press—the *Pittsburgh Courier* and the *Baltimore Afro-American*, for instance—did report the journey. The latter laid out the general plan for the tour on April 12, that is, after it had already started, but only on page 16. The violence or near violence was described, with a bigger headline on April 26, but only on page 37. The Baltimore paper, while following the journey, was more interested in the case that would become the Supreme Court case known as *Sweatt v. Texas*, banning discrimination in state law schools. Of course, the biggest item in any black newspaper was Jackie Robinson opening the season at first base for the Dodgers. In May 1948, a tiny item on page 21 of the *New York Times* reported the conviction of Bayard Rustin and Igal Roodenko for violating the Jim Crow laws of North Carolina. Like other NVDAs in the 1940s, the Journey of Reconciliation acquired its importance later, as a precedent and pioneering application of what would be important in the 1960s. The 1961 Freedom Rides were explicitly a revival of the Journey of Reconciliation.[8] No longer was the purpose "reconciliation," however. Now the aim was freedom, and freedom meant freedom *from* something. Freedom implied conflict with those who prevented freedom. In 1947 the purpose might have been reconciliation, but in 1947 the buses stayed segregated.

Almost a year went by before the trial for violating the segregation laws of North Carolina. In the meantime, the work continued. George Houser's memo of 1944 led to a workshop in Washington in the summer of 1947, with Rustin in charge for July and Houser for August. Again, various restaurants and other facilities were probed, but this time the demonstrations went on for two months rather than two days. The most dramatic campaign was at the YMCA. The YWCA dining hall admitted anyone who appeared. The YMCA coffee shop would only serve whites. "On Wednesday, July 16, an interracial group of eighteen sat at tables and the counter in the Coffee Shop and they were refused service." After a two hour "sit-in," the demonstrators left, but they were back the next day and were greeted with a sign on the wall that read: "What Are the Communists Up to Now?" A black reporter from the *Pittsburgh Courier* was physically thrown out of the coffee shop, but the sit-in continued for eight hours. At one point ammonia was put in the air ducts, and Bayard later wise-cracked that he was among the first victims of chemical warfare since World War I. On Friday, as the demonstrators tried to enter the building, they were met by a delegation of YMCA officials and various athletic men. They were told that only members could enter, but that was clearly not true, since white men were entering and leaving all the time. The demonstrators were afraid that the increasing tensions might lead to violence, so they withdrew across the street. Bayard Rustin and a Washington lawyer talked with the Y leadership about setting up a joint committee. The committee was put together on the spot and after a three-hour meeting agreed to set a resolution before the Y board proposing to end the Jim Crow policy. With that, the protest ceased.[9]

There were other probes. "Methodist House" ended Jim Crow,

but the Washington Zoo did not. The methods for an American version of NVDA were being worked out. It seemed that staying there, "sitting in," a term that had not been used until then, for extended periods had the most effect. As George Houser had suggested, large numbers of people for extended periods of time might make a difference. Simply demonstrating the problem would not.[10] But this was back to one restaurant, one swimming pool at a time, and not even that method was always successful.

That fall, Bayard Rustin started, as he said, to "get the ball rolling" on another front, this one a campaign against segregation and discrimination in the military. The campaign was actually a natural next step for the 1941 March on Washington movement. It was seen as such by its organizer, A. Philip Randolph, who proposed it in May 1945, before World War II was over. But the actual organization of the "Committee Against Jim Crow Military Service and Training" (later called the "League for Nonviolent Civil Disobedience Against Military Segregation") was in response to President Harry S. Truman's 1947 bill reactivating the draft and introducing universal (male) military training—on a segregated basis. Rustin was the executive secretary, that is, the person who actually ran the committee (or "league"). It was Rustin who contacted other black spokesmen and saw to the day-to-day practicalities. Randolph recapitulated his tactics of 1941, calling for an executive order ending segregation in the military, and going all over the country making speeches in behalf of his program. George Houser, Bayard Rustin, and William Worthy, who had also been on the Journey of Reconciliation, proposed a program of civil disobedience, not just for black young men but for all young men. In a press statement, Rustin said, "We know that men will not and should not fight to perpetuate for themselves caste and second-class citizenship. We know that men cannot struggle for someone else's freedom in the same battle in which they fasten slavery more securely upon themselves. A jimcrow army cannot bring freedom."

Randolph had chosen his timing well, for the campaign against segregation in the military came in the midst of a major presidential initiative on civil rights. In 1947 the president's Committee on Civil Rights issued its report *To Secure These Rights*. Its language was clear and its recommendations hard hitting. It called for "the elimination of segregation, based on race, color, creed, or national origin, from American life." There could not be a clearer or more all-encompassing statement of goals than that.

The report could have been shelved and forgotten, but it was not. In February 1948 the president sent a special message to Congress on civil rights proposing protection of the right to vote, a federal Fair Employment Practices Commission, a federal law against lynching, and home rule for the District of Columbia. Significantly enough, he did not mention education, about which his committee had earlier been so explicit. Education was so traditionally a state responsibility that any mention would have provoked even more outcry. Quite apart from the specifics, the clear point, and it was so taken by his opponents inside and outside his own party, was a presidential assertion of the need for federal actions to provide some measure of equality for blacks.[11]

As a portent of things to come, William M. Colmer (D-Miss.) rose to address the House of Representatives. "Mr. Speaker," said Colmer,

> not since the first gun was fired on Fort Sumter, resulting as it did in the greatest fratricidal strife in the history of the world, has any message of any President of the glorious United States provoked so much controversy, and resulted in the driving of a schism in the ranks of our people, as did President Truman's so-called civil-rights message, sent to the Congress several weeks ago. Not only did the message provoke serious racial controversies, but it raised anew the issue of the rights of the sovereign States as against a strong centralized government.[12]

One can dispute how much Truman was motivated by idealism, how much by politics. One can debate about how much he intended really to pass laws and how much was mere posturing. In one sense these debates matter a great deal, but in another hardly at all. Civil rights, race relations, the rights of African American citizens were now on the political agenda in a way they had not been before.[13]

In March 1948, Truman met with a group of Negro leaders, Walter White, Mary McLeod Bethune, Lester Granger, Charles Houston, and, of course, Randolph, to discuss segregation in the armed forces. As in

1941, Randolph made his position clear and would not back down. A week or so later, appearing before the Senate Armed Services Committee, Randolph endorsed the ideas proposed in February by the Houser-Rustin-Worthy group: civil disobedience. In a press release, "Negro and White Youths of Draft Age," which sounded like it may have been written by Rustin, Randolph said, "You ask me whether you should enter the armed forces of the United States under the segregated draft. My answer is this: you should *not* register under this act." Truman had through his civil rights message already determined his course. On July 26 he tried to avoid further infuriating the South by issuing a somewhat ambiguous executive order calling for an end to racial discrimination in the military "as rapidly as possible." Well, did "possible" mean an immediate start, and did an end to discrimination mean an end to segregation? Truman, through an intermediary, replied yes to both questions, and on August 18, Randolph dissolved the league because the president had made "a step in the right direction."

Truman did not satisfy the South. In opposition to the president's civil rights position on a large number of issues and what they regarded as a dangerous direction in the Democratic Party, southern delegates walked out of the Philadelphia convention to form the Dixiecrats.[14] Truman did satisfy Randolph, but just as in 1941, Rustin and some others felt let down. In words probably more restrained than if Rustin had written them, Houser wrote Randolph that "the executive order has little meaning. However, it does have this much meaning—it indicates that the civil disobedience campaign is making itself felt. . . . Only the abolition of segregation itself would have justified this [calling off the campaign]." On August 18, the day Randolph announced at an afternoon news conference that he was dissolving the League for Nonviolent Civil Disobedience Against Military Segregation, the young radicals called a morning news conference to argue that the executive order was inadequate and that the fight would continue. "We want to continue this fight beyond the armed services. We want an executive order eliminating all discrimination in the United States." Randolph and Grant Reynolds, national chairman of the league, issued their own statement in reply. Betraying more anger than he usually did, Randolph said that "a religious pacifist nucleus within the League was intent on using the movement to resist military segregation as a front for ulterior purposes. We had originally welcomed into the League such known pacifists as Bayard Rustin and A.J. Muste whose experience, we felt, would help keep a potentially violent movement non-violent in spirit and action." Randolph went on to argue that the league was set up to oppose segregation in the armed forces, not to oppose the armed forces or conscription in general. The executive order and subsequent explanations achieved what the league aimed at. Having achieved victory, there was no longer a need for the league. In retrospect, Bayard felt terrible about undercutting his mentor, but the older man forgave him. Rustin didn't dare see Randolph for two years, but when he walked into Randolph's office, Randolph greeted him warmly, as if nothing had happened. In fact, nothing much had. No one had noticed the rebel news conference.[15]

In the midst of the campaign against military segregation, Rustin, along with Igal Roodenko, had to stand trial as the result of the Journey of Reconciliation. They were charged with violating the segregation laws of North Carolina. The trial, in March 1948, was one of those semiludicrous affairs that have since become so familiar. The jury deliberated fifteen minutes, and both were found guilty. Bayard was given thirty days, because the judge assumed he was an ignorant manipulated "nigrah." Roodenko, as a New York Jew who had come down to agitate, was given ninety. On appeal, Roodenko's sentence was reduced to thirty days. The lawyer representing Rustin and Roodenko "lost" the crucial evidence of the interstate bus ticket. Rustin was convinced he had been pressured, but without that evidence they had a weak legal base. Besides, FOR was running out of money, and the case was taken no further than the state supreme court.[16] The whole process of appeal took many months, but, as George Houser wrote to Bayard in November of that year, "I am still afraid that you will have to do your thirty days down there in North Carolina, but we'll build it up so that you and the other fellows can be martyrs."

That letter was sent to London, where Bayard had stopped on his way to India. During the time of the appeal and before the jail term, Bayard went on another sort of journey, this one to the source, to

India. The prophet and practitioner of NVDA had just been assassinated. Before he died, Gandhi had arranged a world pacifist conference at Sanitinikatan, north of Calcutta, and invited Bayard Rustin from the United States. After the assassination, Gandhi's son, Devidas, decided to hold the conference as scheduled, and the Fellowship of Reconciliation sent Bayard, who sailed on October 2.

Bayard's guide to and in India was Muriel Lester. A young lady who had grown up in a wealthy family in England, she had taken a vow of poverty and worked as a missionary in London. She traveled to India in 1926, met Gandhi, and became his major advocate in her own country and in the United States. At the time that she and Bayard went to India, she was secretary of the International FOR. She had access to all the important members of the Indian government and the Congress Party.[17]

When George Houser's letter reached him, Bayard was in London for the first of many times. He had traveled extensively around the United States and had once been to Puerto Rico for an American Friends Service Committee summer work camp, but after this trip he would be in Europe, especially London, again and again. He was becoming internationally known in the specialized world of peace advocacy, and A. J. saw in Rustin a figure who could be marvelously effective all over the world. This was a source of tension with A. J., within FOR and within Rustin's own mind. To what extent was he a worker for world peace generally, and to what extent was he specifically fighting for racial justice in the United States?

When he got to London, there was bad news. The Indians had not been able to raise the money for the conference. But after some consultation, the American Friends Service Committee decided they would allow Bayard one thousand dollars to go on to India anyway. On his way he spoke in Cologne and spoke and sang in Le Chambon, France. J. C. Arora of the Indian Information Services in Washington, D.C., had met Bayard at a previous FOR conference and had written about him in Indian newspapers, so his name was known in India. With that preparation and Muriel Lester's endorsement, although the world pacifist conference had not been held, he had time with important Indians and spoke to large audiences. He met the leaders of the Indian independence movement, such as Jaya Prakash Narayan and Vinohba Bhave, and traveled widely around the subcontinent during the next couple of months. With the leaders, he discussed not only broad philosophy but tactics. He learned how one moved people, what plans had to be made, how to set up committees of defense for activists who got into trouble. The leaders, he felt, became extraordinary figures because they were part of an extraordinary movement. The Indian independence movement had, in effect, created them. In the same way, he said later, the civil rights movement had brought out extraordinary aspects of Martin Luther King, which might have remained dormant except for the broad movement.[18] He and Lester were invited to Government House in New Delhi and met with the major Congress Party members, including Nehru. Nehru and Rustin discussed not only the problems of militarism but also those of dark-skinned people the world over.

After his scheduled stay, Muriel Lester requested that he be allowed to stay another month. "Bayard Rustin can do and does at once," she wrote A. J., "three times as much as a white pacifist. His quiet ways, his commanding stature (he really looks a mighty man of valor in his Indian style homespun), irresistible friendliness and his savoir faire endear him to all. He is settling in the very center of power here."[19]

A. J. wanted him back. After all, he wrote, "Bayard's qualities are such that he will practically never be in any country without the demand developing that he stay longer."[20] But A. J. hoped that the new government could be turned toward Gandhian principles, as the independence movement had. FOR eventually extended Rustin's leave for a month, "but then we get to use him for all we are worth after March 15 in the colleges of the United States."[21]

Bayard Rustin's personal standing in the international pacifist movement and in the American branch of the movement were enhanced by his journey to India, but Rustin recognized that, at bottom, the international pacifist conference had failed in that it never came off. He and Lester were convinced that it should be revived in 1949. This conference had failed because, wrote Rustin, "the pacifists in India had largely gone on Gandhi's reputation and depended on his name for raising funds and creating interest." Now they would reorganize on a new basis, and he was convinced that a worldwide pacifist movement could grow from such a nucleus.[22] For the time in India, the center of Rustin's effort was international pacifism.

On returning to the United States, however, he was plunged back into American race relations.

A few weeks after Bayard Rustin had been entertained at Government House, New Delhi, India, conversing with the prime minister, he was on a chain gang in North Carolina for disobeying segregation laws on the bus. The contrast could not have been greater. But in another sense it was a natural sequence. Indian independence had come after many years of nonviolent direct action, and many of its practitioners had served time in prison. Rustin was serving time for a nonviolent action against discrimination. Prison was an inevitable, almost natural part of the process.

"Hey you, tall boy! How much time you got?" called the walking boss, looking directly at Rustin.

"Thirty days," replied Rustin.

"Thirty days, *Sir*," said the boss.

"Thirty days, Sir."

The walking boss took a newspaper clipping from his pocket.

"You're the one who thinks he's smart. Ain't got no respect. Tries to be uppity. Well, we'll learn you. You'll learn that you got to respect us down here. You ain't in Yankeeland now."

Then he handed Rustin a pickax, which Rustin had never worked with before, and told him to get to work. The gang was digging drainage ditches next to a North Carolina road. The work day was seven in the morning until noon, then thirty minutes for lunch, and work again till 5:30. He made a valiant effort to learn how to swing a pickax and how to work a shovel, but Rustin, a city boy, fell into his bunk bed in the dormitory—no single cells here—every night aching and exhausted.

According to Bayard's account—there is no other—he gained the respect of the other members of the chain gang and even a sort of grudging hostility/respect from the walking boss. The guards began calling him "Rusty" (as a few of his friends on the outside did) instead of "hey you" or "tall boy." There was no homosexual incident here. The penalty was terribly harsh, five to twenty-five years added to the sentence. There was no chance for concealment, and anyway,

Rustin was too exhausted for much besides work and survival. Immediately on his release after twenty-two days—he got all his good time—he gave a series of lectures at the university in Chapel Hill, advised the students on what they might do to improve race relations in the state, then hurried back to New York.[23]

From New York he tried to write to some of the "fellows" still inside, but his letters were returned unopened. He did write to some of the wives, asking them to send a pipe or tobacco and emphasizing how important some contact from the outside was. He managed to persuade the *Pittsburgh Courier* to send a free subscription to the camp.[24]

Not only had Bayard Rustin not had anything to do with pickaxes before, but he had not had anything to do with people who had had anything to do with pickaxes. He was a northerner, an intellectual, and a social activist. His medium was words, or maybe words and music, but not pickaxes. Yet he established personal, serious, and mutually respectful communications with the other members of the chain gang. In his account of the inmates there is not a hint of snobbery or condescension. Nor did he rail against large forces like capitalism or "the system." He had quite specific complaints and specific goals.

There was already a movement under way in North Carolina, including at the university, to do away with the chain gang. Rustin sent his account "Twenty-two Days on a Chain Gang" to the interested faculty members. Then, when they indicated that it might do some good, it was published in the *New York Post* later that year. He later gave himself too much credit, as was his habit, when he claimed that his words led to the abolition of the chain gang in North Carolina, but his account was one of the items laid before the governor, and it did add strength to the movement. But the major goal of the Journey of Reconciliation, desegregating interstate travel, was not achieved. Nor did the Journey of Reconciliation make the Congress of Racial Equality a well-known organization.[25]

Think of what had happened to Bayard Rustin since his release from prison in 1946: the Journey of Reconciliation, the developing strategies of sit-ins, the campaign against segregation in the military, the months in India, the time on a chain gang. And what a pace!

He had been in India in January and February 1949. He was on the chain gang from late March into April. By May, he was on a tour of the West Coast. In the fall, between October 30 and November 11, he spoke at a dozen different places in Texas: churches, colleges, YMCAs. In fact, he was constantly on the go during the next few years, speaking at college after college, at one race relations institute after another. At Hartford Seminary, a young divinity student named Andrew Young remembered being awed by an address Rustin gave there. Young recalled the impact one phrase of Rustin's had on him: "Repentance need not be multi-lateral." In other words, don't wait for your opponent to repent. We are all caught up in an evil situation. After the lecture, Young and Rustin talked for a few minutes. Although a communicant of the Church of Christ, Young was very much influenced by two Quaker professors at the seminary and by Rustin. He began attending Quaker meetings in Hartford. He was to begin his ministry in the small town of Thomasville, Georgia, but nonviolent social action was soon part of his mission.[26] Andrew Young became a close associate of Martin Luther King's, an official in the Southern Christian Leadership Conference, later mayor of Atlanta, and U.S. ambassador to the United Nations.

By the mid-1950s Bayard Rustin was clearly the premier theorist and practitioner of NVDA in the United States. But still the question arises: Did that theory and practice lead to any significant social change?

The clear limitations of reasoned nonviolence were illustrated during the summer of 1951, when Rustin and Houser tried to apply their principles to a social explosion. In mid-July, Mr. and Mrs. Harvey Clark moved into their newly rented apartment in Cicero, Illinois. He was a U.S. Air Force veteran and a bus driver, and they were black. The reaction of the community was similar to that of other all-white suburbs in other cities in other years. There was a riot. Up to eight thousand of what the *Baltimore Afro-American* described as "blood-thirsty descendants of immigrants from the Mediterranean area of Europe" (by which the newspaper meant Bohemia) mobbed the house, set parts of it on fire, and shouted "nigger" at the Clarks. Governor Adlai Stevenson had to call out the National Guard to help local police quell the mob, and still it took more than twelve hours. Walter

White was there, and FOR sent Houser and Rustin. The two stayed in Chicago for weeks and drew up an eminently sensible memorandum for the Cicero Committee of the Chicago Council Against Racial and Religious Discrimination. They recognized that "the Clark incident is one of several in the general housing area," so any solution must be communitywide. They argued the need to get strict enforcement from federal, state, and local agencies. "Mob violence," they said, "is not the way of dealing with any situation." The memo was not filled with pious language about the unity of humankind under Christ but rather with hardheaded realistic possibilities. These rational recommendations were completely ignored. The Clarks originally said that they would fight on. "If I shall back out now," Harvey Clark said, "I would be letting down 13 million colored Americans." But less than a month later, they moved out—to Norwalk, Connecticut. Unfortunately, mob violence proved in fact the way of dealing with the situation, and mob violence had won.[27] Bayard resumed his lecture tour, now as a person recently back from India. That he was recently back from Chicago might not have had as much drawing power.

In fact, there were hopeful signs in the Cicero incident that Rustin and Houser did not see. The police chief and several town officials were indicted and tried for not doing their duty. A local jury acquitted them. At President Truman's direction, however, they were reindicted by a federal grand jury, under a seldom-used statute from Reconstruction days. This law was specifically enacted to deal with the case of local juries acquitting people who had acted against the rights of the former slaves. The law made it a federal crime for anyone to deny the federal civil rights of any citizen. Under this law, police chief Edwin Karnovsky and two other policemen were convicted and fined. The housing patterns of the Chicago area were not thereby changed, but this conviction was a sign that the federal government could intervene, if the will was there, to protect black citizens against, if need be, local officials. It was a legal device used frequently during the most active period of the civil rights movement and thereafter.[28]

The implications of the last few years were plain enough, but Bayard Rustin did not draw the conclusions explicitly until some years later. Individual efforts against discrimination might be noble, moral, and brave, but if the morally righteous could find some way to work their way into the political system, as A. Philip Randolph had done, more could be achieved. The demonstrations against segregated buses had failed, but by attaching his own experiences to the campaign against the chain gang, that had at least partially succeeded. Housing discrimination in Chicago continued, but the federal government had moved in, at least a little. Some progress was made against discrimination and segregation in the military. In other words, working entirely outside the political system was without consequences, or at least immediate consequences. Randolph, and later that member of his Brotherhood of Sleeping Car Porters in Montgomery, Alabama, E. D. Nixon, did not compromise their goals or their principles. They found ways of using the system of power to further those goals. It was a lesson Rustin was to learn, but not yet.

If not in Cicero, Illinois, where could the nonviolent method demonstrate its effectiveness? The anticolonial struggle in India had been the only large-scale successful use of NVDA, or at least it was so interpreted by FOR. Perhaps other anticolonial struggles, particularly in the British colonies, could be another success story. This meant Africa. Was South Africa a possibility, or the East African colonies of Kenya and Tanzania? Perhaps West Africa, Nigeria, or the Gold Coast was nearer to independence. A. J. was a bit skeptical of the whole idea. In his essentially Marxist analysis, he felt that Africa had not gone through the necessary stages of development to be ripe for revolution. However, leaders in the South African antiapartheid struggle had heard of FOR and were bombarding Rustin, Houser, and Farmer with their literature. George Houser began corresponding with Walter Sisulu, secretary general of the African National Congress, the major resistance group in South Africa. Houser, Rustin, A. Philip Randolph, Roger Baldwin, Norman Thomas, Conrad Lynn, and others set up the American Committee for South African Resistance. George Houser as secretary actually did most of the work and fund-raising and became increasingly engaged in the African liberation movement. While the activities of the committee were getting under way, Rustin planned a trip to the Gold Coast.[29]

In the summer of 1952, under the auspices of the American

Friends Service Committee and FOR, Rustin again set out, first for a World Friends conference in Oxford, England, then for Paris. Then he would go to the Gold Coast and a meeting with perhaps the preeminent figure at that time in the struggle for a peaceful end to British colonialism in Africa. Kwame Nkrumah was popular in the West. He seemed the very embodiment of a genuine African but Western-, even American-oriented, for he had gone to college in the United States. When the Gold Coast, renamed Ghana, became independent in 1957, the British claimed that their aim all along had been to train Africans to take over leadership in the newly independent countries, and they pointed to Nkrumah as an example.

In 1952 Rustin had long talks in Accra with Nkrumah and in Nigeria with Nnamdi Azikiwe. In the November issue of *Fellowship* he wrote glowingly of Nkrumah's nonviolent campaign against British domination. The nonviolent approach to justice was "the aim and the success of Gandhi and Nehru in India," wrote Rustin. "It is now the hope of thousands of men and women in South Africa. . . . But already in the Gold Coast non-violence has had remarkable success." He then detailed the ways in which Nkrumah's political party had combined with the trade unions and former servicemen to press the British government for a new constitution. A march was organized, carrying a petition to Government House, led by the veterans. "As the veterans, marching slowly and with discipline, reached a spot near the sea about a half mile from the Governor's palace, they were met by a British officer, with a contingent of African police and soldiers with fixed bayonets." The marchers were ordered to stop. They would not, and began singing.

"Shoot," cried the officer.

Rustin wrote that "not one African soldier or policeman fired. . . . They would not fire on their brothers."

Violence did erupt when the officer himself shot four of the marchers. There was pandemonium but no violence against the officer. As a result, Nkrumah was jailed. But at the next election, Nkrumah's party won a majority. The British were forced to let him out to become the nation's and the continent's first black prime minister.

Rustin concluded his article with hope for NVDA. "A handful of black men have demonstrated once again that no array of guns and prison walls can prevent men from pursuing freedom and justice when they have rejected guns and depend on the spiritual power that springs from forgiveness and an indomitable will."[30]

Then in speeches in New York, Chicago, and other cities, he argued that the United States must take heed of the revolutionary struggle going on in Africa. Failure to give moral support to African demands for independence, Rustin was paraphrased in the *Chicago Sun-Times*, will encourage the spread of communism. It is possible that the *Chicago Sun-Times* was giving its own interpretation of Rustin's remarks, but if the summary was accurate, it would be the first time that Rustin was making the essentially cold war sort of arguments that would later put him at such odds with his earlier allies. In all his speeches, Bayard Rustin emphasized the African leaders' commitment to nonviolence.[31]

Azikiwe had been very impressed with Bayard Rustin and asked him to return to edit the West African *Pilot*. There were also other possibilities. A. J. was sixty-eight and would soon retire. At forty-one, Bayard Rustin was an inspiring figure as a speaker and to his colleagues. He was held in high regard by the international peace movement. He was a superb organizer. He was a person who had sacrificed much for his beliefs. He was undoubtedly brave and had experience and ideas within the nonviolent tradition. James Farmer was concentrating his energies on CORE. George Houser was concentrating his energies increasingly on the African continent. There were others within FOR who might succeed A. J. Muste, but was there anyone as widely qualified as Bayard Rustin?

Then he was arrested in California, not for civil rights activity but on a "morals" charge, that is, for homosexual actions.

5

Crash

On January 23, 1953, in Los Angeles, Bayard Rustin was convicted on a "morals charge." The fifties were a period of particularly virulent opposition to homosexuality, epitomized by congressional investigations, disbarment of homosexuals from federal employment, and FBI surveillance. J. Edgar Hoover and others considered "perverts" a potential weak spot in the fight against communism. The American Psychiatric Association had long defined homosexuality as a "mental disorder" and would continue to do so for almost another twenty years.[1] Rustin had been arrested in a car with two other men performing homosexual acts. He was sentenced to serve sixty days in the Los Angeles County jail. David McReynolds visited him in jail. McReynolds was a young Fellowship of Reconciliation member in Los Angeles who had joined largely on the basis of hearing Rustin speak four years earlier at a weekend workshop. He might be called a Rustin acolyte. He had been so struck by Rustin's charisma that for weeks after that first weekend workshop he had mimicked Rustin's way of moving and even his accent. In 1953 McReynolds was shocked by what he saw. "It broke him, it just broke him," recalled McReynolds. "To be in prison but not for something he believed in, but just to be in prison."[2] Rustin later said that the whole episode was trumped up, that the FBI had set him up at a party, but this is unlikely. Rustin was simply not important enough for the FBI or anyone else to have bothered setting him up, and that was not his reaction at the time. As in Ashland in 1945, his reaction was self-criticism rather than defiance. "In God's way of turning ugliness and personal defeat into triumph," he wrote to John Swomley, of the War Resisters League, from prison, "I have gone deeper in the past six weeks than ever before and feel that I have at last seen my real problem. It has been pride in self. In . . . the big ways, I was prepared to give all. I would, I believe, have died rather than join the army. But in the small and really primary ways I was selfish as a child."

McReynolds met Rustin on his release, and they both went down to McReynolds's beach house, or shack. McReynolds was also homosexual, but their relationship was as friends and colleagues, not lovers. They talked about their inner conflict. They were, they were convinced, soldiers in a great moral crusade against war and violence. They were also drawn into what seemed to them at the time something immoral, even dirty. They were not making the connection that the gay liberation movement made later, between civil rights for racial minorities and civil rights for people with divergent sexual orientations. It seemed to them at the time a contradiction. "I know now," wrote Rustin in 1953, "that for me sex must be sublimated if I am to live with myself and in this world longer." He did not say that he would have to sublimate sex merely in order to get along in the world, to seem normal to others, but that he would have to sublimate it in order to live with himself. He would eventually abandon this view, but not in 1953.

"I must tell you," John Swomley wrote to Bayard in prison, "what a real blow this has been to A.J. I don't think I have seen him looking so haggard and upset before. I think you must know that he has to a very real degree looked upon you as an adopted son." A. J. Muste had been betrayed by his foremost disciple and his almost son. Bayard had shown that he could control himself. He had done so for a while in prison in 1946 and after. And "it was made clear that on his part continuance on the Staff [of FOR] involved the exercise of rigorous discipline so that his work would not be affected nor the movement compromised and so that his witness would increasingly be purified and strengthened." A. J. had assumed that the "problem" was under control. Evidently Bayard had been betraying him continuously. A. J. knew that homosexuality was wrong, and he knew that Bayard knew it was wrong. How could he have done such a thing and made FOR so vulnerable?[3]

Within a week, Bayard had resigned or been asked to resign from the Fellowship of Reconciliation. In an executive committee meeting on January 28, FOR concluded a bit ambiguously that "he was not able to continue as an F.O.R. staff member."[4]

Years later, in 1971, according to Dave McReynolds, when McReynolds himself "came out of the closet," Bayard wanted him fired from the War Resisters League. That judgment was purely tactical. McReynolds's admission, Rustin thought, might ruin the organization. Twenty years earlier, Rustin instantly resigned from FOR—and A. J. immediately accepted his resignation—because both thought that homosexuality was inherently immoral. FOR, a religious and moral organization, could not countenance such behavior. And yet a person who had gone through what Rustin had gone through might have been more understanding of McReynolds's dilemma.

When Bayard Rustin had served his sentence and returned to New York, he knew he would have to see A. J. The older man wanted the meeting at his home, on West 122nd street, rather than in the FOR offices. Anna Muste had discussions with A. J. and their son John about whether she should even speak to Bayard when he entered the house. There was no thought of greeting him with love and sympathy, just a deep condemnation and reluctance to have anything to do with this evil. A. J. was something of a puritan when it came to personal conduct. Sex was something that just was not discussed, even mentioned, in the Muste household, certainly not homosexuality. Eventually Anna managed a tight-lipped greeting, and John remembers that after a few minutes, he and his mother were asked to "vacate the premises." They went to their separate bedrooms. Bayard was in for what the French call a *mauvais quart d'heure*, although it certainly lasted longer. A. J. was never one for brevity, on paper or in person. He had, after his visit to Ashland, written to his young protégé about love and admiration. The conversation in his house in 1953 was quite different.[5] It ended with an agreement, but one that the two sides interpreted differently. Both thought that Rustin's "problem" could be "cured" by psychiatry. A. J.'s interpretation of the conversation seems to have been that the Fellowship of Reconciliation would pay for psychiatric treatment if Rustin would give up his homosexuality. Rustin did not think that there was a condition, only that he would seek psychiatric help and that FOR would pay.

A. J. found the psychiatrist through his contacts at Union Theological Seminary. The seminary had a regular arrangement with a senior psychiatrist, Robert Laidlaw. FOR asked him to take on Rustin. When he could not, he referred Rustin to a young man, Robert Ascher, who had just finished his residency. Bayard began seeing Dr. Ascher almost immediately. Clearly he was ashamed of his "crime" because he lied about it to the doctor. He said that the police had found him after fund-raising on behalf of FOR and that he had many small bills on him, so they framed him as—a robber. As late as 1996, Dr. Ascher found it difficult to believe that the conviction was for homosexuality. Bayard talked a great deal about his guilt, even his guilty thoughts. Dr. Ascher tried to tell him that everyone's thoughts are his or her own possession, that they are not something to feel guilty about, but Rustin felt guilty. Rustin talked, sometimes in tears, about needing affection but being unable to accept it and unwilling to give it in more than a fleeting way. Rustin thought that his homosexuality was wrong, but on the other hand, he did not want to change.

Ascher concluded that Rustin was what the doctor called an "obligatory homosexual," a person who would continue no matter what. Bayard had had, said Ascher, hundreds, possibly thousands, of brief encounters. He could hardly go to a meeting without picking up some young lad and bringing him home. Giving up any idea of "curing" Rustin, Ascher and Bayard simply began talking realistically about how Bayard could learn to be more discreet, if he wanted to go on with his other work.

After a while, Muste's payments became more and more irregular. Ascher was only charging fifteen dollars a session, terribly low even in the 1950s, but soon Muste wanted to stop even that. He offered Rustin five hundred dollars as a flat payment and then no more. Ascher had developed a real liking and respect for Rustin and continued seeing him for free. He even tried to get Bayard work, since his FOR job had ended. Ascher had gone to Quaker schools and had Quaker teachers, so he first tried the Friends. He found they were absolutely unsympathetic. When the subject was first mentioned, they were excited about having a person like Bayard work for them. But as soon as they found that he was homosexual, they backed off.

People who preached love and humane tolerance were completely intolerant when it came to sexuality.

Ascher found some work for Rustin in a brewery and then as a furniture mover. Finally, in the fall, the War Resisters League offered him a job at eighty-five dollars a week, which was enough to live on. The War Resisters League was another pacifist organization often with overlapping membership with FOR, but it regarded itself as political rather than religious. By November Rustin stopped regular sessions with Dr. Ascher, though he saw him once in a while for the next couple of years.[6] Gradually he ceased to excoriate himself. He came to accept his own homosexuality and eventually to argue that discrimination against homosexuality was parallel to discrimination against African Americans.

Thus Bayard Rustin, this person who, in his outer role, seemed so supremely confident, had an inner side, more confused and vulnerable. When he spoke or wrote, his thoughts were clear, logical, and forceful. He had convictions and he was convincing. His inner self seemed more uncertain, and possibly that makes the outer self more a matter of conscious construction. And there is the question of that accent, which immediately struck Robert Ascher as affected. Quite apart from its origins, what did the accent mean? On the one hand, Rustin was companionable, liked to go out drinking with his buddies. On the other, there was a side of him that always felt alone, unloved. He knew he was respected and appreciated, but he felt not really loved. He did not find anything that might be called domesticity until late in life. And there was this further hidden side, where he was, in his own terms, sinning and unable or unwilling to stop. He was a highly sexual or sensual being, so that talk of "sublimating" sex was unrealistic.

Bayard Rustin's relationships with the black world were also complicated. He did not, when he had the choice, live in Harlem, but he was moved by and a moving singer of Negro spirituals. Yet he told Dr. Ascher that he did not want to be a "Negro performer." He never had any doubt that he was a black man. Negroes—or black people, the term he began to use in the sixties—were always "we" in his thinking. Yet he would not be anyone's stereotype of what it meant to be black. His longer-term sexual partners were white, though he had had many brief liaisons with both whites and blacks.

People always have inconsistencies in their personalities. In the case of Bayard Rustin the gaps were very wide, yet the gaps did not prevent him from being an enormously effective activist and brilliant analyst. The activism would now be as a staff member of the War Resisters League. Or would it? He had been a member of the WRL for years, and actually a member of the executive committee, so he was not an unknown quantity. But being a regular member of the staff was something else again. Roy Finch, the chairman of the WRL, thought it a wonderful idea. Most of the executive committee were in favor. But A. J. was also a member of the executive committee, and he gave a long and vigorous argument for why Bayard was "unsuitable" for the league and how he would have to make major changes in his life before he would be suitable. He said that if the executive committee hired Bayard, he, Muste, would feel compelled to resign. After a good deal of soul-searching in August 1953, the WRL did hire him, and A. J. did resign. Bayard was rehabilitated. He was once again in "the movement," but A. J. Muste's disapproval still hung in the air.[7] If Muste felt that Bayard had betrayed him, Rustin felt that Muste had deserted him. In only a few years, the two would be working together again, but the ties of affection were broken for a while.

In the course of the next decade or so, Bayard Rustin gradually accepted his own homosexuality with fewer and fewer feelings of guilt. After 1953, it is very rare to find words like "God" or "Jesus" in Rustin's speaking or writing. In 1941, communism had failed him. Now in 1953, in his hour of need, organized Christianity had failed him. After 1953, he became more and more a secular man.

6

Must Converge

In reminiscing near the end of his life, Bayard Rustin was asked, "How do you imagine the face of the black civil rights struggle would have been affected if the March on Washington had occurred in 1941, as originally planned rather than in 1963? Would the struggle be 23 years further along?" Rustin responded, "My own feeling is it would not have been. Simply because I think things outside the civil rights movement, which happened after 1941, were a great contributor to [it]."[1] The political situation changed. The legal situation changed. Demographics of the black population changed. Economics of the black population changed, and thinking, among some blacks and some whites, changed. This convergence of changes made the civil rights movement possible—not inevitable, but possible.

"For example," Rustin went on, "I believe that the number of blacks who fought in World War II and their anger upon returning from overseas, where they had been treated as human beings, had a tremendous effect upon the thinking of blacks in general." The Clarks' move to Chicago was an obvious example. Truman's actions in having the Department of Justice indict police chief Karnovsky, an action the president later bragged about in a Harlem speech, indicated some changes in the country at large. Presidents now had to pay attention to African Americans. There was demographic change. Between 1940 and 1950 the African American population of New York City had gone from some 458,000 to 748,000, that in Chicago from 278,000 to 512,000, with all sorts of consequences. Racism in the North may have increased as the Negro population increased, but it was a less oppressive racism than in the South. For instance, the black population could vote in states with large numbers of electoral votes like New York, Michigan, and Illinois, which meant that presidential candidates recognized them as a significant political block.

The Roosevelt administration had begun to pay attention to the needs of black people, but it had been an ambiguous attention and mostly implicit or behind the scenes. Negroes had not benefited from New Deal welfare and work relief in proportion to their needs, but particularly in the northern states, they had benefited enormously from federal programs, far more than at any time since Reconstruction.[2] But it was Harry S. Truman who put racial issues explicitly on the national agenda. "Harry Truman was the first president to give us the unqualified commitment so necessary to our progress," Rustin said, looking back from the vantage point of 1972.[3]

Another factor "outside" the civil rights movement, said Bayard Rustin in 1986, was that "the NAACP, between 1941 and 1954, was successful in piling litigation upon litigation before the Supreme Court, winning case after case, laying the groundwork for the *Brown* decision, which did not come until 1954. Without that decision, the March on Washington would have been impossible."

The basis for all these decisions, and for the *Brown* decision as well, was the Fourteenth Amendment to the Constitution. That amendment was adopted in 1868 for the express purpose of protecting the freedmen from state attempts to reestablish not the name but the fact of slavery. The amendment required the states to provide "equal protection of the laws" to all people within their jurisdiction and gave the federal Congress the right to enforce that equal protection. In case after case, even as the personnel of the Court changed, the Supreme Court whittled away at segregation in education on the grounds that such segregation denied Negro citizens equal protection. The climax of that process was *Brown v. Board of Education*, declaring the dual public school system, one white and one black, to be unconstitutional. That decision, and the "massive resistance" to it, made necessary the expansion of federal power and made more probable the great upswelling of a popular movement.

So "things outside the civil rights movement" converged: a new attitude among a portion of the black population; an increased attention paid by a portion of the political system; a building of legal doctrine; a consciousness of threat among white supremacists and therefore a hardening of resistance. What was lacking was a broad popular mass movement that could put all these developments together.

What made the popular mass movement was Martin Luther King and the Montgomery bus boycott. Even that might not have produced the civil rights movement had the bus company not been as intransigent as the South as a whole. The initial demands of the Montgomery Improvement Association (MIA) and Martin Luther King were not an end to segregation on the city buses but just that blacks should be seated from the back, whites from the front and no one should have to get up for anyone else. The dividing line would vary and would be wherever it happened to fall on each bus at any one time. If the bus company had agreed to that, the leaders would have had to call off their boycott, and the whole effort might have deserved a tiny item on an inside page of the *New York Times*. After all, this was not the first bus boycott in the country. The *Montgomery Advertiser*, on the second day of the boycott, thought that those demands might easily be met.[4] But the company chose defiance, and Martin Luther King became a national, then an international hero and finally a mythic figure.

Lillian Smith, the woman who had published *Strange Fruit* while Rustin was in prison, knew someone who was experienced in NVDA, as much of an expert as there was in the country. She was a member of FOR, had known Rustin for years, had participated in his workshops, and knew about his time in India and Africa. A few days after the boycott began, she telegraphed Rustin about King and King about Rustin. In a letter to King in March she warned that the movement must remain southern, lest it be condemned as the work of "outside agitators," but she made an exception for Howard Thurman of Howard University and Bayard Rustin.[5]

Not many days after the boycott began, A. Philip Randolph called James Farmer, William Worthy, and Rustin into his office. In his solemn and serious way, he began, "After watching the interesting circumstances in Montgomery, I have come to the conclusion that we ought to find some way that we can help Dr. King. After all, we've been experienced in non-violence. My question is, who should go?"

Farmer spoke up, "I suggest that Bayard go, because he is an organizer, and if there are loose strings in the organizing of the thing, he
can help tie those loose strings up, and if morale sags, Bayard's a good
singer and a good leader of folk songs, and he could lead them in the
singing which would stimulate the morale. Therefore, I think he
would be the best person to send." Randolph smiled and said, "I was
thinking the same thing Jim. I'm glad you said it. Bayard, would you
be willing?" And Bayard said yes.[6] Randolph was in touch with other
civil rights leaders, some of whom, like Roy Wilkins, were opposed.
They thought Rustin's Communist background and homosexuality
would come out and would do the movement harm, but Randolph
was in favor, and so, a few days before Christmas, Rustin went. The
idea was that he might set up some kind of a school for nonviolence.

When Rustin arrived in Montgomery, King was out of town, so
he went to talk with Ralph Abernathy. Abernathy greeted him and
after a few minutes left the room. Without Bayard being aware of it,
Abernathy telephoned Randolph in New York to find out, as Rustin
later said, "if I were kosher." Randolph said he was, and the next day
E. D. Nixon returned to town. Nixon knew Rustin through Randolph,
so Nixon also vouched for him. Abernathy put Bayard right to work,
writing a song for the evening mass meeting and drafting a leaflet.
Rustin accomplished those two tasks quickly. "Well," said Abernathy,
"you gotta stick around until Dr. King gets back, because I think we
need your services very much." When King got back to town, Rustin
and he hit it off immediately. They talked far into the night about
the meaning, theory, and theology of nonviolence. King believed and
yet he didn't believe. He knew something about Gandhi, but his
knowledge of NVDA was not very profound. Rustin later said that
King did not really consider himself a pacifist at that point.[7] Rustin
returned to New York after only a few days, but contacts had been
made that would endure all of King's life. Rustin would soon return
to Montgomery and would try to stay out of the limelight.[8]

As Rustin left, he suggested that Glenn Smiley, his old friend
from the Fellowship of Reconciliation, should take his place. Smiley
was a white Methodist minister, almost Rustin's contemporary. Although living in Los Angeles at the time, he was born in Texas in
1910 and thus was a southerner and might be more acceptable to

other white southerners. He had considerable experience with small-scale nonviolent actions. "Most of the techniques were techniques that I had gotten from George Houser and Bayard," he said. Smiley arrived in Montgomery on February 15. He was a great admirer of Rustin's and wrote about himself that "Smiley is a pore pore substitute, but he is willing, and who knows? Maybe King will latch on to something yet."[9] At that early point, no one could say whether King was going to latch on to something or not. One of the things he did latch on to was Smiley himself. After the Supreme Court invalidated bus segregation and the buses became integrated, Martin Luther King took a ceremonial bus ride in a front seat. He asked the white minister, George Smiley, to sit next to him.

On February 20, 1956, the executive committee of the War Resisters League learned that "a request had been received for Bayard Rustin to go to Montgomery, Alabama." The league did not indicate who made the request or to whom it was directed. Did King or Abernathy want him back? The executive committee voted "unanimously to send Bayard, since he has had considerable experience with non-violent resistance in both the North and South." The War Resisters League saw the potential for the Montgomery Improvement Association and Martin Luther King to create a mass movement, a nonviolent mass movement. King, they said, "is developing a decidedly Gandhi-like view," but he was not all the way there yet. The WRL could do many things to help King, and one of them was to send Bayard.[10] The WRL may have been unanimous, but the Fellowship of Reconciliation had serious qualms. Rustin was vulnerable to being framed. They were worried that perhaps some sort of issue might erupt—were they imagining a homosexual incident?—that would make Rustin a focal point of the opposition. The FOR leadership agreed not to interfere with him but forbade Glenn Smiley from having anything to do with his old friend.[11]

Rustin went back to Montgomery on February 21, with the idea of setting up a workshop "to bring the Gandhian philosophy and tactics to masses of Negroes in the South." Bayard was surprised to find that King's house was still an arsenal. A couple of days after Rustin's arrival, Bill Worthy came down, and Rustin took him to King's house. As they went to sit down in the living room, Rustin admonished,

"Bill, wait, wait, Bill, a couple of guns in that chair. You don't want to shoot yourself." King's MIA was nonviolent, in that it did not plan to hurt anyone, but a full understanding of the nonviolent philosophy, as the Fellowship of Reconciliation, Rustin, and later King would practice it, was not yet really a part of the movement.[12]

On this second visit to Montgomery, Rustin tried to stay out of the limelight, living in "a dingy hotel." "Bear in mind," he wrote back to the War Resisters League, "there must be no talk of my being here and reports should be made confidential in terms of no one here knowing that I am so closely tied in. Already they are watching me closely. . . . So I must be prepared to leave here." King soon gave up his armed guards, but there were lights all around his house. Rustin thought that was a bad idea, and he said King agreed with him, but the Montgomery Improvement Association thought the lights a minimum necessary precaution.

Then Rustin made clear to the WRL that this was a different sort of movement than integrating one restaurant in Chicago or a YMCA in Washington. "How complicated things become in the heat of a struggle—searching for nonviolent answers in a society that accepts so many assumptions of violence." He was encouraged, nonetheless, that the whole movement seemed prepared to assert again and again that its method of protest was nonviolent.[13] He was active immediately. He helped organize a car pool for people who could not get to work. When insurance companies denied insurance for the cars of the black protesters, on the grounds that the cars were being used for something other than private cars, he, with Randolph's help, arranged for the relatively wealthy black steel workers of Birmingham to lend some cars to the Montgomery protesters. He wrote songs to familiar hymn melodies, sang at the mass meetings, and he talked far into the night with King and others about nonviolence.

He might indeed have to leave. Only a week after Rustin arrived, John Swomley, from the War Resisters League headquarters in New York, was reprimanding Glenn Smiley for having anything to do with Bayard, not only because that might make the MIA vulnerable to red-baiting from whites but because he was "also to some degree persona non grata with some of the Negro leaders, or they would not have started the ball rolling with Philip Randolph to have him called back." As the white press began to notice him, Bayard made a mistake. He would not give his name, and although he did not actually claim he was a correspondent for the *Manchester Guardian* and the Paris newspaper *Le Figaro*, he said he was writing articles for those papers, which was taken as a claim that he was on their staffs. Perhaps he thought that would be hard to check. In fact, it was easy. Someone made a call to *Le Figaro*, which said that the unidentified Negro with a clipped British accent was not the paper's correspondent in Montgomery.[14] So the police began inquiring, finding out about his background.

By the end of February, Rustin himself was feeling he might have to leave. "This afternoon [February 26], I received word that the white community has learned that I am in Montgomery, that I am being watched, and that efforts will be made to get me out of town. I was warned under no circumstances to go into the white areas of the city."

On February 29, there was a meeting in New York including Norman Thomas, Randolph, and various FOR members, and "it was the feeling of this group that Bayard should be urged to leave Alabama and return to New York." Randolph felt that the people in Montgomery were doing fine and didn't need "any of our so-called nonviolence experts." Farmer heard about the growing problem and consulted with Randolph. It seemed obvious to both that Rustin had better get out. Randolph, who had originally suggested that Bayard go to Montgomery, now deputized Farmer with the awkward task of getting him back to New York.

Smiley reluctantly agreed that Bayard should leave but argued that Randolph was wrong in his estimate of what was happening in Montgomery.

> Montgomery leaders have managed a mass resistance campaign, but it was petering out until 1. the indictments and arrests, 2. King suddenly remembered Gandhi. . . . Altho [*sic*] the protest had been going on for 9 weeks, little help if any of consequence, had come from the outside until the announcement of the non- violent features, and the quotation of King's magnificent address. When that hit the press, simultaneous with the arrests handled

with a non-violent response, help began to flow in. Hundreds of telephone calls, letters, checks etc. . . . We can learn from their courage and plain earthy devices for building morale etc. but they can learn more from us for being so new at this, for King runs out of ideas quickly and does the old things again. He wants help, and we can give it to him without attempting to run the movement or pretend we know it all.[15]

The "non-violent response" Smiley talked about was that the leaders of the boycott, when they were indicted for conspiracy, responded to their arrest warrants by giving themselves up instead of waiting to be arrested. E. D. Nixon walked into the police station and said, "You are looking for me? Here I am." Soon hundreds of Negroes gathered outside the police station and applauded the leaders as they entered, one by one.[16] The magnificent speech had in fact been written by Rustin, although no one could write King's eloquent delivery.

> We have known humiliation, we have known abusive language, we have been plunged into the abyss of oppression, and we decided to rise up only with the weapon of protest. It is one of the greatest glories of America that we have the right to protest. . . .
>
> If we are arrested every day, if we are exploited every day, if we are trampled over every day, don't ever let anyone pull you so low as to hate them. We must use the weapon of love. We must have compassion and understanding for those who hate us.[17]

No matter how obvious it may seem in retrospect that the Montgomery bus boycott was the start of a mass nonviolent campaign, that was only a hope for advocates of NVDA in late 1955 and early 1956. The *New York Times* did not mention the boycott in 1955, but the *Baltimore Afro-American* did. The Baltimore paper ran a large picture of Mrs. Rosa Parks and E. D. Nixon, plus some remarks by King, whose initials they got wrong in that first interview. For the first couple of articles on the boycott, Ralph Abernathy was featured as prominently as King. After a couple of months, by February 1956, the white press also began paying attention.[18]

By the first days of March, Bayard and Bill Worthy did leave town. They went first to Birmingham, where a federal district court had just issued an order that the University of Alabama must admit Autherine Lucy, who was attempting to become the first black student at the University of Alabama. The university trustees immediately expelled her for, they said, making unfounded accusations against the university. The court order was ignored by the state of Alabama and President Eisenhower. Eventually Lucy married and withdrew her application. The university would remain segregated for another seven years.

Then Rustin and Worthy returned to New York. As a result of what they had done in the past few weeks, the pacifist movement saw in the Montgomery campaign a route for making NVDA a major, even a mass, method for social change. For King, the church was of course his bulwark, the NAACP the legal arm, but he also saw the Fellowship of Reconciliation, the War Resisters League, the American Friends Service Committee, certain labor unions, and individuals like A. Philip Randolph, Bayard Rustin, and Glenn Smiley as major sources of inspiration and support. For example, it was through Randolph that the United Packinghouse Workers were connected to King. They gave one thousand dollars to the Montgomery Improvement Association in April 1956, before any other union, and eventually they virtually supported the first year of the Southern Christian Leadership Conference.[19]

Support there was. Bayard knew he could not, at least for the moment, help on the spot in Montgomery. He could, however, have a major role in organizing northern support for the southern effort. That became his central task for the next several years. In a series of marches and demonstrations, climaxing in the great March on Washington in 1963, he would prove his skill in organizing such support. His experience and reputation increased with each march. Back in New York in March 1956, he joined with Ella Baker and Stanley Levison to form In Friendship, a northern support group for southern civil rights activists who suffered economic harm because of their activity, which also served as a fund-raising device for King. Ella Baker, a tough-minded, hard-drinking NAACP activist with a leftist past, would in 1960 be the inspiration for founding the Student Nonviolent Coordinating Committee (SNCC) at her alma mater, Shaw University, in Raleigh, North Carolina. She was a person of incredible energy, firmness, and strength, suspicious of all sorts of hierarchy, with an almost mystical faith in the ability of groups of untrained people to find, form, and act on their own definition of their own needs.[20] Levison, whom Rustin introduced to King, became one of King's closest advisers, from New York rather than Montgomery. He was accused of having been a member of the Communist Party, which he may have been, and he was certainly Jewish and an "outsider." He was therefore vulnerable, and made King vulnerable, on many counts. The result was that Levison remained somewhat out of view, but King consulted with him constantly.[21]

Another sort of support was simply publicity. The pacifists in New York, essentially Muste, were setting up a new magazine called *Liberation*. Not officially an organ of the War Resisters League, it nevertheless had Muste, Dave Dellinger, Roy Finch, and Rustin as co-editors. There was some sort of apology from A. J., and a reconciliation with Bayard. A. J. and Rustin reestablished the "Rusty-Muste" axis, as it was called, and from early 1956 on, the two worked cordially together. That is, they worked cordially until a final split over Vietnam in 1963. There was no longer a father-son sort of relationship, however. Now they were co-workers. They complemented each other. A. J. would have some large flowing theoretical idea, and Rustin would bring him back to earth. "AJ, that's the stupidest thing I ever heard," Rustin would say, but in good humor. Muste would consider, pause, then say, "You're right, Bayard." On some other issue, Rustin might be too prone to favor a practical result over what Muste regarded as principle. Muste would keep Rustin's eyes on the larger questions.[22]

The second issue of *Liberation* (April 1956) was entirely devoted to the emerging nonviolent civil rights movement. There was an article by Rustin, "Montgomery Diary," and one with King's name, but drafted by Rustin, called "Our Struggle." Rustin's article described and analyzed the Montgomery campaign day by day from February 21 through 27. He described the magnificent heroism of the leaders. Whites, he said, especially whites who had always considered themselves liberal, were in a state of "psychological confusion." They were "immobilized by fear" of the violence that they expect "will break out sooner or later." So white actions became dominated by the haters. Rustin quoted a handbill passed out by the thousands that said, "When in the course of human events it becomes necessary to abolish the Negro race, proper methods should be used. Among these are guns, bow and arrows, sling shots and knives."

The Negro community was not intimidated, Rustin reported. King's church was packed for Sunday services. King told the congregation, "We are concerned not merely to win justice in the buses but rather to behave in a new and different way—to be non-violent so that we may remove injustice itself." After another meeting the next day, Rustin wrote, "As I watched the people walk away, I had a feeling that no force on earth can stop this movement. It has all the elements to touch the hearts of men."

King in his article, more in Rustin's logical than King's rhetorical style, asserted that the Montgomery boycott was creating a new psychology in the South. Negroes had been accepting the white view of themselves. They had, through repression, forgotten that it was oppression that created their inferior position, not any lack in themselves. Even many who joined the boycott predicted that internal weakness or white pressure would cause it soon to crumble. Yet it persisted. "42,000 Walk" each day, rather than ride the buses, shouted the *Afro-American* in huge headlines, after the boycott had been going on for three months. And, as King—or Rustin—wrote, every white attempt to stop the boycott only strengthened black resolve. At one point, "two policemen on motorcycles followed each bus on its rounds through the Negro community. This attempt at psychological coercion further increased the number of Negroes who joined the protest." At a conference with city officials, the mayor said, "'Come the first rainy day and the Negroes will be back in the buses.' The next day it did rain, but the Negroes did not ride the buses."

Now "WE BELIEVE IN OURSELVES," King wrote. "In Montgomery we walk in a new way. We hold our heads in a new way." The article included scorn for the "enlightened white Southerner, who for years has preached gradualism" and was really counseling subservience. William Faulkner had spoken for this group in *Life* by urging that the demonstrators "stop now for a moment," that is, accept injustice.

"We do not wish to triumph over the white community," concluded King. "But, if we can live up to non-violence in thought and deed, there will emerge an interracial society based on freedom for all.[23] The bus boycott had now become much more than a battle over who should sit where on the buses of Montgomery. It was not only a challenge to the whole system of Jim Crow in the South but a remaking of black and white consciousness of themselves and each other.

At the same time In Friendship was organizing more tangible support for the Montgomery effort. A major fund-raising and also consciousness-raising event was a rally in Madison Square Garden in May. It was Rustin's first stab, with Baker and Levison, at mass organization. Organizing for this rally was also the first contact Rachelle Horowitz and Tom Kahn had with Rustin. They were members of the Eugene V. Debs Society at Brooklyn College. Horowitz and Kahn were to be close allies of Rustin for the rest of his life, working hard for all his major events including the March on Washington in 1963. One day in March or April 1956, as Horowitz recalled, they walked into the Young Socialist League (soon to merge with the Young People's Socialist League, or YPSL, "yipsel") office on Fourteenth Street, where Michael Harrington was in charge. He said to both of them, "'You're going to West 57th street and you're gonna help Bayard with a rally to support the Montgomery protest.' And we said 'okay.'" Harrington, not well known at the time, was to become a national figure when he published *The Other America* in 1962. The book shocked readers by detailing the poverty in presumably prosperous America. That shock was one of the factors allowing Lyndon B. Johnson to start his "War on Poverty" in 1964 and 1965.

Kahn and Horowitz went to that little office on Fifty-seventh Street where Bayard was working. There he was, with something like ten thousand handbills piled all around him, all printed with the wrong date for the Madison Square Garden rally. Kahn and Horowitz and Rustin sat there for hours, crossing out the wrong date, putting in the right one, Thursday, May 23. At the same time, Bayard regaled them with the theory and history of and his hopes for the civil rights movement. This was typical of Rustin. He was thinking about the big ideas, but he was also willing to do the little details, like crossing out a wrong date and putting a right one on ten thousand handbills.

Rachelle Horowitz and Tom Kahn were enthralled and became, in effect, his acolytes.[24]

The Madison Square rally was a great success. The *Baltimore Afro-American* estimated the crowd at twenty thousand, the *New York Times* a more conservative sixteen thousand. "In Friendship" was not mentioned, although they had done the organizing. The official sponsors were the Brotherhood of Sleeping Car Porters, the NAACP, the International Ladies' Garment Workers, and some smaller unions. A. Philip Randolph, the connecting link between King and organized labor, presided. Mrs. Franklin Roosevelt, as she was called in the press accounts (rather than Eleanor Roosevelt), interviewed Autherine Lucy, now married and so Mrs. Foster. There were speeches by Roy Wilkins and, significantly enough, Charles F. Zimmermann of the International Ladies' Garment Workers Union and chairman of the civil rights division of the Jewish Labor Committee. During the 1960s, that union and that committee would be major supports for Bayard Rustin and his civil rights work.

The most fiery speech was given by Adam Clayton Powell—a speech featured first in the *Afro-American* and last, almost an afterthought, in the *New York Times*. Powell came into the hall late. In fact, Bayard was afraid he wouldn't appear. As the rally went on, Powell did not show up, and continued not to show up. Randolph was getting worried. He said to Rustin, "You've gotta find Adam, you've gotta find Adam." So Bayard went over to his friend Harry Belafonte and asked him to sing another number. "My God, Harry," said Bayard, "you gotta help us, Adam's not here." Belafonte answered, "Oh, Adam's just across the street. He's sitting at the bar." "Will you for God's sake send your brother to tell Adam to get over here." Suddenly the lights went out. Randolph called, "Bayard, Bayard, what's happening?" Bayard was stumbling around backstage trying to find out, when a spotlight hit the back of the auditorium, and there was Adam Clayton Powell. He came down to the stage waving to his friends and working up the audience. He mounted the stage, where Randolph rose to introduce him. The crowd was now repeating, "We want Adam. We want Adam." Randolph couldn't even introduce him. Adam began speaking.

Powell denounced Eisenhower, who was, he said, "a President in exile, a commander in chief of the armed forces stripped of his stars, a leader of the people insulated and isolated from them, the most commanding figure of the free world captured by his own palace guard," a palace guard controlled by Eastlandism and the White Citizen Councils. After Powell had been speaking for some time, Bayard went up and laid a note on the podium asking him to cut his speech short. Mrs. Roosevelt had not yet spoken, and the bill for the Garden would mount up after eleven o'clock. Powell looked at the note. "I've got a note here from somebody," he said to the crowd, peering at the note, "Bay-ard Rust-in. Anybody ever hear of him?" Of course, Powell knew perfectly well who Rustin was. The crowd roared back, "No!, who's he?" Powell said, "He tells me that if we're not out of here by eleven o'clock, it's going to cost a thousand dollars every minute. Can I ask you a question? Do you have to pay for freedom?"

"Yes," answered the crowd.

"Do we believe in paying for freedom?"

"Yes."

"Does anybody think we should stop having this important meeting because it's going to cost us something?"

"Yes, Adam," meaning that he should go on.

"I will tell this what's his name, Bay-ard Rust-in," throwing the note away, "I will stand here and we will stand here all night if necessary to tell the world, to tell the government, to tell the President of the United States, we want freedom and we're willing to pay for it." And the crowd went wild.

Powell did go on for a good while, ending up costing the organizers an extra five thousand dollars. He promised that the Abyssinian Church would pay, but it did not, so the NAACP finally ended up with the bill.

Finally, after eleven o'clock, Mrs. Roosevelt spoke, interviewing Mrs. Lucy Foster. It must have been an anticlimax after the show Adam Clayton Powell had put on.

From that time on, Powell seemed to have it in for Rustin. It is not clear why. Rustin presented no threat to Powell at the source of his power. Rustin was not part of the Harlem political scene. Powell would later denounce Rustin and force him out of his position with Martin Luther King's Southern Christian Leadership Conference.

Maybe Powell feared being eclipsed by King. Later still, Powell would be angry that he was not on the podium at the March on Washington. Yet in 1966, when Congress tried to expel Powell, Rustin supported him. Bayard in his "Reminiscences" used the incident at the Madison Square Garden rally to point out that no one could upstage Adam. At the rally, all the speakers emphasized that racism was a national, not a southern, problem, but most of the proceeds went to the Montgomery Improvement Association.

Rustin was now intertwined with a national movement as he never had been as merely a pacifist.[25]

7

From the "Spirit

of Montgomery"

to SCLC's

First Campaign

During the first years of Martin Luther King's growing prominence, Bayard Rustin supported the Montgomery Improvement Association, then the Southern Christian Leadership Conference (SCLC) in three ways: direct advice and service to King, arousing northern consciousness of what SCLC was trying to change, and raising money.

Not usually in Montgomery or Atlanta but from his New York outpost, with only occasional visits south, Bayard kept in constant communication with "Martin," a communication that would keep up, even when the two disagreed, until King's assassination in 1968. In the fall of 1956, Rustin sent King a series of questions asking how the Montgomery Improvement Association was doing. King needed the kind of northern support Rustin could supply and was grateful for Rustin's advice and concern. He answered with warmth and in detail. The MIA was doing all right but had to have outside help for its five thousand dollars per month expenses, mostly for the transportation system.[1]

Rustin had told northern readers of *Fellowship* about the boycott. Now he had to tell them about the systematic terror that maintained segregation. In the fall of 1956 he went into what he called "Till Country," and in *Fellowship* for October he told the story in "Fear in the Delta." Repression was so great in the Mississippi Delta and other parts of the Deep South, he said, that if change was to come at all, help had to come from outside.

He told how in a church near Bobo, Mississippi, on September 30 he had related the story of the Montgomery boycott and said it was like Moses walking with the Hebrew children out of slavery. The audience was enthusiastic, but as soon as Rustin sat down, the pastor was on his feet saying that God alone in his good time could lead the Negro to freedom. Then the pastor left in his Cadillac. In most places, Rustin wrote, the black church was bought and owned by the White Citizens' Council. He told how vigorous black leaders suddenly left town; how anyone who openly resisted might turn up the next day dead in a local creek. He quoted one Citizens' Council leader as saying, "You niggers can't live unless we let you. Your food, your work and your very lives depend on good-hearted white people." And Rustin had to agree, as he told the tale of Amzie Moore, head of the NAACP in the Delta. Moore had built up a solid group of small businesses: gas station, beauty parlor, restaurant. As soon as it became known that Moore was resisting the system, local credit dried up. He was able to survive only with help from the National Sharecroppers Fund and the American Friends Service Committee. Even so, by the fall of 1956, when he took Rustin on a tour of "Till Country," he was on the edge of bankruptcy.

They started out in Le Flore County. Here was the little town of Money, where in the previous year Emmett Till, a Chicago teenager visiting his uncle, had taken a dare from his cousins and said to a white woman, "Hey, baby!" That night he was kidnapped. Rustin and Moore then went to Sunflower County, where Till was killed, then to Tallahatchie County, where his killers had dumped his body in the river. Amzie Moore was the one who found out about the case and telegraphed the New York NAACP. Till's murderers were known. They were tried and acquitted by a local jury in a farcical trial, and the case became a national sensation. So when the Negroes of Mississippi talked about "Till Country," everyone knew what was meant: Terror Country.

The two drove out in the country. "I want you to see the barn where they murdered that boy," said Moore. "It's just the other side of Ruleville—on a farm where Milam's brother [one of the killers] used to live. He ain't there no more; white folks drove him out. A man named Wyman lives there now. He's a mean cuss—don't let nobody go near that barn. But I think we can see it from the road."

"You mean," asked Rustin, "that we have to go close to a white man's farm to see it?"

"Well, I'm not sure. I think, if I remember right, there's a public road that goes by it."

But there wasn't. They turned up what they thought was a public road and found themselves on Mr. Wyman's driveway. They saw the barn all right, with Mr. Wyman standing in front of it with a shotgun.

Amzie Moore brought the car to a slow stop. Slowly he got out and approached a woman who appeared at the kitchen door. He tipped his hat and politely asked the way to Ruleville, which of course he knew perfectly well. The woman was nervous but pointed out the road to him. They turned the car around and slowly drove back to the road. "Man," said Amzie Moore. "If we had turned back or looked nervous, we'd sure have got shot."

As they drove on, Rustin asked Moore why the white people had run the killers out of the county. "Well," said Moore, "white folks is hard to explain. For one thing, they are all tied up inside. Seems as if they considered what he'd done a bad thing—but at the same time, mind you, they were defending him for all they was worth."

Bayard Rustin returned to New York to tell the readers of *Fellowship* of his experiences. King, and what was soon to be a "movement" in the South, needed northern help—help to help themselves.[2]

The Montgomery experience had also shown that mass protest, mass nonviolent protest, could create a new spirit among southern blacks and could arouse the country. The *Montgomery Advertiser* during the boycott complained that the city was getting a bad name throughout the nation. The editors were astounded when a reporter from a *Japanese* newspaper showed up among the throng of "outside" newspeople asking for aid from the local press. Montgomery was getting a bad press throughout the whole world!

From the point of view of the protester, of course, that "bad press" showed that what had begun as a wrangle about seating in buses in one southern city could have enormous ramifications. The protests in Montgomery were in fact being echoed in a few other cities, notably Tallahassee, Florida. On one visit to Montgomery, in the fall of 1956, Bayard and King were sitting in the latter's basement "family room," where they often went to chat and drink beer. Talking about the protests in other cities, Bayard said, "I think Gandhi would very definitely conclude that Montgomery cannot win unless satellite protests take place all over the South, not in one or two places, but a couple of dozen places. And if Montgomery wins, then these satellites win." They chewed over the idea for a bit. "What are you saying, practically?" asked King.

"What I am saying practically is that you need to set up a South-wide organization, which will support Montgomery AND simultaneously all these other places. And you've got to bring the leaders of all these other [protests] in."

Rustin later claimed that this was the origin of the Southern Christian Leadership Conference. More likely, several people were thinking along the same lines. Rustin had been discussing some sort of larger organization than the Montgomery Improvement Association for the past weeks with Ella Baker and Stanley Levison in New York.[3] Clearly the "Spirit of Montgomery" could not be allowed to die, merely if the bus lines in Montgomery eliminated segregation. Something more permanent than the Montgomery Improvement Association should be created.

Toward that end, Rustin, at about the same time as the article in *Fellowship* about "Till Country," was writing Working Papers for what was styled the "Southern Negro Leaders Conference on Transportation and Non-Violent Integration." This was to be a workshop in Montgomery on nonviolence, like so many other workshops Bayard had organized, but this one was to be followed by an organizational conference in Atlanta. This time the workshop was not just going to be a matter of small probes into racism. This time it was held in the midst of a large, internationally known mass nonviolent protest, just what FOR had been hoping for. This time, a larger movement might develop.

In his first Working Paper, undated but probably written in October 1956, Bayard carefully analyzed why the blacks of Montgomery had been able to sustain the boycott for all those months, summer and winter, rain and shine. Rustin would use these essentially psychological insights in his later protests.

[1. The boycott is] directly related to *economic survival,* since the masses of people use buses to reach their work.

2. These people *know* that in bus segregation they have a *just cause.* No one has to arouse their social anger.

3. In refusing to ride the buses the people pledge a daily rededication. This *daily act* becomes a matter of *group pride.*

4. Unlike many problems, such as integrated education, there is no administrative machinery and legal maneuvering that stands between the people and the act of staying off the buses, or sitting in front seats. The situation permits *direct action.*

5. The action is *based on the most stable social institution* in Negro culture—the church.

6. The protest requires *community sharing* through mass meetings, contributions, economic assistance, hitchhiking etc.

7. The situation permits and requires *a unified leadership.*

8. The method of non-violence—Christian love, makes humble folk noble and turns fear into courage.

9. The exigencies of the struggle create a *community spirit through community sacrifice.*

Rustin added that the nine underlined qualities were required for any mass movement, but when "a group of people have developed them in one area," these qualities can be transferred to another through *"education by action."* A better summary could hardly be imagined for how Richard Gregg's *The Power of Non-Violence* could be adapted to the American racial scene. The means might be Christian love, but the motivating force was not any abstract principle but economic survival. A rededication, which might be completely secular, was required each day. The church was regarded not only as a spiritual base, maybe not as that at all, but as a stable social institution.

In others of the Working Papers, he developed more fully the ideas and problems of maintaining a nonviolent discipline. He knew, even expected, that the protesters would sometimes be met with violence. To maintain the nonviolent discipline he suggested continuous active daily involvement by the demonstrators; leaders refusing to carry arms; mass meetings on nonviolence; and assigning important nonviolent duties to the more militant. He also suggested that perhaps there was a need for a small disciplined group of nonviolent volunteers. "These persons should receive intense training in spirit technique. They would serve as 'non-violent shock troops' in time of danger and accept the consequences. . . . Their courage would inspire the community and show those who might resort to violence."[4] One thinks immediately of the Student Nonviolent Coordinating Committee (SNCC), whose members often spoke of themselves as the shock troops of the movement. Rustin's co-worker from "In Friendship," Ella Baker, would be instrumental in the establishment of SNCC in 1960.

On November 13, 1956, that is, between the time he wrote the Working Papers for the conference and when the conference took place, the Supreme Court affirmed a lower-court ruling that the segregation of Montgomery's buses was unconstitutional. Segregated buses and the boycott continued until all the paperwork was done, but essentially the protesters had been successful! At a mass meeting in King's church on the evening of December 20, the boycott was called off. After the meeting, a training session was held on how to react nonviolently in case there was violence the next day. On December, 21, 1956, Martin Luther King rode symbolically in the front seat of a bus with Glenn Smiley beside him.

There is nothing so fatal to a popular movement as victory. The "Spirit of Montgomery" had carried the boycotters through many months. Could that spirit be maintained when the specific enemy had been beaten? Further crusades could certainly be envisioned. If in Montgomery, why not throughout the South? And if buses, why not other municipal facilities? And could municipal facilities also be broadened to include places licensed by the municipality? The questions could be asked, but were the psychological requisites that Rustin had analyzed in his Working Papers going to be present?

The workshop on nonviolent social change met in Montgomery on the anniversary of Rosa Parks's arrest, December 6, 1956. Church bells pealed from the bell towers of the black churches. Many Montgomery blacks fasted in honor of the day. December 6 was a Thursday, so most people had to go to work, not yet riding the buses that the city insisted were to remain segregated until it had final word from Washington. Rustin was not at the workshop, but it was his kind of workshop, with his kind of people. Lillian Smith, described by the *Montgomery Advertiser* as the "controversial white southern novelist," argued that the bus boycott and nonviolent methods were giving whites and blacks their freedom. Glenn Smiley gave a speech entitled "Non-violence and Social Change." Ralph Abernathy spoke for the ministers on the social implications of Christianity, and while King was there, he is not recorded as speaking.[5]

Glenn Smiley regarded the workshop as successful. It gave King a chance to meet other southern ministers, because outside Montgomery, most of his activities were raising money in the North. But Smiley regretted profoundly that this workshop did not produce a lasting integrated organization. Within a few weeks another meeting was held, also in Atlanta, but this one was all black.[6]

This organizational meeting of the "Southern Leaders Conference on Transportation and Non-Violent Integration" was held at Martin Luther King Sr.'s Ebenezer Baptist Church in Atlanta in January 1957. Sixty "leaders" attended; in fact, they included only one sort of southern leader, ministers, but representatives of labor unions also took part. There were three representatives from the Packinghouse Workers, including the union's vice president, and one from the Amalgamated Meat Cutters.[7] This was the small start of something big, but no one knew that in 1957. No one in either the black or white press paid any attention. It was, after all, a small group of black preachers getting together for some vague purpose.

In the midst of the conference in Atlanta, Ralph Abernathy's home in Montgomery was bombed. Abernathy rushed home, accompanied by King. The meeting was adjourned and reconvened the following month in New Orleans. It was at this February meeting, attended by almost one hundred people, nearly all ministers, that the Southern *Christian* Leadership Conference was formally inaugurated.[8] It was going to be an organization of black ministers throughout the South whose aim was to keep alive and broaden the "Spirit of Montgomery."

In one of his Working Papers, Rustin made clear what he thought the next area should be. "The time has come," he wrote, "to broaden the struggle for Negroes to register and vote. . . . Until the Negro votes on a large scale, we shall have to rely more and more on mass direct action as the one realistic political weapon." Right then, he felt "direct action is our most potent weapon," but that might not always be the case. After all, he said, industrialism had come to the South; Republicanism might follow. A two-party South might emerge, with competition for the Negro vote. To a degree this foreshadows Rustin's most famous and much criticized 1965 article, "From Protest to Politics." He was, from the very beginning, not working to replace the American political system with some more direct democracy but to open it up to Negro—and other liberal—influence. It was only in the face of a system closed to blacks that they were forced into direct action. Others of his allies would see it differently. Julian Bond in 1970 would judge that Rustin had sold his soul to the Democratic Party. But Rustin was arguing in 1956, as he would in 1964 and more strongly thereafter, that party politics, more specifically Democratic Party politics, in concert with the labor movement, could be a rational next step after protest demonstrations had brought the subject into public debate.

The decision of SCLC on its first project made its purposes less vague. The presidential election of November 1956 had shown signs that Bayard Rustin's political predictions might be right. Eisenhower won more southern votes than he had in 1952 and a greater proportion of the black vote, although the black gains came more in the North than in the South. Adam Clayton Powell broke from a Democratic Party in which white southerners, he said the White Citizens' Council, had such a large influence, and he supported the Republican ticket. The one-party South might indeed become a two-party section, and the black vote might be decisive. So Bayard Rustin's proposal in his Working Paper, emphasizing the black vote, might be a way to maintain and broaden the "Spirit of Montgomery."

The first project of the new Southern Christian Leadership Conference was therefore a march on Washington but with a twist. Since ministers sponsored it, it was to be a Prayer Pilgrimage in May 1957. Thousands of Negroes would converge on Washington and prayerfully urge federal protection of the right to vote where it was denied, and they would urge black voters to exercise their right where they could. Plans were made for fifty thousand people to assemble peacefully and drive home their point. The Reverend Martin Luther King was now a national figure, whether temporary or permanent one could not say. The Southern Christian Leadership Conference was trying to break new ground in the struggle: pressing the federal government on voting, an area traditionally left to the states. A demonstration with a religious tone, albeit the secular goal, seemed a logical next step. Randolph, Wilkins, and King were co-chairs, and Ella Baker and Bayard Rustin organized it. They established contacts all over the eastern half of the country: Philadelphia, Baltimore, Newark, Chicago, Boston, New York, and, from the South, Richmond, Greensboro, Charlotte, Raleigh, Montgomery, Mobile, Birmingham, Atlanta, Savannah, Tallahassee, Jacksonville, Baton Rouge, and more.

The Republicans had made at least a gesture toward the black vote by introducing a civil rights bill. A weak bill, more designed to seem than to be significant, it nevertheless offered support for SCLC's contention that increasing black registration and voting might make a difference. The civil rights bill of 1957 proposed the creation of the United States Civil Rights Commission, proposed a Civil Rights Division within the Department of Justice, and permitted the attorney general to seek injunctive relief in the case of a denial of voting rights by local officials. Whether the Civil Rights Commission or the Department of Justice would be effective would depend on the people appointed and on the intent of the administration. The provision on voting rights did not deal with the mass denial of rights in the South. Each person would have to complain individually, and in a provision added at the behest of the southern senators, local officials could have a jury trial—in each instance.[9] The process would be so protracted as to be of no political significance whatever. But the bill was better than nothing. If enacted, it would become the first civil rights act since Reconstruction, and it might be a beginning.

The Prayer Pilgrimage office in New York, that is, Rustin, aided by Rachelle Horowitz, Tom Kahn, and Sandra Feldman, issued a stream of upbeat press releases.[10] Important people backed the pilgrimage, and fifty thousand were expected to show up. The

Baltimore Afro-American had huge headlines. "They're on the way," proclaimed the paper, and an editorial cartoon pictured Congress in fear of the coming fifty thousand people. On May 18 the *Afro-American* ran a special section with photographs of the pilgrims.

The Prayer Pilgrimage demonstration, on the third anniversary of *Brown* on May 17, was in a sense a rehearsal for the great March on Washington in 1963. In 1963 there was a major civil rights bill before Congress, and the purpose of that march was at least partly to urge action from the Congress. In 1957 a civil rights bill was also before Congress, and the Prayer Pilgrimage was partially intended to show support for the bill. The pilgrimage took place in front of the Lincoln Memorial, like the 1963 march. King delivered the major speech, as in 1963. A. Philip Randolph opened the speeches, as in 1963, and Martin Luther King came last. "Give us the right to vote!" he cried. "Give us the ballot and we will transform the salient misdeeds of bloodthirsty mobs into the abiding good deeds of orderly citizens. Give us the ballot and we will fill our legislative halls with men of goodwill." With the ballot, he predicted, Negroes would elect to Congress men who would not sign "southern manifestos," elect just judges, and implement the Supreme Court decision against segregated schools. He criticized the executive for being "silent and apathetic" and the Congress as "stagnant and hypocritical."[11] Rustin had gone over what Martin Luther King would say, line by line. Having seen a draft of the speech, perhaps prepared by Levison, Rustin thought that there was not enough "spiritual content" in it and not enough emphasis on nonviolence.[12] Rustin, the increasingly secular man, had advised the man of God to be more spiritual. The man of God had ignored Rustin and given an almost entirely secular speech that emphasized not nonviolent direct action but traditional politics.

To many participants, the Prayer Pilgrimage was a success. Andrew Young, then pastor of a small church in Thomasville, Georgia, recalled that his parishioners were quite fearful of attending. He persuaded two carfuls to go, but they began dropping out during the last days before the march, and he and another pastor from Thomasville ended up going alone.[13] When they got there, the crowd looked big— it was big—but not as big as predicted. The speeches were brave words, defiant words, but they did not have much behind them. The organizers of the pilgrimage estimated the crowd at some twenty-seven thousand, and the park police said only some fifteen thousand. Whatever the number, it was far less than the fifty thousand predicted. The *New York Times* did notice the pilgrimage with a small item on the bottom of the first page. *Life* magazine ran a two-page spread in its "Speaking of Pictures" section. The focus was on "interesting" faces: Mahalia Jackson belting out a chorus, a Negro patriarch. The brief text totally misconstrued the purpose of the pilgrimage, saying it was for integrated schools. The vote and the substance of Martin Luther King's speech were not mentioned. *Time* magazine did not even mention the Prayer Pilgrimage. The final version of the bill was passed in August. It would be difficult to find any influence from the Prayer Pilgrimage on the Civil Rights Act of 1957, which *Time* characterized, when it finally passed in August, as "a compromise with a compromise with a compromise." If the federal government was going to be pushed, it would have to be harder than this.[14]

With the help—or at least the hope of help—from the Civil Rights Act, SCLC could now embark on a "Crusade for Citizenship," to vastly increase black registration and voting. Because the later Voting Rights Act of 1965 came after the Equal Accommodations Act of 1964, it would be easy to conclude that voting rights were a later goal of civil rights activists. Because the Kennedy administration tried to talk civil rights activists into emphasizing voting rights rather than ending Jim Crow in other spheres, it would be possible to regard voting rights as an easy subject that would calm the waters. The Kennedy people hoped for and the activists feared that result. In fact, however, the protection of voting rights was a goal of the NAACP and SCLC right from the beginning, and it turned out to be as explosive an issue as any other challenge to white supremacy. But the voting rights campaign was not to be led by either organization.

The "Crusade for Citizenship" was to be a natural follow-up to the Prayer Pilgrimage, designed to make real the hopes expressed by King in Washington. The idea was to hold rallies in as many southern cities as possible, on February 12, 1958, Lincoln's birthday, to encourage registration and voting by black southerners. The rallies would be followed up by letters to officials in Washington and by workshops in each locality to ready people for the process of registering and voting. The hope was to raise two hundred thousand dollars to continue the efforts.[15]

In his continuing service to King, Rustin helped organize the effort from offices in New York, while Ella Baker worked from Atlanta. Twenty rallies, not dozens, were held in cities from North Carolina and Tennessee to Texas and Louisiana. In some cities, the NAACP saw the rallies as a threat to their own dominance in the civil rights effort and tried to discourage them.[16] Yet rallies were held. Ministers preached in one another's churches. King spoke at a Miami rally. Reverend C. K. Steele, who had run a bus boycott in Tallahassee, Florida, spoke in Atlanta. Rustin prepared resolutions and a form telegram for each rally to send to Attorney General William Rogers. It was a weak telegram but perhaps all that was possible under the new law. It urged Rogers merely to inform citizens of their rights. The crusade planned an ambitious continuing program of education for registration, but that never materialized, and the hoped-for two hundred thousand dollars was never raised.[17]

Even enthusiastic rallies, but in only twenty cities, did not change things. The rallies faced in the wrong direction. The problem was not black citizens not knowing how or wanting to vote. The problem was with white registrars who resisted registering them and the whole systematic terror campaign on the part of whites to discourage black registration and voting. Significant changes in black voting did not occur until the federal government, in the Voting Rights Act of 1965, forced local registrars to obey the Constitution.

The Prayer Pilgrimage might have been smaller than expected, the Crusade for Citizenship a statistical failure, SCLC an uncertain organization, but Martin Luther King was now a world figure. It was not only that he was helping to turn the civil rights movement, which had been mostly a legal battle, into a mass movement; he was joining the worldwide revolution of darker-skinned people against oppression by lighter-skinned Europeans. He was urged to travel to the home of NVDA, India, and to the soon-to-be independent nations of Africa. He was invited to be present at the ceremony of Ghanian independence in the early spring of 1957. Bayard Rustin was the person with contacts in both places, so he was the natural person to arrange the trip. As it turned out, India and Nigeria fell out of the itinerary, and King went only to Ghana and to Europe on the way home. "Bring along your mandolin," wrote Bill Sutherland from Accra, Ghana, to Bayard, "and we can do some singing." Sutherland was now assistant to the Ghanian finance minister and married to a Ghanian poet, playwright, and head of Ghana's theater. But Rustin had regretfully to tell his old friend that he was not coming. He would remain supporting the cause in New York. "Is it the same old story of your 'past' again?" asked Sutherland. "Who gave you the axe this time?"[18]

Discretion might mean that Rustin should not too obviously be close to King, but that did not mean that Bayard's international efforts would cease. In April 1958, he and four other pacifists set out on a "Mission to Moscow" to try to get the Soviets to renounce nuclear weapons. The effort could have no hope of success but would serve the argument that pacifists were not just making their point to a West that would then be a toothless opponent of Communist expansion. The five first went to London, where they left a message at 10 Downing Street and took part in the first Aldermaston March of the Campaign for Nuclear Disarmament (CND). The CND was organized by some of Britain's most eminent intellectuals, including Bertrand Russell, asking for British unilateral nuclear disarmament. Each Easter weekend after 1958, the CND organized a fifty-mile march from Trafalgar Square to Aldermaston, the British Los Alamos. The CND had an impressive first few years but then declined, only to be revived again in the late 1970s. On that first march in 1958, the five pacifists were encouraged by participation of what Rustin described as "hundreds upon hundreds of young people." In Britain, as well as later stops in France and Germany, the five found that all major political parties favored retention of atomic weapons, so the nuclear disarmament campaigns would have to be waged outside party politics. When they reached Finland, they found that their visas for the Soviet Union had not arrived. They waited from the end of April to the middle of May and then were told informally that they could wait forever; no visas would appear. Leaving an open letter to Premier Khrushchev, they returned home having "borne witness," perhaps, but with nothing much else accomplished.[19]

8

Marching,

Marching

Only a few months after Bayard Rustin returned from the fruitless "Mission to Moscow," he was organizing in the cause of school integration in the United States, and not only in the South. Here his efforts seemed to have a payoff greater than five pacifists merely "bearing witness" in Helsinki against the powers in Moscow. The civil rights movement was given its great initial impetus by the Supreme Court's decision in *Brown v. Board of Education*. Challenging Jim Crow on buses, extending the challenge to other institutions, increasing the black vote—all these were central to Rustin's and King's efforts. But the integration of southern public schools had set off that great hope and that great reaction that together made the movement. The question in the late fifties was whether the hope or the reaction would triumph. The outcome was not at all clear and would depend in large part on what the federal government did. The Prayer Pilgrimage and the Crusade for Citizenship were attempts to push the Eisenhower administration, neither with much effect on national policy.

Federal reluctance and the possibilities of pushing were further illustrated later in 1957. The federal court had ordered that Central High School in Little Rock, Arkansas, be integrated. The attempt of nine Negro children to enter the high school was met with mob violence. The conflict, like the Montgomery boycott, became a national, even an international news sensation. The indomitable head of the Arkansas NAACP, Daisy Bates, was absolutely firm and unwavering in her support for the nine schoolchildren, no matter how many threats she received or how large the mob might be outside Central High. Governor Orville Faubus cast his political lot with the most intransigent racists. All petitions of the state for delay, because of violence and the threat of violence, were turned down by the Supreme Court. President Eisenhower very reluctantly sent troops to enforce not so much the limited integration but obedience to the order of a federal court. Here was a crisis of conscience for the pacifists of the War Resisters League and a sign of things to come in Bayard Rustin's odyssey from protest to politics: armed troops being used to support justice.[1]

Rustin was now on the staff of the War Resisters League (WRL) and an editor of what was unofficially its journal, *Liberation*. The league's crisis of conscience was expressed in a series of articles in the magazine in November 1957, "Little Rock: Are troops the answer?" Only Lillian Smith answered with an unambiguous yes. Other articles talked around, over, through the central issue or simply deplored the fact that things had been allowed to reach such a stage. The official position of the WRL was against the use of troops. Its members wanted Eisenhower personally to lead the black students into Central High. That being out of the question, they had no further position.

It was notable that Bayard Rustin did not join in the debate. He was an editor of the magazine, the one with greatest experience in nonviolent action and race relations. But his was not the position that the WRL took, and he wrote no article in that issue of *Liberation*. He had already discussed the difference between a police force and troops in his Working Paper #6 toward the formation of SCLC. "Police power is the power to arrest individuals who break the law. There police power ends. Such persons are then brought before courts. . . . Army power may be indiscriminately directed toward groups of people who are not involved in wrong doing in a situation where the army become[s] judge, jury and executioner. The police power should and can respect the individual: the latter cannot." But he went on to say that when the military comes into a community and acts as a police force, "leaders of non-violent campaigns may cooperate with such agencies to the degree that they cooperate with the police." Rustin saw the use of troops in Little Rock as exactly that: an army used as a police force when the local and state policing forces would not control the mob. "You've got to get those kids in there," he said to the editorial staff of *Liberation*. He was not interested in all too much theoretical agonizing. He wanted real things to happen in the real world.[2]

Over the next several years, this would put Rustin increasingly at odds with his friends in the international peace movement. A series of efforts at controlling atomic testing or nuclear proliferation had virtually no effect. On the other hand, nonviolent direct action was pushing toward measurable progress on race relations in the United States. Rustin preferred to work in that sphere where something was happening rather than the sphere where it was not.

What was clear to Bayard Rustin and Martin Luther King and others was the key role of the federal government. Individual or small group actions could be thwarted or had very limited effects. Local power could not or would not act to change race relations, whether in Chicago or Montgomery or Little Rock. When federal power was exercised, something happened—not perhaps enough, but something. The judicial branch of the federal government had taken the lead. The legislative branch had been quiescent and was at the mercy of local politics. Only the executive branch had the power to enforce orders of the courts, so it was the executive branch that had to be pushed. But was pushing possible, and if so, how?

Although there were small pockets of at least token school desegregation in the border states, the late fifties were the age of "massive resistance," as Virginia called its program. Every fall, popular magazines like *Life* and *Time*, and the increasingly widespread television, would bring pictures of a few brave black children trying to be the first to enter a previously all-white school. But the progress was painfully slow, and the opposition found device after device to delay implementation of *Brown*. Little Rock was simply one in a long series of states and towns that petitioned federal courts for delay after delay. Little Rock was only one in a long series of towns where mob violence was the response to tiny attempts at obeying court-ordered desegregation. The Supreme Court's carefully chosen phrase "all deliberate speed" was taken to mean "never."

Martin Luther King was becoming a national figure, but after the Prayer Pilgrimage and the failure of the Crusade for Citizenship, SCLC was, in the words of David Garrow, King's biographer, "moribund."[3] King published *Stride toward Freedom: The Montgomery Story* in 1958, sending the chapters to Rustin and Levison for suggestions as he wrote them. The book was a detailed account of the situation in Montgomery before the protest, including factional tensions in the Negro community, then a detailed account of the boycott. It was not a best-seller and received important but relatively few reviews. The civil rights movement seemed to pause, and the initiative seemed to pass to the resisters against change.

Social reformers in the United States have often had more success if they focus the issue on children rather than posing the issue as reforms for adults. School integration was an issue that led naturally to an emphasis on children. Randolph and Rustin had seen marches or threatened marches on Washington work and had seen at least one, the Prayer Pilgrimage, not have much effect. If, however, a march could be made up of school children, maybe that would capture national and hence politicians' attention. The two, along with Stanley Levison, started to organize the Youth March for Integrated Schools. Like the marches that weren't, like the Prayer Pilgrimage, the Youth March was to bring thousands of people, mostly black people, to Washington. The hope was that their numbers would make it impossible for the president and the Congress to ignore them and that the national press, maybe even television, would pay attention.

The first of what turned out to be two Youth Marches for Integrated Schools was to take place on October 11, 1958, and planning began only about a month earlier. Rustin and Levison were "coordinators," that is, the people who really put out the effort, with the help of Rustin's young acolytes like Rachelle Horowitz and Tom Kahn. A. Philip Randolph was the chairman. Though he did not do the day-to-day work, his was not merely a titular post. He signed letters of solicitation, was the contact with labor unions, and lent the enterprise an air of respectability and reality. His first solicitation letter spoke only of a delegation of one thousand young people, but the organizers' ambitions soon exceeded that.[4]

The Prayer Pilgrimage had had some northern participation but was mostly a campaign of southern clergymen. The Youth Marches, on the other hand, were largely northern events, with something like half the participants coming from New York, primarily Harlem. The organizational work was done in offices on 125th street, just a few doors down from Randolph's office. This was the local office of the Retail, Wholesale and Department Store Workers Union, the office of its president, Joe Overton.[5] The technology was mimeograph machines and envelope stuffing. Rachelle Horowitz later recalled that she became a superswift proficient envelope stuffer.

But the work was not at all solemn. There was joking and horseplay. After a day of telephoning and mimeographing, Rustin and the young people might have supper together at some restaurant that seemed exotic to the Brooklyn College students, like one with soul food, or East Indian. There would be drinks and laughter. Tom Kahn called Rustin a nonchemical antidepressant. Bayard was always making jokes, often on himself. Even a racial protest could also be a joke. For example, New York cabs would often not stop for a black man, especially if accompanied by a white woman. Rachelle Horowitz would sometimes hail a cab, and then Rustin would rush out from behind a doorway, join her in the cab, and say something like, "Take me to the police station!"

Of course the fun was in pursuit of serious ends. The young people felt that they were in touch with making history. They organized rallies at colleges. They arranged speaking dates in aid of the march. Rustin, often with Jackie Robinson, went to various colleges in the New York area selling tickets and drumming up support.

The whole thing was a shoestring operation, costing about $17,000, ending about $1,000 in the black. Indeed, all of Rustin's demonstrations ended up with an ever-so-slight surplus. Most of the support came from labor unions, primarily those unions in which black workers were an important part of the membership: Packinghouse Workers, Hospital Workers. The United Auto Workers (UAW) contributed $25. This was the beginning of a long and growing relationship between the UAW and Rustin. Horace Sheffield of the UAW in Detroit was a member of the short-lived Negro American Labor Council set up by A. Philip Randolph and had been an NAACP youth leader. He was important in a black faction within the UAW staff trying to get the union to observe its own nondiscrimination by-laws. It was Sheffield who connected Rustin to the UAW. That very large union, under its president, Walter Reuther, contributed to a variety of liberal organizations and would in time support several of Rustin's projects with major contributions.[6] There were also Jewish organizations, like the Jewish Labor Committee (JLC) and the heavily Jewish International Ladies' Garment Workers Union (ILGWU). The JLC and the ILGWU would also turn out to be long-term backers of Rustin's projects. Individuals also contributed: Jim Peck of the WRL, heir to the Peck and Peck chain of fine ladies' sportswear, and even Adam Clayton Powell. Organization was mainly through churches, with many churches arranging for their own buses for the March.

As with subsequent marches, the organization was tight and detailed. There was a precise time and place for boarding the buses: precise instructions for a "marshall" in each bus, instructions for dress (girls with dark skirts and white blouses, boys with dark suits and white shirts—"if possible"), elementary school children to be accompanied by a parent, at least five adults per bus. Arrangements were made with a Washington hospital to handle any emergencies. Groups were to make their own signs, but only with approved, and strictly nonpartisan, slogans.[7]

As preparations were going forward, Martin Luther King was traveling around the country on a promotional tour for *Stride toward Freedom*. On Saturday, September 20, he was signing books at Blumstein's department store in Harlem. A black woman, later shown to be deranged, stepped into the line directly in front of King. She asked whether he was Martin Luther King, and when he nodded, she stabbed him in the chest with a letter opener. King was rushed to Harlem Hospital, was operated on, and was soon out of danger, but it had been a near thing! He would have to recuperate in the hospital for two weeks, then at home for several months.[8]

Would this tragedy mean that the Youth March for Integrated Schools should be called off? King was to have been one of the main speakers and perhaps the greatest attraction for participants. The march organizers decided that the march should go on but be delayed until October 25. Randolph's form letter to supporters announcing this delay betrayed a worry of the coordinators that the call for the march was having only a lukewarm response. Perhaps King's brush with death could increase enthusiasm.

"The attack on Reverend Martin Luther King Jr., beloved leader of the integration struggle, has added a new dimension of importance to the Youth March for Integrated Schools," wrote Randolph. "As a constructive expression of sympathy for him, many groups are planning to enlarge their participation in the March. To give the opportunity for the fullest participation of all and to increase its effectiveness, the March Committee announces the postponement of the date to Saturday, October 25, 1958."[9]

The march did take place on that date. The keynote speech was given by Randolph. Coretta Scott King read her husband's speech, while he remained at home in Montgomery. Harry Belafonte, Roy Wilkins, and Jackie Robinson spoke. But there could be no denying that the crowd was less than what had been hoped for: perhaps six or seven thousand or so from out of town, joined by a couple of thousand from Washington. A preselected delegation of five white and six black young people was to go to the White House and present a statement to President Eisenhower. The five white members were all from the South. All but one were students in the North. Five of the six Negro members were veterans, sometimes bloodied veterans, of the integration struggle. Minniejean Brown was one of the original Little Rock nine, who had been driven out of the school and was now at the progressive New Lincoln School in New York. Paula Martin was the eleven-year-old on whose behalf a suit against Norfolk, Virginia, had resulted in a court order to integrate that city. Norman Braileu and Leon Thompson were two of the first Negro students to attend an integrated school in Baltimore. Fred Moore had led a student strike at North Carolina State in defense of the NAACP, been expelled, and was, at the time of the march, a student at Howard. Offie Wortyham, leader of the Peekskill Youth Council, was the only northerner.

Randolph had written the president several weeks before, informing him of the planned delegation, but had received no reply. The delegation, led by Harry Belafonte, went to the White House, hoping to present the president with a statement asking for, among other things, "an explicit moral as well as legal commitment of the full resources of the Federal Government to the objective of achieving orderly, effective and speedy integration of the schools." When they got there, they were met not by the president—that was too much to hope for—not by an aide or indeed anyone but the guard at the entrance. Bayard later said that they weren't even permitted to slip the statement under the gate—true symbolically but not actually. They left the statement with the guard. The delegation felt totally rebuffed and returned to the crowd in front of the Lincoln Memorial.

"Although he didn't receive us, or one of his officials," Belafonte told the cheering crowd, "there are millions of people in Asia, Africa and Europe who will be fully aware of his behavior to the group this afternoon."[10]

The president did not respond to the march, but he did in fact respond to the issue, or at least one narrow part of it. In July 1958, Eisenhower, together with Attorney General William Rogers, met with Randolph, Wilkins, King, and Lester B. Granger of the National Urban League. Randolph did most of the talking for the delegation, and the conversation centered on a stay that the district court in Arkansas had granted to the Little Rock schools, allowing a two-and-a-half-year delay in starting integration. Eisenhower listened "with deep attention," in the words of E. Frederic Morrow, Eisenhower's black staff member. The meeting was scheduled for thirty minutes and actually lasted an hour. But there is no evidence that the Youth March had any influence.[11] Later that year, the Supreme Court vacated the stay and insisted on the immediate start of school integration.

The whole purpose of the Youth March, however, was to arouse public opinion, and there was no aroused public. Certainly the participants felt they had done something significant, but in any larger sense the march must be judged a failure. The crowd was too small, the spiritual inspiration was not there, the media had not noticed, the political leaders had not noticed. But perhaps with more time to organize and a bigger turnout, there would be more notice.

The same group of people began to work on a second Youth March for Integrated Schools. It all seemed part of the same effort. The same people, the same office, the same goal. The suppers at exotic restaurants, going together to bars after work, all that resumed. There was also time to recruit support from far corners of the country. Early in

1959, Bayard went out to Chicago and there made an inspiring speech to the Young Peoples Socialist League at the university. A graduate student in sociology, just out of the army, heard him. "I'd never heard anybody talk like that, about social change and civil rights," remembered Norman Hill. Then Bayard took Hill to meet A. Philip Randolph, which awed the young Hill, and Rustin and Randolph talked about the first Youth March and the next one they were organizing.

"What can I do to help?" asked Norman Hill.

"Organize Chicago," answered Rustin.

Hill had never done anything like that before, but he was in touch with a dissident group of the Chicago NAACP, those who opposed the political machine of Mayor Richard Daley, and he was in touch with various labor unions. The leader of the anti-Daley faction of the NAACP was also an official of the local United Auto Workers. There was already a close connection between the incipient civil rights movement and the United Packinghouse Workers. So Norman Hill was able to build on his associations with socialist students, the NAACP, and the labor movement. Hill did what Bayard had asked: he organized Chicago. There were rallies and speeches and solicitations. Hill ended up sending eight busloads from Chicago to the second march, April 18, 1959: church groups, union groups, students, activists from the NAACP.

Norman Hill was a friend and close associate of Bayard Rustin's from then on. Hill dropped out of graduate school, and soon he and his wife, Velma, moved to New York and joined the Congress of Racial Equality. It was not long before he became program director. Eventually Hill left CORE, under strained circumstances, and first worked as deputy to Rustin at the A. Philip Randolph Institute and then succeeded Rustin as director. The association started with the second Youth March.

This second Youth March was different. It was held on April 18, 1959. This time more than three hundred buses rolled into Washington, half of them from outside New York, and some participants flew in from as far away as California. This meant that more people came to the march from outside New York than the total number of people who had come to the first Youth March from anywhere. There were some twenty-six thousand at this march. Harry Belafonte and Jackie Robinson were cheered. Tom Mboya of Kenya, chairman of the All Africa People's Conference, received a standing ovation. Martin Luther King, just back from a visit to India, spoke in person: "As I stand here and look out upon the thousands of colored faces and the thousands of white faces, intermingled like the waters of a river, I see only one face—the face of the future."

King told the young people that they would soon be participating in government by voting. The white young people would have no difficulty voting, but for black southerners, denial of the vote was only one of the many attempts at degradation. But things were changing, he said.

> The southern Negro is learning to transform his degradation into resistance. Non-violent resistance. And by so doing he is not only achieving his dignity as a human being, he is helping to advance democracy in the South. This is why my colleagues and I in the Southern Leadership Conference are giving our major attention to the campaign to increase the registration of Negro voters in the South to 3 million. Do you realize what would happen in this country if we were to gain 3 million southern Negro votes? We could change the composition of Congress.[12]

The march was ostensibly to support school integration, but King, in emphasizing the vote, made clear that a broader integration effort was at stake. Did King consciously leave the word "Christian" out of the title of his organization, in view of the large Jewish support for the march?

This time a delegation of the marchers was received in the White House—not by the president, who was in Augusta, Georgia, but by Gerald P. Morgan, deputy assistant to the president, and by presidential aide E. Frederick Morrow, the only black member of Eisenhower's White House staff. Morgan accepted their statement and answered them with soothing words: "The President is just as anxious as you are to see an America where discrimination does not exist. To reach this goal we have a long way to travel, but in the past six years, we have also come a long way." Morgan went on to say that much of the progress had been made under Eisenhower's leadership but that the president would not be satisfied "until the last vestige of discrimination has disappeared."[13]

There was no point arguing with a deputy assistant who was just telling people what they wanted to hear, but at least the existence of the march had been recognized. The delegation returned to the march reporting at least some progress. A cartoon in the *Baltimore Afro-American* showed a cowering Congress under a sign that said "1958, 7,500. 1959, 26,000. 1960?." "We'll be back," shouted the crowd again and again.

Bayard Rustin had kept himself in the background at the first march, but in April he jubilantly told the crowd, to supportive cheers,

> We came with 10,000 in October and we didn't get inside the White House.
>
> We have more than doubled our forces and this time we received an audience, but not with Eisenhower.
>
> When we come back with 50,000, I promise you, the President will be in Washington. And when we bring 100,000, Congress will sit in special session.[14]

Rustin's prediction was not that far wrong. When, in 1963, more than 250,000 people showed up for the great march, a different president and a Congress not that different did indeed listen.

Black newspapers covered the Youth March. The *Amsterdam News* ran an editorial titled "The Triumphant March," which mentioned the names of the prominent leaders, but not Rustin or Levison, and claimed thirty thousand participants. As far as the white press, there was a story in the *Washington Star*, but once again the national media did not notice. It is possible to say the event got into the halls of Congress, but only sort of. On April 20, Elijah Forrester of Georgia inserted into the *Congressional Record* a story about the march from the *Daily Worker* to prove that the march was part of the international Communist conspiracy. He was indignantly answered a month later by Charles Diggs of Michigan, who inserted a speech defending the march and providing materials on sponsors and statements made at the march. The contrast between the two congressmen could not have been more striking. Forrester was born in 1896 and had read for the bar not at law school but in the office of his cousin in Leesburg, Georgia. Diggs, born in 1922, was from a heavily black Detroit district and was one of the few black representatives. Their speeches were inserted in the *Record*, however, not actually delivered.

Clearly there was progress, but more would be needed to put the civil rights movement at the top of America's political agenda.

9

Serving Two

Masters

Bayard Rustin's actual job for the period of the Youth Marches was as an editor of *Liberation* and a member first of the staff and then of the executive committee of the War Resisters League. The WRL was happy to "lend" him from time to time to the civil rights movement, but the league, or at least A. J. Muste, felt that it was always a loan and that Bayard had an ongoing responsibility to the international peace movement. Bayard's other mentor, A. Philip Randolph, could see his value to the peace movement, but for Randolph action for racial justice was far more pressing. During the years between 1959 and 1963, Rustin tried to satisfy both mentors. He was often out of the country on various projects for international pacifism, but this work was increasingly interrupted for civil rights activities. After late 1962 or early 1963, the civil rights activity pretty much pushed international pacifism aside.

A. J. had an irrepressible hope that somewhere, somehow, NVDA would find a locus or an issue that would galvanize the world and make people see that violence must be banished from God's earth. Surely nuclear arms would be able to terrify humankind into good sense, he thought, if anything could. And perhaps the recently free or soon-to-be free countries of sub-Saharan Africa could lead the world to what for A. J. was a self-evident conclusion.

In early October 1959, Bill Sutherland was on a brief visit to the United States accompanying his boss, the finance minister of Ghana. He reported to the WRL executive committee that a group of English pacifists planned to leave London in a few days for Ghana, and from Accra, with the full approval of the Ghanian government, to march across West Africa and the Sahara to protest French nuclear testing there. He requested that the American branch of the WRL lend its support, by which he meant Bayard. Here, just maybe, was the campaign for which the WRL was looking. The executive committee agreed that Rustin should participate in what was soon known as "the Sahara Project." Within two weeks he was in Accra, first attending an All Africa Trades Union Congress, then on to peace work.[1]

After he had been in Africa a few weeks, his friends in the civil rights movement began to get impatient. They, that is, A. Philip Randolph, Stanley Levison, and Tom Kahn, converged on A. J. and asked that Bayard come back to the United States. The result of this conversation was an official-sounding telegram to Rustin saying that the group could not agree. Randolph felt the struggle at home needed him, while A. J. argued that the Sahara Project had worldwide implications. Tom Kahn put it more bluntly in a private letter: "COME HOME YOU SON-OF-A-BITCH OR I'LL NEVER TALK TO YOU AGAIN (not really, but I hope I've made my position clear.)."[2]

Rustin stayed in Africa another month, leading the detailed organizing of the Sahara Project: arranging trucks, gasoline, food. A. J. came to Accra to witness the departure of the team on December 6: eleven Ghanians, two other Africans, one person from France, three Englishmen, and Sutherland and Rustin from the United States. "As daylight came," wrote Muste in *Liberation*, "the two landrovers (British version of jeeps), the truck to carry water, gasoline and food, and an extra jeep left the bungalows belonging to the Ghana government, in which the Team members from abroad had been housed for some weeks. Ghanians walking the roads waved to the caravan. Everybody in this city knows about the Team." Muste called the project "the most significant in the series of direct-action civil-disobedience projects" in recent years.

It took the team three days to reach the border between Ghana and Upper Volta (now Burkina Faso), singing their songs and welcomed at each stop, according to Muste, by enthusiastic crowds. Rustin recalled that it was "such wild country that even the Ghanians didn't know where their country left off and Upper Volta began."

Each morning, they went to the baker in whatever village was nearby to buy a kind of breakfast roll that was common in that part of the continent, something like a doughnut without a hole. One morning they came back with rolls that "were light as a feather." "'Uh huh,' said one of the caravan, 'we are now in French territory.' Because the ones that the British made were just like British cooking—like rocks!"

Meanwhile, the French authorities in Upper Volta had discovered where the team was. The next morning its members were surrounded, arrested, and dumped back across the Ghanian border, still some seven or eight hundred miles from their goal. At this point Bayard returned home, but a select group of seven, including Bill Sutherland, tried again, on a series of byways they were told were used by smugglers. They got caught again and again were transported back to the Ghanian border. With that, the "most significant direct-action" against nuclear testing ended—brave people following their moral principles with unlimited energy and in some danger but ultimately without effect. The French exploded a dozen nuclear devices. Atmospheric nuclear testing was eventually ended not because of pacifist demonstration but because the leaders of the nuclear powers became convinced of the dangers of radiation. After the Sahara Project, an international conference on NVDA was held in Accra. Bayard did not attend, although Ralph Abernathy did. There was talk of setting up some sort of training school in Ghana for nonviolent direct action, but nothing came of that either.[3]

Back in Alabama, Martin Luther King had been arrested on patently phony charges of evading Alabama state income taxes. In early March 1960, Rustin, as executive director and with Randolph as titular head, organized the "Committee to Defend Martin Luther King." The committee worked out of Randolph's office, and its task was to raise money. Rustin solicited the pastors of the churches where King had spoken over the last few years and well-known liberals like Corliss Lamont. The greatest single source of funds, however, was a concert by Harry Belafonte in Los Angeles, which raised eighty-five hundred dollars for the cause, some 10 percent of the total amount of money raised by the committee.[4]

A young math teacher at the private Horace Mann School had been inspired by the sit-ins. During spring break at Horace Mann,

Bob Moses went down to Hampton, Virginia, and joined the picket lines there. He heard that SCLC was setting up a New York Office, and he asked Wyatt T. Walker of SCLC whom he should contact. Walker gave Moses Bayard Rustin's name, and when Moses got back to New York, he attended an organizational meeting of the Committee to Defend Martin Luther King and volunteered to help. This was not the first time Moses had met Rustin. Back in 1953, Moses had turned eighteen and decided to register as a conscientious objector with the Selective Service System. At the suggestion of a Quaker professor at Hamilton College, he had gone to see Bayard about the philosophical complexities and legal process. He walked into Bayard's apartment on Mott Street and was astounded to find a black man speaking with an English accent. "I had never heard a black man speaking with an English accent. I thought it was way out there." He eventually received not a CO status but a student deferment, which was good enough.

By April 1960, the "Committee to Defend Martin Luther King" had added "and the Struggle for Freedom in the South" to its name. That committee, by April, had become essentially a New York branch of SCLC. Besides aiding the defense of King, it was to support the pursuit of school integration and voting rights under another compromise Civil Rights Act, this one signed in May 1960.[5] In May, the committee ran a celebration in honor of the anniversary of *Brown v. Board of Education*, at the 369th Armory, in Harlem at 142nd Street and Fifth Avenue. As it happened, Moses' father had been caretaker there for decades and had taken his son all over the building. So Moses knew every nook and cranny and could be a big help. Harry Belafonte was to be the major draw at that event, too, and Moses remembers that the evening before the celebration, when everything that could be done had been done, the staff relaxed backstage and Rustin sang for Belafonte. After the event, Moses said he wanted to work with SCLC in Montgomery. Bayard said no, it was Atlanta, and wrote a letter to King saying that Moses was coming. So Moses went down to Atlanta, met Ella Baker, toured the South, and joined the students in what was becoming an organization separate from SCLC, the Student Nonviolent Coordinating Committee.[6]

At about the same time, another unknown young person came

to see Bayard and offer her help. Maya Angelou, not well known for nearly another decade, had been uplifted by a speech Martin Luther King gave at a Harlem church. At the time, she thought of herself as primarily a singer, and she and Godfrey Cambridge, also an unknown who would become a famous comedian, decided they could put on some sort of a show to raise money. She had heard of Bayard Rustin, knew he had led demonstrations against racism in the 1940s and had been to India. She was nervous going to see such an important personage and had a speech rehearsed. Unfortunately he was out of the office, and the speech did not quite fit Stanley Levison, who greeted her. She stammered through the parts that were relevant, and soon Bayard came in. Angelou, like Moses, was struck by the British accent. He gave cautious approval to the idea and a contact at the Village Gate nightclub. Within two weeks the "Cabaret for Freedom" was playing there, as a special Sunday matinee, and according to Angelou, to packed houses.[7]

King's indictment in Alabama was so ludicrous that he was acquitted in early June by an all-white Alabama jury. Almost immediately after King's acquittal, Randolph, again with Rustin as chief administrator, announced a march on the Democratic and Republican conventions. Both King and Roy Wilkins were scheduled to appear before the platform committees of both conventions anyway, but the marches were supposed to bring up to five thousand Negroes, including heroes of the sit-ins, to pressure the parties further. The leaders demanded that both parties unequivocally endorse *Brown v. Board of Education*, that both repudiate the segregationists within their own ranks, that both endorse the spirit and tactics of the sit-ins.[8]

Adam Clayton Powell was furious that there should be a march on the Democratic convention, especially without consulting him, and furious that the upstart King should be more prominent than Powell. The *New York Courier* suggested that Powell was under pressure from southern Democrats, whose support he would need to become chairman of the House Labor and Education Committee, to squash the march.[9] Even Powell could not attack Randolph, however. That man was indifferent to personal attacks and had such prestige that the attacker would be diminished by the very act of attacking. King might be vulnerable, however, not directly, but through Bayard

Rustin. Accordingly, on June 25, Powell claimed that "certain Negro leaders are captives of behind the scenes interests." King had been "under undue influence ever since Bayard Rustin of the Fellowship of Reconciliation went to Alabama to help with the bus boycott."

Rustin could have expected that King, who was on a trip to Brazil at that moment but was kept informed of events in North America, would wave aside Powell's accusations and issue a vigorous statement in support of Bayard. Three years later, when Rustin was attacked by Strom Thurmond, A. Philip Randolph would demonstrate what such a statement might look like. In 1960, however, no such statement from King was forthcoming. King, rather than talking to Bayard personally, delegated a group of ministers to suggest to Rustin that he really ought to leave. "And that's the only time Martin really pissed me off," Rustin said later. "He didn't have the courage to come to me." Several years later, King, talking about the incident, said, "We had to let him go." It was not Powell threatening to expose a nonexistent relationship between King and Rustin, said King, but Rustin's homosexuality. "When he drinks," said King in a telephone call to Clarence Jones, "he would approach these students . . . and there was something of a reflection on me."[10] The question of homosexuality was simply one that King was too embarrassed to talk about.[11] Bayard was not without ego, but he did not seek glory by closeness to King, as so many others did. He retained enough of the Quaker modesty to keep himself out of the limelight, if that would serve the cause for which he was working. To avoid making problems for Martin Luther King—as he had in Montgomery during the boycott—he resigned as special assistant to King and as head of the SCLC New York office. In his statement of resignation, Rustin criticized Powell, recalled his own long service in the civil rights struggle, but added, "I cannot permit a situation to endure in which my relationship to Dr. King and the Southern Christian Leadership Conference is used to confuse and becloud the basic issues confronting the Negro people."

In fact, however, he was deeply depressed by King's action. Years later he told the historian August Meier that King knew about his homosexuality and assured him that he still wanted Bayard as head of the New York office of SCLC. So not only was Bayard depressed, but he felt betrayed. He knew that the civil rights movement was accelerating. He knew that King was finally making NVDA a major force in American society, and he was afraid he was being pushed to one side. He was also distressed that his presumed friend Stanley Levison had not supported him.[12] There were other parts of the civil rights movement besides SCLC, however—the "sit-inners," as they were still called, soon to form SNCC and CORE—so leaving SCLC was not the same as being excluded from the civil rights movement in general. Still, King's action was both somewhat out of character and somewhat inexplicable. Was he that worried about conflict with Adam Clayton Powell?

Ella Baker had mused a couple of years earlier, "How can Bayard not be included in the leadership of discussions of non-violence?"[13] Evidently King agreed, for he continued to talk with or see Rustin frequently. On one occasion, Rustin and King discussed the probability that civil rights activists, including King, probably could expect to spend time in jail. King was very reluctant about going, perhaps frightened of jail. Rustin advised him not to seek jail, like some of the young "militants," but simply to be prepared to accept it as a consequence of doing what he thought was right. Rustin cautioned King over and over again not to do something just to please the young radicals. They would often be distressed at King's caution, but Rustin urged King to make decisions on the basis of the situation SCLC faced, not on the basis of satisfying the more radical members. Rustin's constant urging that "we have to be sensible" was a foretaste of more open splits in 1964 and later.[14] Eventually King established what was called the "Research Committee," a group of people in New York who might constitute a point of vulnerability for King but who King wanted as advisers. The committee was an informal group, with somewhat shifting membership, not all of whom were always enthusiastic about one another, but it always included Stanley Levison and Harry Wachtel, New York lawyers; Clarence Jones, publisher of the *Amsterdam News;* and Rustin. King was a person who would ultimately make his own decisions, but he wanted first to consult with people he trusted. He was constantly on the phone with this Research Committee, as FBI phone taps show.[15]

There were only a few days until the Democratic Party convention, and no one expected anything from the Republicans anyway, so there was no point in having Bayard resign from the March on the Conventions Committee. Nothing like the five thousand marchers King and Randolph said they hoped for showed up. A few did march, and a picture, but no story, appeared in the *New York Times* on July 14. The Democrats adopted such a strong civil rights plank that the southerners filed a dissenting minority report. But there does not seem to have been any relationship between the marchers and the platform positions.

What was clear was that the civil rights movement was changing beyond the ability of any governmental action or the established civil rights leaders, even Martin Luther King, to control. There had been sit-ins before, but the one at the Greensboro, North Carolina, Woolworth's in February 1960 started a wave of student protests and white resistance like nothing since the *Brown* decision. Most of the students at North Carolina A&T, and most of those from Fisk or Vanderbilt University who formed the "Nashville Movement," did not know much about the philosophy of NVDA. Some of the leaders had heard Rustin at a meeting in Atlanta during the summer of 1959, but most had not heard the names A. J. Muste or Bayard Rustin. It was James Lawson who was more important in bringing the message to Nashville. NVDA had swirled into the center of the movement in ways that the longtime prophetic minority from FOR hoped but did not anticipate.[16]

The four students who began the sit-ins in Greensboro may not have heard of Rustin, but the founders, and the founding mother, of the Student Nonviolent Coordinating Committee, had. Ella Baker, during Easter vacation of 1960, called a group of young activists to a meeting at Shaw University in Raleigh, North Carolina, to form some sort of youth branch of the movement. King at first thought they might become an offshoot of SCLC, but Baker urged the young people not to be a branch of anything but to form their own organization. The result was the Student Nonviolent Coordinating Committee. At that initial meeting, the students adopted a statement of principles that began, "We affirm the philosophical or religious ideal of nonviolence."[17]

Rustin was not at that Easter meeting, but, as special assistant to

King, he helped raise the money that made it possible. He raised money also for a more inclusive meeting that fall in Atlanta. He was to be one of the speakers at that "General Conference," where there was deep discussion of the philosophy and practice of NVDA. Since he had by then resigned from SCLC, he was identified in the program as the executive secretary of the War Resisters League. At the last moment one of the main sources of funds for the conference objected to a person who was a former Communist and a homosexual. There were long discussions that ended with Rustin being sent a telegram disinviting him. SNCC was struggling to be born and not concerned with civil liberties issues. If there was a choice between funds for the conference and Bayard Rustin, Rustin had to go. Jane Stembridge, a white southerner who was in many ways the organizational backbone of the emerging SNCC, argued heatedly against the decision and resigned in protest. Who had done the deed is unclear, but there were people in the central office of the AFL-CIO who did not like Rustin, and probably it was an informal telephone call from one of them, rather than a formal decision, that was the source of the disinvitation. The big attraction at the conference was, of course, King, who still hoped that SNCC might be a youth branch of SCLC. After the General Conference, SNCC participated in a get-out-the-vote drive for the 1960 election. Bayard was not exiled for long. In subsequent years he was active in a variety of SNCC meetings and projects.[18]

As the national presidential election approached, an editorial in *Liberation* in October, perhaps by Bayard, said that neither party was very good on civil rights but that most Negroes would support the Kennedy-Johnson ticket. Whether it was the strong support of the Negro press, the equivocation of Nixon on civil rights, the well-publicized telephone call by candidate Kennedy to Coretta King, the civil rights plank, or something else entirely, most Negroes did vote Democratic, and the tiny margin of John Kennedy's victory made at least plausible the argument that those votes made the difference. Whether there would be any policy changes at the center of the federal government was, however, unclear.[19]

During the first few months of the presidency of John Kennedy, the civil rights movement was relatively quiescent, but in May 1961, CORE set out on what was explicitly a revival of the Journey of Reconciliation. This was the Freedom Ride, and soon the newspapers and television screen were again filled with news of the movement. The only Freedom Rider who had been on the 1947 Journey of Reconciliation was James Peck. Had NVDA now moved out of the reach of its pioneering generation and been captured by a new generation of pioneers? Would Bayard Rustin, who had done so much to bring NVDA to the civil rights movement, now be left behind as a monument: honored but only as active as the marble Lincoln in the memorial? Possibly so, because soon Rustin was out of the country again on international pacifist campaigns.

Almost immediately after the election, the WRL sent him to India for the meeting of the War Resisters International. Then, after a few months in New York, he was off again, this time to London, to help with a project of the British Committee on Non-Violent Action: a San Francisco–to–Moscow march against nuclear war. He loved London and was there as often as he could arrange it. The march actually took place, and a few marchers got to Moscow, but Bayard himself did not go along. In early May, he went from London to Dar es Salaam in the newly independent Tanzania (formerly Tanganyika). "I went to Africa," Bayard later recalled, "for the same reason I went to Montgomery, Alabama after the bus protest began, because I saw this as an opportunity not only to help black people get their independence, but a way for me to justify a method of peaceful change that I think is going to be essential throughout mankind's history."[20]

In Tanzania, he met President Julius Nyerere for the first time and developed a close working relationship with the president of the new country. Rustin was trying to establish some sort of training center for nonviolent action, for the WRL still saw a great potential for black Africa as a place where nonviolence could catch fire. Kenneth Kaunda and Nyerere had both written and spoken out for nonviolent social change. Nyerere, for example, had written, "Colonialism is an intolerable humiliation to us. We shall wage a relentlessly determined battle against it until we are free. We shall use no violence. We shall stoop to no dishonest methods." These leaders seemed to be people who could combine a version of African socialism with nonconfrontational tactics. Perhaps the theory and practice of nonviolence, which had had its first victory in one anticolonial struggle, could be widened by another. A. J. and others saw a potential not only for a broader nonviolence but also for combining nonviolence with a more just social system. Robert Gilmore, Rustin's old friend and supporter from the American Friends Service Committee and a man of great wealth, was now on the executive committee of the War Resisters League. He showed some interest in a training center, and Dar es Salaam seemed a logical location. More preliminary work was needed, and so by June, Rustin was back in the United States.

In October 1961 students at Howard University, Courtland Cox, Tom Kahn, Stokely Carmichael, and others, formed a group called Project Awareness to bring prominent people to campus to debate national issues. The Howard student body was, for the most part, made up of well-dressed, well-behaved young members or aspiring members of the black middle class. The first debate was between Bayard Rustin, arguing for integration, and Malcolm X, for separatism. The two debated several times in the early sixties and, though differing fundamentally in social philosophy, seemed to respect each other. The debate at Howard was revealing about Bayard's functioning as a teacher, for after he had spoken for half his allotted time, he told the students, "You hear my view about integration all the time. You never hear the argument about separation. I'm going to give some of my time to Malcolm X to speak." Most of the buttoned-down Howard students had not heard Malcolm or his ideas. They were stunned. His speech was sharp, funny, yet uncompromising.[21] The students did not necessarily change their ideas, but they were exposed to a way of looking at the world that most of them had not taken seriously up to then.

Just before Christmas 1961 Bayard went to Beirut for the founding of another one of those extravagantly named pacifist campaigns: the World Peace Brigade. This was before Beirut descended into civil war. There was a renowned international university there and, in a suburb called Brummana, a Quaker high school that served as the headquarters. A. J. raised most of the money from FOR supporters, but some undoubtedly also came from Robert Gilmore. The founding meeting took place during the school's Christmas vacation of 1961–1962, when students were not there. Fifty-five people attended, more from the United States than any other country, including A. J., Rustin, Robert Gilmore, Norman Hill, and Ann Morrissett. There was a contingent from India, one from Britain, and a few from other European countries, but no one from Africa. Lebanon would not admit Israelis or anyone with an Israeli passport stamp. Bill Sutherland, now divorced from his Ghanian wife and no longer resident in Ghana, was not aware of this restriction. He was in Israel and invited Martin Buber. Buber, however, got furious and said he certainly would not go to a place where Jews were unwelcome. The conferees reluctantly accepted the Lebanese limitation but resolved never again to meet where there were such restrictions. The founding conference established three divisions: Europe, Asia, and Africa. They knew they wanted to make a great gesture against war, but what that gesture should be was uncertain.[22]

As the World Peace Brigade fumbled at its very founding, it was invited to be an observing organization at a meeting in Adis Ababa, Ethiopia, of the Pan African Freedom Movement East Central Africa (PAFMECA) to be held in February 1962. The observers from the World Peace Brigade were Bill Sutherland; Bayard Rustin, back in Africa again after briefly returning to New York and London; Michael Scott, who had been one of the British originators of the Sahara Project; and Siddharaj Dhadda, a representative from India. Nelson Mandela sneaked out of South Africa and was also there.

While parts of the independence movement had decided on "armed struggle," as the African National Congress had after the Sharpeville Massacre in March 1960, the question was still open at that February meeting. The delegates from Ghana and Egypt, although neither was from East Central Africa, argued the necessity for violence. The World Peace Brigade, Kenneth Kaunda, and Julius Nyerere argued for nonviolence. The final resolution simply said that independence should be achieved "by various means." At that meeting, the African division of the World Peace Brigade became incorporated into the African organization, renamed African Freedom Action, with headquarters in Dar es Salaam, Tanzania. African Freedom Action included African leaders like Kenneth Kaunda and Julius Nyerere and had as its immediate goal elections in Northern Rhodesia, the future Zambia. The African Freedom Action part was to be a great march of thousands on the Northern Rhodesian border, and even across it if possible. Bayard Rustin went all over Tanzania speaking for the movement and organizing the march. On February 20 he met with Kaunda, Nyerere, and ministers of the new government who agreed to the march and the establishment of a nonviolent training center in Dar es Salaam. Thus Bayard became more than an observer. He was now a participant in the East African independence movement. Whether he gained a deep understanding of the politics of that part of the world would later become a controversial issue. The great plans, or at least hopes, came to nothing. The march never happened. There were a great many pressures on the British, and for reasons having nothing to do with the World Peace Brigade, they agreed on a constitution for Northern Rhodesia and elections to be held in the fall of 1962. It was clear that the elections would give a majority to Africans and would mean that Northern Rhodesia would become Zambia. African Freedom Action faded away.[23]

The other project of the World Peace Brigade was a training center for nonviolence in Dar Es Salaam. It fared no better than the march. It could gather neither funds nor volunteers and, after only a few months' struggle to be born, was abandoned.[24] The only lasting legacy was that Bayard got his old friend Bill Sutherland a job with the new government of Tanzania. Sutherland, at this writing (1998), lives in Dar still.

Rustin in future years would occasionally go to a pacifist meeting. He continued until 1965 as executive secretary of the War Resisters League and on the editorial board of *Liberation*. He did not realize it at the time, but these campaigns in Africa in 1961 and 1962 were the last of his serious pacifist actions. It was clear to him that these actions were simply not effective. Exactly when he stopped being a pacifist is hard to say, but certainly by 1966 his old pacifist friends realized that they had lost him for their cause. There might eventually be some potential for NVDA in East Africa, but Rustin clearly felt that the civil rights movement was not merely potential.

It was actual, and it was on the move. For the next years Rustin put his efforts increasingly into the civil rights movement. In mid-1962, he returned to the United States, nominally to *Liberation* but soon to work for his old mentor A. Philip Randolph and on that project that would lead to his and Randolph's picture on the cover of *Life* and make Bayard Rustin a name of national significance.

10

Convergence

Ralph DiGia, one of Bayard's old friends from the War Resisters League, remembers walking into the four-story headquarters of the March on Washington in July 1963. There was Bayard, in the midst of seeming chaos: phones ringing, people running in and out, and Bayard making decisions, one after another, with almost machine-gun rapidity. Someone would run in with a question about transportation, and Bayard would answer, another would ask about placards, and Bayard would answer, about jurisdictional disputes in the organization, and Bayard would decide. "I don't know if it was right or wrong," recalled DiGia, "but he wouldn't hesitate. . . . He was a whirlwind up there." And in fact, Rustin loved it. He was no longer in the little offices of the WRL, with only two or three other people, where each decision would be agonized over, from a moral, political, religious, and who knows what point of view. Here things were happening thick and fast. "It was bedlam," Bayard recalled. The results were soon going to be clear, not at some distant date in a millennial future but on August 28, 1963: the movement of a great many people into and out of Washington. And the purpose was clear: to put pressure on Congress to pass President John F. Kennedy's civil rights bill and to overcome any attempted filibuster.[1]

What a contrast to the offices DiGia was used to. Here were four floors filled with activity. On the first floor were Bayard and Tom Kahn, on the second the receptionist, the office in charge of volunteers, and another for supplies, mailings, and the physical plant. The third floor was a particular hub of activity: Rachelle Horowitz and Eleanor Holmes. Horowitz, on the organizational chart, was in charge of transportation, but in fact she did a bit of everything: contact with community groups, helping with the newsletter and manuals. There were also Roy Tempero, for liaison with labor, Courtland Cox from SNCC for liaison with the South, and his assistant, Joyce Ladner. There was Norman Hill, in charge of fieldwork, and two bookkeepers. The fourth floor, at this early point in the process, was for fundraising and press relations, but those offices soon moved to the first floor, and the fourth floor became what was known as "the police station," where Bayard trained New York black policemen from a black police fraternal organization called the Guardians in techniques of nonviolent crowd control.[2]

This was the headquarters of the March on Washington of 1963, in some ways the high point of Bayard Rustin's life. By 1963, he was already well known, but only among a tiny fringe of American society: those people who would recognize the initials NVDA. After the march, he, along with A. Philip Randolph, would have his picture on the cover of *Life*. He would be interviewed in newspapers, and at least the outlines of his life would be widely reported. He moved from being a fringe idealist to being a national figure. This change in reputation meant as well a change in role and tactics.

Yet it all started out as something quite different. Back in December 1962, A. Philip Randolph began thinking about some sort of demonstrations on Negro unemployment. Surprisingly, the Bureau of Labor Statistics did not keep figures on unemployment by race, but the New York office of the BLS estimated that the Negro and Puerto Rican figures were from two and a half to five times the citywide rate.[3] Randolph did not need the figures to know the reality. Rustin was chatting with him in his office and suggested that maybe a march on Washington would be a good idea. Rustin and Tom Kahn prepared a memo for Randolph, and he circulated the idea to other civil rights leaders. He received encouraging replies from organizations without any financial resources, CORE, SNCC, and SCLC, and a lukewarm response from the NAACP and the National Urban League. He was already thinking that Bayard would lead the march, because he asked the War Resisters League to "release" him. A. J. Muste replied that they had reluctantly concluded that they could not, but of course ultimately Bayard went where he wanted to go.[4] On April 23, Randolph called a meeting in his office of the Negro

American Labor Council, an organization that he had formed and of which he was president. Here he repeated his call for an "Emancipation March for Jobs." The NAACP representative who was supposed to be there did not show up, and there was no one from the National Urban League. Randolph insisted that he was determined to go ahead with the march anyway and appointed Norman Hill to "begin immediately to set up a conference with community leaders, including all ministers in New York." Randolph himself would send letters to social, fraternal, and religious groups. The call for the march was from only the Negro American Labor Council, the Southern Christian Leadership Conference, the Student Nonviolent Coordinating Committee, and the Congress of Racial Equality. The NAACP and the Urban League were conspicuous by their absence. Cleveland Robinson of the Retail Clerks Union was to be chairman. Thus the genesis of the 1963 March on Washington was economic, and, though support from whites was obviously welcome, it was essentially a black, northern, labor effort.[5] The story of the next three months is how this pinpointed effort was transformed into that great March on Washington.

The transformation came from the South. The sit-ins, CORE, and SNCC had renewed momentum in the movement, or maybe even changed its nature. Then in April Martin Luther King and SCLC became part of the renewal and change, with Project C (for Confrontation) in Birmingham. There were children marching and being battered by water cannons. There was "Bull" Connor and his policemen. There was King's "Letter from a Birmingham Jail." At the end there was victory, at least as the demonstrators defined it. The most blatant forms of segregation were ended in Birmingham. "Our campaign in Birmingham," wrote Andrew Young, looking back, "proved that a sustained and comprehensive non-violent, direct-action effort could bring about change under the most difficult circumstances."[6]

The sense of victory in Birmingham brought exhilaration to King and SCLC. James Bevel wanted to continue the "Children's Crusade" in Birmingham by young people *walking* to Washington, a distance of more than seven hundred miles.[7] Clarence Jones, King's lawyer, on May 15 and again some three weeks later, suggested to Randolph that the march the Negro American Labor Council had been planning for the fall could be moved up and broadened in scope. Randolph, realizing that any march devoted only to unemployment might be eclipsed by a larger demonstration, was willing to consider the idea. The momentum for a more comprehensive march gathered steam over the next few days, and on June 9, in a conference call with Stanley Levison and others of his advisers, King almost took it for granted that there would be a march, but he wanted advice on what form it would take and whether it should be centered on the president or the Congress. King (in the indirect discourse of the FBI telephone tap transcripts) said that "Phil should come around and let them have this one big thing for Civil Rights which would include the three points that they have been going for: 1. Desegregation of public facilities, 2. Jobs and 3. To vote." The conversation compared this march to the Prayer Pilgrimage, so that the thought of some sort of involvement of Bayard Rustin was not far from anyone's mind.

Then there was President Kennedy's response to Birmingham. He had been supportive of changes in race relations, at least verbally, at the same time holding back or trying to mollify southern white supporters. The ambivalence in deed continued, but the nature of his words changed, and when a president changes words, the words are themselves deeds. On June 11, that is, two days after the conference call between King, Levison, and the other close advisers, Kennedy introduced what was to become the Equal Accommodations Act of 1964, essentially ending legally sanctioned segregation throughout the nation. His words brought the relationship between the administration and the movement leaders to a new plane. We are faced with a moral issue, he said, "as old as the scriptures and . . . as clear as the Constitution." How different from Eisenhower's commitment to merely "enforcing the law of the land," or the need to touch hearts and minds before the law should be changed. Now there was a moral commitment from the administration. King was ecstatic. He and Levison were convinced that the president could no longer be put in the position of being the enemy. He was on the side of the movement. The enemies were in Congress.[8]

The next day, June 12, 1963, Medgar Evers was assassinated in Jackson, Mississippi.

King may have had some initial hesitation about the march, but pushed by Fred Shuttlesworth, he became an enthusiastic supporter. With that support and Randolph already in motion, the other leaders of major organizations were drawn in inexorably. During that conference call on June 9, the King group had considered, probably only in jest, announcing the march at a news conference without telling Roy Wilkins, to force him to agree. That did not prove necessary, and so on July 2, at a luncheon at the Roosevelt Hotel in New York, the "Big Six"—Randolph, King, John Lewis from SNCC, Whitney Young from the National Urban League, James Farmer, and Roy Wilkins—met. Dorothy Height of the National Council of Negro Women was not at that meeting. The NCNW was listed in the *New York Times* article as one of the original sponsoring organizations. The stationery of the march, however, did not list it. The addition of the National Council of Negro Women, as an afterthought, was typical of the whole march effort. It was as though the organizers came to the thought "Oh, we mustn't neglect the women." But they were not included as fellow planners or, as it turned out, as speakers at the march itself.

According to John Lewis, he, King, Farmer, and of course Randolph assumed that Bayard would be director of the march. Rustin had the ability, the experience, and the time. He came to the meeting as Randolph's deputy. Norman Hill was there as Farmer's program director. Fred Shuttlesworth, an important figure in his own right, was there as a fellow member with King of SCLC.

Wilkins, perhaps anticipating what was to come, commanded all but the six principals to wait in the hall. He went around the room, "You stay. You go," so the meeting would be just of leaders. When that was settled, Wilkins expressed skepticism that, as James Farmer recalled, a march would be the best way to help Kennedy's bill but said that he'd go along if the others wanted it. Randolph, who had wanted the march for more than twenty years, insisted that this was the time and suggested that Rustin should head it. Roy Wilkins, in John Lewis's words, "went into a rage." He went through Bayard's vulnerabilities: draft resister, former Communist, conviction for homosexual activity.[9] The march should not be burdened with all that. James Farmer's recollection was that Whitney Young also opposed Rustin. Obviously "Phil" should lead it, Wilkins said. Randolph, after all, was "Mr. March." Randolph agreed but said that of course he would name his own deputy director, which would be Bayard Rustin. A. Philip Randolph had not been intimidated by Franklin Roosevelt or Harry Truman, so Roy Wilkins was not going to move him. Bayard was the person to pull it off. If there was criticism, and there would be, Randolph would know how to meet it.[10]

At that luncheon at the Roosevelt Hotel, then, the Big Six agreed on a march to be held at the end of August. There would be no "Emancipation March Against Negro Unemployment," but so that Randolph's original emphasis should not be completely lost, the march was to be called the "March for Jobs and Freedom." In fact, the "jobs" component was overwhelmed by the need to support the "freedom" component in general and the Kennedy bill in particular. During the course of the next few weeks, the economic aims of the march were further diminished. The original demands for a two-dollar minimum wage and a federal public works program were explicitly dropped.[11] Randolph and Rustin would try to reemphasize economic needs after the march when they came to consider "next steps."

Immediately after lunch, there was a meeting of the larger Leadership Conference on Civil Rights, augmented by representatives from the National Catholic Welfare Conference, the National Council of the Churches of Christ, and the Synagogue Council of America. The march would thus be a demonstration not by civil rights organizations alone but by other groups, too, including whites with a strong commitment to racial equality.

In announcing that the march would favor a civil rights bill "stronger, if possible, than the President's proposal," Roy Wilkins and Martin Luther King "stressed that the Washington demonstration would not involve any 'civil disobedience' or sit-ins in the halls of Congress in case of a filibuster on the bill." There were some CORE members who wanted major disruptions in Washington, and the original proposals, drawn up before the July 2 luncheon by Norman Hill and Bayard, had included the possibility of some direct action, but the idea was rejected. Civil rights activists were accustomed to being labeled Communist, and the publicity for the march made clear that "We expressly reject the aid or participation of totalitarian or subversive groups of all persuasions."[12]

In fact, the march as a whole was very tightly controlled. Rustin planned every detail to avoid a backlash. The records of the march reveal almost as much attention to caution as to impact. According to the march manuals, each bus or car of a train was to have a marshal, identified by an armband. Rustin himself carefully trained several thousand black policemen in crowd control. They were to be unarmed, but their identified presence, it was hoped, would maintain order. Rustin was continually in touch with the Washington police; he made sure that they understood all the arrangements and that the march organizers understood the police. Bayard knew that if there was some sort of counterdemonstration it would come from outside the march itself, so he arranged with the Washington police that white policemen would be stationed around the periphery and on approaches to the city in Virginia and Maryland.[13] That way, whites coming to the city for counterdemonstrations would be arrested by white, not black, policemen. In 1963 and later he was acutely aware— some would say too aware—of the growing national appeal of conservatives. George Wallace and Barry Goldwater would demonstrate that his fears were justified, for both built their appeal mostly or partly on reaction against the civil rights movement.

Bayard was an old hand at marches on Washington. This one would be like the Prayer Pilgrimage and the first and second Youth March for Integrated Schools—but on a different scale of magnitude. Stanley Levison had guessed that they would have to have one hundred thousand marchers to be considered an effective demonstration, and that became their target and their repeatedly announced goal. Subsequent decades of huge marches may make that number look modest, but it was far larger than anything yet seen in Washington. And it all had to be done in under two months.

The organizers found a new headquarters in a brownstone belonging to one of the churches at 170 West 130th Street. The official organization was that Randolph was director, Rustin deputy director, but it was Bayard who ran things for his old mentor. There were six "Founding Chairmen," James Farmer, Martin Luther King, John Lewis, A. Philip Randolph, Roy Wilkins, and Whitney Young. By the middle of August, four others were added to the list: Matthew Ahmann (Catholic), Eugene Carson Blake (Protestant), Joachim Prinz

(Jewish), and Walter Reuther for organized labor, or at least a part of organized labor. The staff would consist of Bayard as deputy director, Tom Kahn as his assistant, some paid typists, and a host of volunteers, but regular volunteers: Rachelle Horowitz, Eleanor Holmes (later Norton), Sandra Feldman, and many others. Volunteers they were, but they would be expected to show up every day, as if for a paying job but for no pay. Norton and Horowitz set up their desks facing each other with a phone between, and when a church leader from one place or an activist from another would ask for one or the other of them, with a question on transportation or other details, they would each answer, playing the part of whomever the caller wanted.

Bayard later recalled working on the march as the high point in his life. He loved it. He always enjoyed younger people and recalled that the enthusiasm of the young people made up for the makeshift facilities: not enough desks, telephones, or typewriters and such. And what a group of young people—many still in college—they were. Many of them went on to influential positions in what might be called the establishment, but always a reform element of the establishment. Sandra Feldman was later head of the American Federation of Teachers. Eleanor Holmes became New York City commissioner on human rights and then member of the House of Representatives from Washington, D.C. Joyce Ladner became a well-known professor of sociology. Courtland Cox, from SNCC, is now (1998) head of the Minority Business division of the Department of Commerce. Tom Kahn had many jobs, but one was foreign policy aide to Lane Kirkland at the AFL-CIO.

The central office of the March on Washington had three main objectives: raise the money, get marchers to come, arrange the hours—and even minutes—in Washington. Bayard was doing all three simultaneously, although Randolph was of particular importance in raising the money.

Funds were needed mostly for the office, for publicity and communication in New York, and for the events and facilities in Washington. For example, the public address system alone cost $16,000 to rent. Each group or individual was supposed to pay their own way to and from the march, but Bayard hoped that there would be enough money to pay transportation costs for some of the unemployed. Initial contributions came from the major civil rights groups: NAACP gave the most, $10,000; SNCC, which essentially had no funds, the least, $500. More money came from labor unions than from the civil rights organizations: $6,500 from the International Ladies' Garment Workers Union, more than $6,000 from the United Auto Workers.[14] The largest single contribution was given by the Archdiocese of Washington, D.C., $15,000. This was clearly not a march merely of civil rights groups. Many people made smaller individual contributions. Harold Stassen gave $100! The total cost was just over $133,000, and receipts as of a little more than a year after the march totaled about $146,000, with a few matters still in dispute. Thus accounts were kept very carefully, under Cleveland Robinson's supervision, so there could be no hint of financial scandal.[15]

Bayard Rustin in later years was criticized for being too close to organized labor. But his experiences were that organized labor had vigorously backed the civil rights movement, with its participation and with hard cash. There was, of course, A. Philip Randolph, but also the Packinghouse Workers support for SCLC, and cash and hard work for the March on Washington from many unions. Rustin's ties to organized labor were not simply a theoretical hangover from days with the party of the proletariat, or influenced by scheming from "Shachtmanites," but based on the realities he had experienced.[16] He did not fully realize the depth of racism within many parts of the labor movement.

Certainly large elements of organized labor opposed racial equality, and many were slow coming to pro–civil rights positions. George Meany and the executive council of the AFL-CIO did not come out in favor of or in opposition to the march, which amounted almost to the latter (although Donald Slaiman reported that Meany later regretted his decision).[17] The building trades particularly, such as electricians and plumbers, had a very closed system that excluded black craftsmen. Their members often walked off projects rather than work with black workers. Yet Bayard, aware of this, was sure that on balance organized labor was a progressive force. The reality was somewhat more ambiguous than he hoped.

As with the Youth Marches, Bayard could write broad goals for

"Manual #1" of the march while also paying attention to the small-est details, like how many buttons had been sold, how many tank trucks with how many drinks of water should be available, how many portable toilets. Portable toilets were, in fact, a big issue. John Lewis recalls that he happened into the march headquarters and heard Bayard say in his broadest English accent, "We *cawn't* have any unregulated pissing in Washington."[18] At first the police wanted the buses to wait somewhere other than where they let off the passengers, but Bayard insisted that they had to stay in one place so that people could find their way back to their bus after the march was over.[19] A list, un-dated but fairly early in the process, headed "Bayard to do" included, for that day, thirty-two tasks:

> Arrange Randolph trip, Unity House, Baltimore, Chicago,
>   August 15
> Do total revision of budget
> Reach Dave Apter
> The Newsletter
> Second Organizing Manual
> Call Rush Stack, the Masons on separate meetings
> Appointment with Reps of CORE, NAACP on unemployed
>   seating
> Rustin letter to 10 top chairmen and advisers re Friday meet-
>   ing agenda
> Brief Wash. police and Jackson on marshall plan
> Clear with Randolph and Cleve on Overton bill
> BR letter to Emma Lazarus people

and the list went on and on.

All in all, the attention to detail was meticulous.

The manuals and all subsequent instructions kept the march under tight discipline. All placards were furnished by or had to be approved by the march committee. They had to contain only a spe-cific list of approved slogans: "We March for Jobs and Freedom," "End Segregation Now." "We Swear This Oath, America Will Be Free," "Catholic, Protestant, Jew, White; In The Struggle for What Is Right," "Fair Employment Makes Free Citizens." Groups could make their own signs that identified the group, but the slogans had to be the approved ones. Rustin wanted to be certain that groups with their own purposes, however worthy, would not dilute the unity of the march. There was a long debate at the leadership level about whether "Home Rule for Washington" was allowed. The compromise was that it was not listed as a goal of the march but it was allowed on placards.

All policy statements had to be made by the central committee, and no one was to schedule television or radio appearances without clearance from Rustin, Kahn, or the volunteer director of publicity, Seymour Posner.[20]

The Kennedy administration at first opposed the march, arguing that it would do more harm than good. Something like a month before the march, convinced that they could not stop it, they tried to capture it. Roy Wilkins came to the office on 130th Street with the message that the president wanted to be one of the speakers. According to Courtland Cox's recollection, Bayard knew right away that they could not have that. If Kennedy spoke, the march would be Kennedy speaking to the people. The march was supposed to be the people speaking to Kennedy—but how do you refuse a president? While the discussion was going on, Bayard excused himself for a few minutes to go the bathroom. When he came back, he announced to Wilkins and the others, "I understand from some Negroes, that if Kennedy comes to the march, they will stone him." He had made that up in just a few minutes on the spot. There was no threat from anyone, but Rustin had contrived to use white fears of Negro violence to raise the specter of security. Wilkins took the message back to the administration, and the request from the White House dissolved.[21]

A dozen days before the march, Randolph received a letter from Anna Arnold Hedgeman, on the board of SCLC and a member of the administrative committee of the March on Washington, pointing out that women were not being recognized. In response, Randolph, or maybe Bayard, suggested to the ten speakers that since they "were all men and since it is imperative that the role of women in the struggle be made clear," important women should be invited to participate. Randolph suggested Rosa Parks, Mrs. Medgar Evers, Mrs. Daisy Bates, Mrs. Gloria Richardson, Mrs. Diane Nash Bevel. "The difficulty of finding a single woman to speak without causing serious problems vis-a-vis other women and woman's groups suggests . . . that the chairman should introduce these women and tell of their role in the struggle and tracing their spiritual ancestry back to Sojourner Truth and Harriet Tubman," that they should be applauded, not speak, and then sit down. The male speakers and Rustin all agreed, and that is in fact what happened. Not one woman spoke from the platform.[22]

Much of the opposition to the march was predictable. The South Carolina congressional delegation was particularly vociferous. Congressman William Jennings Bryan Dorn wrote, "I cannot endorse your mass pressure technique to force through Congress unnecessary Federal legislation. This attempt to force Congress to bow to the demands of the demonstrators is a dangerous precedent and could some day lead to the overthrow of free government and destroy the liberties of our people. Our individual freedom can best be preserved by free local and State government."

Senator Olin Johnston (D-S.C.) was sure that "criminal, fanatical and communistic elements as well as crackpots will move in to take every advantage of this mob." The *New York Herald Tribune* on July 25 editorialized that "The March Should Be Stopped" and two days later that "Crude Tactics Won't Help the Negro." Arthur Krock in his syndicated column deplored, without identifying them, "super-aggressive Negro leaders." Clearly the prospect of thousands of Negroes gathered in one place scared some people. Franklin D. Roosevelt Jr. talked to A. Philip Randolph at a gathering honoring Julius Nyerere in mid-July and expressed serious worry about "trouble and violence," which Randolph assured him would not occur.[23]

And there was outrage at Bayard himself, epitomized in the attack by Senator Strom Thurmond (still Democrat, S.C., although he switched parties later) on the Senate floor on August 13. Obviously on the basis of reports from J. Edgar Hoover, Thurmond went through the litany of calling Rustin a draft dodger, a former communist, and a person without personal morality, by which he meant homosexuality. Rustin himself answered the charges, explaining his Quaker opposition to war, his joining and then leaving the Young Communist League. The most important defense, however, came from

Randolph, a reply that had been drafted by Tom Kahn and Bayard Rustin himself.

> I am sure I speak for the combined Negro leadership in voicing my complete confidence in Bayard Rustin's character, integrity and extraordinary ability.
>
> Twenty-two arrests in the fight for civil rights attest, in my mind, to Mr. Rustin's dedication to high human ideals.
>
> That Mr. Rustin was on one occasion arrested in another connection has long been a matter of public record, and not an object of concealment. There are those who contend that this incident, which took place many years ago, voids or overwhelms Mr. Rustin's ongoing contribution to the struggle for human rights. I hold otherwise. . . .
>
> We are not fooled, however, into believing that these [accusers] are interested in Mr. Rustin. They seek only to discredit the movement.[24]

That was the sort of firm, unambiguous endorsement that Martin Luther King did not give to Rustin in 1960. Now, three years later, Randolph's rocklike support did not make criticism vanish, but Bayard could continue his work without worrying about protecting his back.

And the work continued. Endorsements, money, and the promise of sending people came from dozens of organizations: the Alabama Christian Movement for Human Rights, Catholic Interracial Conference, Ethical Culture Society, Jewish Labor Committee, Presbyterian Interracial Council, Washington, D.C., Civil Liberties Union (which promised to take care of any legal problems at the march), the Medical Committee for Human Rights (which would take care of medical emergencies), the Fellowship of Reconciliation (which arranged a special prayer meeting for clergymen before the march), the Emma Lazarus Foundation of Jewish Women's Clubs, Women's International League for Peace and Freedom, National Federation of Settlements, and dozens of labor unions. Hamish Sinclair, of the Hazard, Kentucky, miners, wrote to Randolph that some of their number would come to the march "provided that they are not the only white workers present." Bayard assured Sinclair that the National Council of Churches would bring forty thousand people, predominately white, and the Catholic groups were committed for ten thousand, so the miners would not feel they stood out in the crowd.[25]

The heavy lifting of getting people to come was done by the major civil rights organizations. Roy Wilkins may have been reluctant about the project to begin with, but once it was under way, it was the NAACP, first among equals, that organized much of the crowd in Washington that day. Brooklyn CORE organized in the New York City area. Norman Hill, still in CORE but soon to leave for Bayard Rustin's new organization, traveled throughout the Midwest. Maurice Dawkins was on the West Coast. Labor unions did quite a bit, as did church groups.

Rachelle Horowitz kept as close a tally as she could on how many people were to come. So many buses were chartered in the New York area that not enough were available for all who wanted to ride.[26] Entire special trains were chartered from some places. Would they reach their one hundred thousand goal? As march day approached, Horowitz began making up daily estimates. Just before the march, she could assure Bayard of only sixty-seven thousand. The actual number might be larger, but how much larger no one could tell.[27] Two days before the march, a few key organizers and Bayard Rustin moved down to Washington.

Rustin could plan the transportation, keeping order, and slogans, but what happened on the speakers' platform would have to depend on the speakers themselves.

Suddenly a controversy erupted. Texts of major speeches, not King's or Randolph's, had been prepared in advance. People in the Kennedy administration objected to some of the anger in John Lewis's speech, and they contacted Patrick Cardinal O'Boyle of Washington, who was to give the invocation. Lewis had earlier shown the speech to Rustin, Horowitz, and Kahn, and they all thought it was wonderful.[28] O'Boyle said that if Lewis delivered the speech as written, he, O'Boyle, would not agree to be on the platform. Lewis planned to say, for instance, that he could not support the administration bill because it was too little and too late. He promised that the civil rights movement would sweep through Georgia like Sherman. But the march was supposed to support the administration bill, and Sherman was hardly a devotee of nonviolence. The night before the march, while Bob Moses and other SNCC members were out picketing the Justice Department, there was a meeting of the "Big Six" (without James Farmer, in prison in Louisiana) chaired by Bayard. They were all of one mind, but it was Randolph who asked Lewis to change the speech. "You couldn't refuse a man like A. Philip Randolph," recalled Lewis in his congressional office some thirty-four years later, and so he agreed. But what should the changes be? The exact alterations were being negotiated, with Tom Kahn doing much of the revising in a little office under the Lincoln Memorial, right up to the moment of the speech. Meanwhile Julian Bond was outside distributing copies of Lewis's original speech. Bayard was in and out of the room. He was simply concerned with holding things together, not the details of what was said.[29]

None of it mattered. Can anyone now remember a word of any speech but Martin Luther King's, and then only a few choice phrases and cadences?

As the controversy about Lewis's speech was going on, people were arriving in Washington. Early on the morning of the march, Bayard was terrified that not enough people would show up. At five in the morning, with only a few thousand there, reporters asked Rustin on the mall what was going to happen. Bayard extracted his pocket watch, then glancing at a yellow pad, which was in fact blank, he announced in his upper-class British accent, "Gentlemen, everything is exactly on [then using the British pronunciation] shedule."[30] Bayard, Horowitz, and Randolph himself, as they heard about traffic jams on the roads into Washington, as they saw the multitudes pouring in on buses and trains, put their anxieties away. Not 100,000 but twice that many, maybe as many as 250,000 people, showed up. It was a beautiful day, clouds in the sky, warm, but not hot for summertime Washington. The crowd surged toward the Washington Monument, where signs were being frantically handed out from large piles around the monument.

I was one of the quarter million people and simply accepted a sign as it was thrust into my hand. It read "We March for Jobs and Freedom," but I had already moved well down the mall before I looked at it because the flow of the crowd was irresistible. I remember being surprised at the "jobs" part. I knew I was marching for "freedom," but "jobs"? I noticed a small black man with an orange-and-red tam-o'-shanter moving along the edge of the crowd, sometimes with, sometimes against the current shouting, "We shall overcome not some day, but *to*day, *to*day." The mood was joyful, courteous, laughing, and orderly. Whites were polite to blacks and blacks to whites.

Bayard could remember the crowds at the Youth Marches. From the Lincoln Memorial, at the most they stretched back to the reflecting pool. Here, when he and Rachelle Horowitz and Sandy Feldman and Tom Kahn looked out from the memorial, they could see the crowd stretching way back along both sides of the pool. There was that mass of white and light-colored shirts, and white and black faces—more black, but many white too.

In fact, the crowd was so large that back in the mass it was hard to see or hear what was going on at the front. "What?" asked people to their neighbor. "Who was that?" When a breeze rustled the tree leaves, even the sixteen-thousand-dollar loud speaker system was not good enough to reach all the listeners. Some people who were there did not really hear "I have a dream today" until the evening news.

There was the entertainment, organized by Harry Belafonte, the introduction of the women, then the speeches.[31] Bayard has been criticized for putting Martin Luther King's speech last, but he knew, as he said, that once King had spoken, the march would be over, which it was. After the "I have a dream" rhythm and after King had received the roars of approval, Randolph read out a pledge that the marchers would dedicate their lives to justice. Those who were paying attention agreed, but people were already moving back toward their buses, and within a little while, the park police were cleaning up the trash.

It was a triumph. It was a triumph for Rustin, who now became a person to write about, photograph, analyze. Andrew Young was sure that the march made civil rights into a national not just a southern issue. The southern civil rights goals, not the economic ones, were now on the national agenda. Martin Luther King moved a step closer to becoming a mythic figure. A. Philip Randolph had finally seen what he had been planning for more than two decades. Rustin was convinced that both President Kennedy and George Meany changed their attitudes toward the civil rights movement because of the march, not so much its fervor but its good order. Bayard said, "It proved that we were capable of being one people."[32] This was Rustin's goal throughout his life: one people. Any sort of "identity politics" or "multiculturalism" was for him anathema. We were one people.

There were stories about the march in newspapers in many other countries. In Ghana, Bayard's co-worker from three years before, Maya Angelou, helped organize a simultaneous march in Accra, where she was then living. As the marchers were about to start, one of the organizers announced that W.E.B. Du Bois, now a Ghanian citizen, had died that night.[33]

The march was a utopian moment, a peaceable kingdom where whites and blacks joined hands and swayed back and forth singing "We Shall Overcome." There were Congregational ministers from New England and black Baptist ministers from Georgia. There were white coal miners from Kentucky and black auto workers from Detroit. Jewish textile workers from Brooklyn were there, and thousands of Negroes from Harlem. There were wealthy employed and poor unemployed, those scarred by experience in the movement, and those participating for the first time. Most of the marchers were fairly young, but there were the elderly, too. All were exalted by their own presence and the presence of one another.

Utopian moments are rare and can serve a purpose. They reveal what might be, in some world as fictitious as Edward Hicks's painting. They can inspire idealists to keep pushing against reality toward that peaceable kingdom. But the moments are evanescent. To be useful they have to be used. That was what Bayard Rustin—others too, but Rustin more directly—tried to do in the days after the buses had returned home and the sound equipment removed from the mall.

The march was also a manifestation of the kind of coalition that Rustin would later insist, again and again, was necessary for progress toward a less racist society. Liberal politicians, mostly Democrats, moved toward explicit support. Integrationist whites were joined by integrationist blacks. All religions were represented, but Jewish groups were particularly important.

And yet, did the march achieve its specific aims? Was the president's civil rights bill moved forward? There would soon be five murders, four in Birmingham and one in Dallas. There would be the longest filibuster in history before the bill passed on July 2, 1964, nearly a year after the march. So the role of the march is unclear. Was it simply a picnic in the park, as some CORE people thought? Were the leaders of the movement just dreamers, as Anne Moody said about Martin Luther King's speech?[34]

Bayard had only a few days of pleasure and rest. Letters poured in congratulating him. To well-wishers he replied with thanks but added, "The big job remains to be done." On the Friday of the week after the march he invited the whole staff and volunteers to a party at Cleveland Robinson's offices on Astor Place.[35] The celebrations and congratulations were limited, however, by the need to get on to the next steps. The next step was supposed to be bringing one thousand people to Washington for every day that the southern senators filibustered. Within a few days of the march, Rustin was trying to organize for this "People's Congress," but soon he had to recognize that the idea was unworkable.[36] What, then, was workable?

On September 15, before Bayard had time to formulate his thoughts on the meaning of the march, the Sixteenth Street Baptist Church in Birmingham was bombed, and four girls attending Sunday school were killed. Within twenty-four hours, he was writing local committees of the March on Washington that the ten chairmen called on all Americans to observe the next Sunday, the 22nd, as a national day of mourning. He, James Baldwin, the Reverend Thomas Kilgore, and Norman Thomas observed the day by speaking at a mass meeting in front of the Department of Justice in Foley Square, in lower Manhattan. Two days later Rustin flew to Richmond, Virginia, where King had asked him to speak on nonviolence, because, as he said, the Birmingham bombing placed the whole "concept of non-violence on trial."[37] King so valued Bayard's counsel that he had never been willing to cut himself off entirely from Rustin. After the march, Rustin was such a public figure that King did not have to hide the association.

So when Bayard came to sum up the march, he had to put the bombing into the mix. "We were bombed," he wrote, "because we were winning, not because we were losing." He then emphasized two major points that he would refer to in various ways over and over again for the remainder of his life. One was that "we need allies." The other was that the problems were at base not racial, or not mainly racial, but economic. To face them realistically meant facing the whole distribution of wealth and power in the United States. "The March was not a Negro action; it was an action by Negroes and whites together. . . . It began the process of focusing attention where it belongs: on the problem of what kind of economic and political changes are required to make it possible for everyone to have jobs." But this was certainly more hope than analysis. There was a focus on the economic origins of racism in the Kennedy administration, and there would be more when Lyndon Johnson became president, but it would be hard to demonstrate that the march focused attention on those issues.

Then Rustin allowed himself to get angrier than he usually appeared in print. Kennedy, Rustin wrote, says nice things to Negro leaders. "Then he turns and bows to the Dixiecrats and gives them Southern racist judges. . . . On the one hand he blesses the march and on the other hand he reassures the segregationists and sabotages the aims of the March [sic]." Rustin even seemed to anticipate the "Black Power" slogan. "The need of the civil rights movement is not to get someone else to manipulate power. They will not do it in our interests. Our need is to exert our own power, and the main power we have is our black bodies, backed by the bodies of as many white people as will stand with us. We need to . . . create a situation in which society cannot function without yielding to our just demands." But he made clear that this disruption could not be violent. "If violence could ever be justified, it would be justifiable now." But the aims of the civil rights movement cannot be reached with guns. "We need to go into the streets all over the country and to make a mountain of creative social confusion until the power structure is altered." His emphasis would be very different only a few months later in the article "From Protest to Politics." And this program of mass action, he said in 1963, had to be pursued by the coalition that organized and led the March on Washington.[38]

Would it be the coalition that organized the march, or did Bayard have to find a new home?

Bayard Rustin's grandmother, Julia Rustin, date unknown. *Courtesy of the Bayard Rustin Fund.*

Bayard Rustin as a member of his high school football team, 1931. *Courtesy of the Bayard Rustin Fund.*

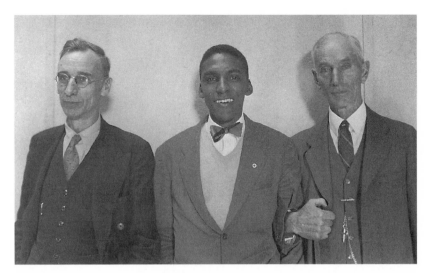

Left to Right: A. J. Muste, Bayard Rustin, George Payne, vice president of the Fellowship of Reconciliation, early 1940s. *Courtesy of the Bayard Rustin Fund.*

Cover photograph for a CD of Bayard Rustin singing, produced by the Bayard Rustin Fund of New York City. Photograph from the later 1940s. Rustin learned to play the lute while he was in prison as a conscientious objector during World War II. *Courtesy of the Bayard Rustin Fund.*

Bayard Rustin organizing the March on Washington for Jobs and Freedom, August 13, 1963. *CORBIS\Bettmann.*

Bayard and two uniden-
tified men during the
Harlem riot of 1964.
*Courtesy of the Bayard
Rustin Fund.*

Left to right: Tom Kahn, James Farmer, Ernest Green, Rachelle Horowitz during a demonstration at the opening of the 1964 World's Fair against the opulence of the Fair as contrasted with the plight of the poor. Rustin is not pictured with his colleagues, but he was a participant in the demonstration. All were arrested for violating a court order against the demonstrations. April 22, 1964. *CORBIS\Bettmann.*

Left to right: Bayard Rustin, Jack Greenberg of the NAACP, Whitney Young, executive director of the National Urban League, James Farmer, national director of CORE, Roy Wilkins, executive director, NAACP, Martin Luther King, president of SCLC, John Lewis, chairman of SNCC, A. Philip Randolph, head of the Negro American Council, Courtland Cox of SNCC. July 30, 1964. *CORBIS\Bettmann.*

Bayard Rustin with A. Philip Randolph arguing for the Freedom Budget before the Senate Government Operations Committee, December 6, 1966. *CORBIS\Bettmann.*

Rachelle Horowitz and Bayard Rustin, San Francisco, 1975. *Courtesy of Rachelle Horowitz.*

Bayard Rustin with Golda Meir, probably 1976. *Courtesy of the Bayard Rustin Fund.*

Rustin in a yellow roadster, given to him, which he drove mostly in the country. He was a city boy and in the words of one of his friends, "was a terrible driver." *Courtesy of Bayard Rustin Fund.*

Bayard Rustin with Lech Walesa, Warsaw, Poland, April 1981. *A Philip Randolph Institute. Photograph © by Adrian Karatnycky.*

Rustin with Afghan refugees, Pakistan, 1982. *Courtesy of the Bayard Rustin Fund.*

Part II

Things fall apart.

—Chinua Achebe, after W. B. Yeats

11

Transitioning

Physically Bayard had a new home. Late in 1962 he moved into what would be his apartment for the rest of his life, on Twenty-eighth Street and Eighth Avenue in Manhattan. Rachelle Horowitz found an apartment in the same complex. Tom Kahn, who had been Bayard's partner for some time, moved in with Bayard for a few months until the relationship ended. However, the two remained friends and close colleagues for the rest of Rustin's life. Rustin's apartment, perhaps counted by New York standards as five rooms, was actually a tiny living room, two tiny bedrooms, and a mini-kitchen, on the ninth floor of one of ten identical twenty-two-story high-rises built by the International Ladies' Garment Workers Union (ILGWU). Tenants either had to have some connection with the ILGWU or had to have been in the buildings torn down to create the complex. Horowitz's grandmother was a member, so she got in, but Rustin did not fit into either category. He was close to the union leadership, however, and was allowed in as the start of an informal sort of affirmative action program that eventually included A. Philip Randolph, Norman and Velma Hill, and Ernest Green. Tenants paid in proportion to their income. If the income went up, so would the rent. When they reached a maximum, they would either have to leave or pay a premium. Eventually Rustin did the latter, because during the last years of his life he was quite prosperous.[1]

The living room seemed ever tinier, because over the years Bayard gathered a large and somewhat eclectic art and antique collection. He had begun studying antiques in prison, starting with a lute he learned to play there. He would often hobnob with the antique dealers in the neighborhood and learned more. He gradually developed quite an amazing knowledge. Decades later, on the border of Afghanistan and Pakistan, he amazed his fellow refugee relief workers by discussing a small statue that turned up in a flea market there. It was Greco-Roman, he explained, and had come on the old silk route! Whenever he went to Europe, he would buy antiques for local Manhattan dealers. Instead of a commission, he would ask for this or that piece. Or he might see something under a pile of junk in an antique dealer's showroom on Seventeenth Street. He would begin rubbing it to see what was under the grime and find, perhaps, something from the fifteenth century. At first he concentrated on Victorian art but then decided he did not like Victorian art and switched to Russian icons and African art. But that was only a concentration. If he saw a large Madonna, say, that he liked, that would be added to the collection on Twenty-eighth Street.

Besides the art, the apartment would frequently be crowded with friends—young people mostly. He liked having people around, and they enjoyed being with him. Not that his apartment was a perpetual party. He would often give serious fatherly advice, if that was wanted. He would go out of his way to help his friends. Sandra Feldman, one of the band of devoted volunteers working on the march, recalled that when her marriage was under strain, it was Bayard she turned to for serious advice and comfort.

In these and subsequent years, Bayard and some of his young friends would often take a ride on the Long Island Railroad out to Floral Park to spend Sunday afternoons with Max and Yetta Shachtman. Yetta was secretary for Albert Shanker, head of the New York City teachers' union. If the weather was fine, they'd walk from the station to the Shachtmans' house. If not, Max would meet them at the station with his car. Shachtman was the former Trotskyist who had spoken at City College of New York while Bayard was there.

Tom Kahn and Rachelle Horowitz had originally connected Shachtman and Rustin. Kahn and Horowitz had been enthusiastic "Shachtmanites" since college. In 1956, at the time of the Hungarian revolution, Shachtman spoke at Brooklyn College, where Kahn and Horowitz were students. The two of them, still holding illusions about the Soviet Union, heard him rail against the tyrannical nature of Moscow. It was important not only who owned the means of production, Shachtman argued, but who owned the state. The polity, he insisted, had to be democratic, and the Soviet Union, in which he had invested a good deal of hope in the 1920s, had become simply a repressive dictatorship. He and a group of "ex-Trots," as they were called, had formed a faction of democratic socialists called Shacht-manites. Shachtman spoke for some three hours, and for Kahn and Horowitz it was revelatory. They retained their critical stance toward American society with its profound inequalities but gave up any illusions about the Soviet system. They looked for some "third force" in the world and some possibilities for a democratic socialism within the United States. In subsequent years, Rustin was certainly thought of as a Shachtmanite by many people.

On those Sunday afternoons in the sixties, the talk would be long and serious, punctuated by beer and snacks. Was it sensible to support a socialist ticket in a national or local election? Could the civil rights movement be the basis for some version of socialism? The labor movement in the United States ought to be seen as a potentially progressive force, not simply another interest group in American capitalism. Sandra Feldman remembered that in those Sunday afternoon discussions, there was a complex of ideas that enabled her to be what she wanted: a patriot and social critic. Love of country was, for her, combined with a critical stance toward its shortcomings. And it was always fun to be with Bayard!

Shachtman's approach to social questions was highly theoretical, according to Rachelle Horowitz. "Bayard brought me back to the United States of America," recalled Horowitz. For instance, Max Shachtman retained a hope for some form of nationalization of basic industries, but that was never a part of Bayard's agenda. For Bayard, the issue was always what could be done here and now about, say, the realities of school segregation in New York. He enjoyed a verbal tussle and was good at it, but his goal was always to do something about hard, usually economic, realities, not to construct an impregnable verbal analysis.[2]

However, Bayard needed not so much a new physical home as a new organizational one. The March on Washington had come and gone, leaving him prominent but without a home in the civil rights movement. Martin Mayer in the *Saturday Evening Post* called him

"The Lone Wolf of Civil Rights" and "a leader without followers." There were two obvious possibilities where Rustin had a long-standing but on-again, off-again prominence: the Congress of Racial Equality and the Southern Christian Leadership Conference. CORE was in perpetual turmoil, with James Farmer as an inspirational figure but not really a leader. Some members saw him as a windbag who could make speeches but not much else. It was not simply a matter of getting the right correspondence in the right files—Alan Gartner, as his assistant, could do that. The question was what direction would the growing organization take? CORE had not been a "membership organization." If a person was taking part in a CORE action, that person was in CORE, otherwise not. Nor had it been "left wing" in the sense of having a political or economic agenda.

A group of Manhattan members who called themselves the "East River CORE" centered around Norman Hill, believed a transformation was needed. They thought that CORE should make a major effort to expand its membership, finances, and goals. It should forge an alliance with the liberal wing of the labor movement and broaden its own agenda. The pro-Farmer members thought of the labor unions as one of their major problems, not as potential allies. In late 1963 and spring 1964, the rebel group, with Hill, A. J., and Rustin as the organizers, started not a movement exactly but some beginning conversations, secret from Farmer, about somehow changing the direction of the organization. Farmer discovered the "conspiracy" and interpreted it as an attempt by the conspirators to replace him with Rustin. It was indeed an attempt to push CORE in a direction Farmer had not chosen, but probably Rustin did not actually want to replace him, although rumors to that effect did circulate. Rustin was simply not the kind of person who could have functioned in an organization that was not his own. He was too freewheeling. In any case, Farmer considered the effort an attempt to stab him in the back and was ever after furious at Rustin.[3] Three years later President Lyndon Johnson tempted Farmer with a position heading a new federal agency promoting black literacy. Farmer resigned from CORE, but the federal agency never materialized. At that point, Rustin was offered the national directorship, but he turned it down.[4] Of course CORE by that time had become something quite different from what it was in 1963.

The other possibility for an organizational home was SCLC. During the fall of 1963 and the first couple of months of 1964, Rustin and Martin Luther King toyed with the idea of Bayard becoming executive secretary, succeeding Wyatt T. Walker, and bringing some order to office procedures and fund-raising. But if Ella Baker had been out of place in Atlanta, Bayard Rustin would have been more so. King was aware that Rustin's homosexuality would horrify some of SCLC's leadership, but he concluded that "he controls himself pretty well until he gets to drinking." Rustin had now, in effect, legitimized himself through the March on Washington, so King felt that he could be open about employing him.[5] But by 1963, Rustin was a thorough New Yorker, far more at home with white left/liberal secular Jews than he would have been with southern black Baptists. So even as he and King reestablished a working relationship, it was clear that the Atlanta office of SCLC was not going to be his organizational home. Andrew Young, far more at ease with the SCLC preachers, succeeded Walker.[6]

But King wanted Bayard somewhere in SCLC. Perhaps he could head the New York office, essentially a fund-raising arm of SCLC, as In Friendship had been. Here Rustin ran directly into Walker, who thought he himself was the obvious choice for the New York office. Walker would take the job only if Bayard would be his subordinate. Bayard would work in the office only if the two were co-leaders. In addition, the FBI leaked photographs of Rustin entering the Soviet embassy for a reception, reigniting the charges of pro-communism. The whole thing would probably not have worked out anyway. Early in 1964 the NAACP also offered him a job, but he turned it down because he thought "it was an effort to control me." So by spring of 1964, the only position Rustin had was still executive secretary of the War Resisters League, frequently on loan to the civil rights movement. This was the same job at about the same salary that he had had before the March on Washington.[7]

When explaining many years later why the Mississippi SNCC people had not been more interested in the March on Washington, Bob Moses said, "We were transitioning." He meant that they were transitioning to Freedom Summer, but there was a broader "transitioning" going on during the precisely 365 days between the March on Washington and the end of the Democratic convention of 1964. The civil rights movement was veering in one, or perhaps several, directions, and Bayard Rustin was veering in another. Rustin had been a hero, a teacher for the nonviolent protest movement, but by August 1964, some members of Mississippi SNCC would think of him as a traitor. He was terribly distressed at finding himself rejected by the very people he regarded as his protégés. At the same time, in New York, he would find that he was becoming irrelevant to new forms of radicalism in the protest movement, both within and outside established civil rights organizations. As for Rustin's own position, he would argue that with Lyndon Johnson in the White House, and even more with Hubert Humphrey as vice president, more could be done within the political system than by railing against it. He became, in effect, a liberal, perhaps very liberal, Democrat. Those differing courses would lead to a widening separation within the movement and between the movement and Rustin over the next several years. Rustin's new course would also lead him to a decisive break with his pacifist friends.

Freedom Summer, which became one origin of the split, actually had its beginning in the summer of 1963. SNCC had for some time been working at a voter registration campaign in Mississippi. Progress was incredibly slow in the face of Mississippi repression. If black citizens of the state could not register for regular elections, perhaps as a desperate gesture they could form a new party, the Mississippi Freedom Democratic Party (MFDP). Allard Lowenstein, a brilliant young idealist of irrepressible energy but with trouble keeping that energy focused, had persuaded a group of white college students to come down to help with the registration drive during summer vacation of 1963. The results of white northerners "helping" black southerners were not clear, but Lowenstein was pushing the idea of a sustained and broadened effort the next summer. Perhaps the MFDP could even challenge the regular Mississippi delegation at the Democratic National Convention in Atlantic City in the fall of 1964.[8]

Rachelle Horowitz went to Mississippi (after Bayard arranged to have the rent paid for her new apartment) to help with the organizational work. She arrived just after the Kennedy assassination and stayed for some two and a half months. She found the situation terribly complicated, already with a growing sentiment against whites.[9] Rustin himself did not go to Mississippi until the spring, but Horowitz was frequently on the telephone with him and wrote a report to him after she returned to New York. Rustin, in a phone call in December, said he "hoped that SNCC wouldn't go the way of the Wobblies, who were full of energy, ready to go to jail, ready to die, but cutting themselves off continually from the body politic."[10] Horowitz, in other phone conversations, shared her doubts with Rustin about the idea of bringing a large number of white students to Mississippi. What would the implicit message be to the black students who had been working and facing danger and death if hundreds of white northerners came south? Wouldn't it imply that the danger, the violence, and even the murders that black young people faced were not worth anything in the eyes of the nation unless whites also were exposed to them? By February, "I decided I was white," she recalled with a chuckle, and she concluded that the project was a black southern effort that those young people should organize on their own. With the MFDP still unsure of its future course, Horowitz returned to New York just in time for the school boycott.[11]

The New York school boycott again raised the issue of school segregation in the North. For Rustin, the boycott was a triumph, but it also showed how campaigns in the North were probably going to veer into a direction in which he did not want them to go. As Bayard and others pointed out repeatedly, there were more children in segregated schools in 1964 than at the time of the *Brown* decision. The first and second Youth March for Integrated Schools had come and gone, with no apparent effect. Perhaps if the schoolchildren themselves could be visibly brought into the process, their presence might be persuasive—hence a one-day boycott of the city schools, with "Freedom Schools," a term also used in Mississippi that summer, instead of regular school. The boycott was organized under the auspices of the Emergency City Wide Committee for Integrated Schools, which included the teachers union and local NAACP and CORE chapters, and was headed by Milton Galamison. Galamison was a black Brooklyn minister who had been a leader in the school integration fight in the city for several years. But as with the March on Washington, Bayard Rustin actually organized the boycott. The effort started in January, with the boycott day set for February 4. Bayard asked churches and civic groups to help by urging their members to keep the children out of school. There were circulars in Spanish and English, so the effort was both black and Puerto Rican. There were clear guidelines for picketing to keep everything orderly, and there were suggestions about what the alternative Freedom Schools—some in churches, some actually in the school buildings—might teach.[12]

The whole issue became highly emotional, with debates on radio and television. James B. Donovan, president of the New York City Board of Education, in a television debate with James Farmer, denounced the boycott as a "lawless course of action" and vowed that he would not "react one inch" to the pressure. Yet just before boycott day, Donovan announced a plan of school pairing: black and white children would go to one school for early grades and another for later grades. The plan involved only a few schools, and the City Wide Committee denounced it as inadequate. Parents at white schools refused to contemplate sending their children to black schools, so the plan was dead the moment it was announced.

There was a final rally the night before the boycott, at Concord Baptist Church in Brooklyn, with more than a thousand people in attendance. They sang "We Shall Overcome" and "We Shall Not Be Moved"—both also labor songs. Bayard told the crowd that what happened the next day would be significant for the white leaders of the nation. "They know that this is the black capital of the Western world and whatever we do will be felt in every hamlet and . . . " Applause and cheers drowned out the rest of his remarks.[13]

Bayard stayed at the boycott headquarters at Galamison's church in Brooklyn, all day and all night on the day before the boycott, snatching a few hours' sleep on the couch in the office. He emerged, rumpled and sleepy-eyed in his pajamas, bathrobe, and slippers, in the morning. "Where do you think you are, Bayard, at home?" said one of the volunteers. "Yes," answered Rustin, and in a way he was. Someone told him that Harlem was pretty well closed down. "Of course, what did you expect?" he replied.[14] In fact, more than 350,000 students stayed out, but the numbers varied widely from school to school. Sandra Feldman, the person who eventually became head of the American Federation of Teachers following Albert Shanker's death, was teaching at a school on the lower east side. She remembered that she was the only person from that school, student or teacher, to stay out that day and that she formed a picket line of one. Shanker and the union promised that they would defend any teacher who was disciplined for joining the boycott.[15]

Yes, the boycott was highly successful. Yes, a great many students stayed out of school. But the New York schools and schools in every other major northern city remained and remain segregated. Every attempt to change the system has been met with white resistance or white flight or both. A March on Albany, with three thousand people in the snow, tried to get the state to do what the city would not or could not do. And the schools remained segregated.

Almost immediately, Galamison was talking about a second boycott in March. Rustin did not see any utility in a second boycott and was becoming leery of Galamison.[16] The NAACP and most Harlem ministers withdrew their support from the City Wide Committee, which Galamison was trying to turn from a coordinating agency into his own organization. Galamison did organize a second boycott, but without the assistance of Rustin, CORE, or the NAACP, it was much less successful than the first. Angrily, he said that Rustin, Norman Hill, and Frederick Jones of the NAACP had "no roots in the New York City community," which was pretty much true. Galamison was the kind of person Bayard would repeatedly clash with in the future, a person who combined a desire for racial change with voluble self-promotion.[17]

Things were not going much better in Mississippi. There was such slow progress on voter registration that Bayard had serious doubts that the MFDP could fulfill its hope of mounting a plausible challenge to the all-white Mississippi delegation at the convention in Atlantic City. A couple of months after the New York boycott, Rustin went to Mississippi. At a meeting in Jackson in the living room of the home of Edwin King, the white pastor at Tougaloo College, Rustin told Bob Moses and others of his doubts and offered to mount a major national demonstration in support of the new party. Ed King remembered that Bayard was talking about demonstrations all over the country, through churches, NAACP chapters, and other Negro groups, and "he would have both coordinated, managed it and controlled it," said King. In fact, many people had doubts about the local MFDP and wanted to control and manage their movement. There was Allard Lowenstein and his northern white students with their self-confidence, hi-fis, and competence. Lowenstein even wanted to bring in William Sloan Coffin, pastor of Yale University. Now here was Bayard Rustin, also trying to control and manage. A few of the MFDP people knew Bayard personally, Bob Moses and Stokely Carmichael from New York and Eleanor Holmes from Washington, but most only knew of him as the organizer of the March on Washington. Yet for all of them he was an outsider who, black or white, wanted to define his own role instead of asking the Mississippi people what they wanted him to do. Moses gently told him, "But that wasn't what we had in mind."[18]

There was also a heated discussion about whether to accept help from the National Lawyers Guild, a group heavy with Communists. James Forman, who later would call himself a "black revolutionary," and John Lewis favored an open-door policy of accepting help from anyone who wanted to give it. Bob Moses was "leery of the Stalinoids." Rustin, of course, supported Moses, saying that when the Communists came in, "things were messed up," and at one point he actually walked out in anger, "almost red-baiting us," as Ed King put it.[19] The result was that the National Lawyers Guild was not excluded, and Rustin's idea of a national campaign that he would organize was rejected.

Perhaps it was reasonable for Rustin to think of himself as a leader rather than a subordinate. After the March on Washington, he was famous enough so that he could earn several hundred dollars per lecture on the college circuit. In May 1964, back from Mississippi, he spoke at Bowdoin, a mostly white New England men's college, for the opening of an exhibition, *The Portrayal of the Negro in American Painting*. Besides praising the civil rights bill then before Congress, he defended nonviolence—but carefully planned, not thoughtless, nonviolence. He told how a group of young activists had come to him and said they were going to blockade a bridge into Manhattan with garbage during the night, as a way of protesting inadequate garbage collection in black neighborhoods. Rustin advised against it. Protests, he said, have to be directly related to the evil being protested and have to target the evildoers. But the activists said they were going ahead anyway, and Rustin said OK, people have to learn on their own. They did, he reported, and the first to cross the bridge in the morning was a black man going to work in Manhattan. As the barrier builders started to explain, the driver kicked the garbage out of the way, climbed back into his car, and drove to work. Thus ended the demonstration. Rustin thereby illustrated the distance between his brand of controlled demonstrations and a growing anger in the black community that could lead to what he regarded as irrational and self-defeating demonstrations.

Another group of activists, continued Rustin in his talk at Bowdoin, this time from Brooklyn CORE, planned a "stall-in" on the Long Island Expressway on opening day of the World's Fair, April 23, as a demonstration contrasting the affluence at the fair and the poverty of blacks. Rustin had tried to get them to instead "have a program based on sanity." Again, he made the point that "when you have direct action, it should be against the evil, not against something twice removed, like the bridge." The stall-in failed, with traffic moving freely. Only a couple of small cars showed up, and they were easily pushed aside by the police.

One of the few black students at the college rose and in a stammering, anguished voice asked, "You . . . you are so rational. How can you tell me to act rationally in the face of an irrational situation. Why do you tell me this? . . . Why can't there be stall-ins, garbage on bridges? Why should you tell me to be moderate? How can you ask me to believe in non-violence?"

Rustin paused in thought, though he must have been asked that question many times in the past. "You must not push a man so far into a corner that he becomes desperate. You, you and I," and with his arms he made a gesture indicating that he and the student were one person,

you and I must do more than react. . . .

And of course you say, But why should Negroes be treated this way and still have to be super nice people? I say, because we are a chosen people . . . chosen to help free everybody, black and white from the curse of hate. . . .

But you are young and I am old, and I have talked too long. But do not think that just because there is snow on the roof there is no fire in the furnace.

And the audience applauded, aware that they had been present at a special moment of insight and feeling.

After the talk, Bayard stayed for hours sitting in an armchair, long legs stretched out, slender fingers gesturing to emphasize a point, often with a cigarette, or pressed together as he thought. Students sat on the floor or leaned against the wall. Those who heard him would remember the evening for decades, and this was only one of many such evenings for Rustin.[20] The stammering young student, though, had perceived a fundamental aspect of Rustin's thinking that at times was a hindrance. He was indeed a rational man, so rational that he could not really empathize with the nonrational. People should not worry about how they wore their hair or courses in racial identity; rather, they should be concerned with programs of social and economic change.

By the actual Freedom Summer, Rustin had begun to do what SNCC wanted. He participated in the June training session for the volunteers, in Oxford, Ohio. He was still a little worried about what "those youngsters" might do, however, and wanted to bring Martin Luther King, A. Philip Randolph, and James Farmer in to help "get things under control." In mid-June, he called Bob Moses to say that the three leaders were getting behind the project and could bring both prestige and money.[21] At the end of June, Marian Wright called Rustin asking him to go to Mississippi to see what was going on. Scorched by his experiences in Ed King's living room a few month earlier, Bayard did not want to push himself into a situation where he was not wanted. He told Marian Wright that he would not go unless Moses and James Forman invited him—"If you're positively certain that there will be no resentment." In a call the next day, Bob Moses assured Rustin that he was wanted. For various reasons, Rustin could not arrange to come to Jackson right away, and in the meantime Harlem experienced the type of violence that would become familiar over the next few years.

On June 18, 1964, only about two weeks after Johnson signed the

Equal Accommodations Act, a white policeman in Harlem shot a young black man who may or may not have brandished a knife, and Harlem exploded. Bayard Rustin had been expecting it, as he had told the Fellowship of Reconciliation's National Council meeting in April, that is, while southern senators were still filibustering the equal-accommodations law. Before the phrase was common, he called his talk to FOR "Hot Summer." Rustin went through the litany of frustration in the South and increasing economic desperation of northern blacks. "The move to violence is not a move from one spiritual platform to another," he said. "It is the move which always occurs in a situation where the tactics that have been advocated and used are inadequate for dealing with the objective needs." And nonviolence had not been adequate. "The Negro community is no longer taking Martin Luther King's brand of nonviolence. . . . No Negro leader if he wants to be listened to is going to tell any Negroes that they should love white people. . . . They don't love them, they have no need to love them, no basis on which they can love them."[22]

When the riot broke out on July 19, Rustin, in a speech at a large church in Harlem, tried to argue that nonviolence could achieve more than a riot. He was booed and threatened, whereas five months before, at the time of the boycott, his speaking had been drowned out by cheers. After his talk, he was surrounded by a threatening mob. Some in the audience agreed to help him, however, and Rustin and his supporters walked the streets of Harlem for four nights, aiding the injured and arguing for nonviolence. He realized that he did not know anybody. He was black, he was a New Yorker, but he was not of that community, and he had no channels into it. "He couldn't reach these kids," wrote M. S. Handler in the *New York Times*. Bayard was appalled by the level of violence and feared worse. He was told that two men, and the two were pointed out, were storing dynamite in their basement and might use it for some unknown action. Using all his persuasive power, Rustin persuaded them to give up their plan and dump the dynamite in the river. He called the FBI to report three cars in a caravan distributing handbills accusing the policeman of murder and calling for retaliatory action. He did not realize that he could have dialed any number whatever from his office phone and told whoever answered about the three cars and the FBI would have been informed through its wiretap on his office phone. The FBI had been keeping watch on him since the 1950s. It began tapping his office phone in November 1963 as part of J. Edgar Hoover's obsession with Communist influence in the civil rights movement.[23]

From the explosive atmosphere of New York, Bayard flew down to a different sort of tension in Mississippi. In Jackson on July 23, Bayard asked the MFDP not to plan any direct action at the Democratic National Convention, such as a sit-in, that might cause a southern bolt and add strength to Barry Goldwater. Moses assured Rustin that they were not (although in fact there were some small demonstrations). Back in New York, Rustin called King. "I wouldn't say this to those youngsters, but we—all our friends are in this convention. All of our friends don't want anything to happen that would damage Johnson and help Goldwater. We simply have to be sensible."[24]

A week after the disorders broke out in Harlem, Martin Luther King called Rustin from Atlanta, asking about how he should react to the violence. "I thought you could help me on this, and also should I come to New York?" Bayard suggested King say that law and order do not exist in a vacuum and that "to the degree that you have justice, to that degree, law and order can be maintained." The next day King did come, as Mayor Robert Wagner had requested, but New York was not Birmingham, where the sides were black against white. New York had prominent black political leaders and officials, and some of them resented King trying to appoint himself peacemaker. King was in New York probing the idea of extending his movement, not just fund-raising for it, into northern cities. On July 27, King, Rustin, Cleveland Robinson, and others met with Wagner asking for a civilian review board to receive complaints about police violence. No such board was established, and King got a taste of the ambiguities and complications of racial politics in the North. Rustin and Hill advised against SCLC moving north. What was clear from the whole experience was that the movement against oppressive race relations had now proceeded on to another stage. People like Rustin, and even King, were simply irrelevant. Rustin knew that the social structure of racism in New York was not the same as that in Alabama. "Martin can win victories in the South," said Bayard to Harry

Wachtel, "but there are no victories for him to win in the North," which was prophetic.[25]

Bayard further distanced himself from the more radical wing of the movement when he joined with others arguing for a moratorium on demonstrations until after the election. Two days after the frustrating meeting with Wagner, Rustin, Jack Greenberg, Whitney Young, James Farmer, Roy Wilkins, Martin Luther King, John Lewis, A. Philip Randolph, and Courtland (the *New York Times* said "Courtney") Cox of SNCC met in New York to discuss a moratorium. Wilkins chaired the meeting but quickly turned it over to Randolph, who spoke about the disaster that a Goldwater victory would mean. He then asked Bayard to read a statement pledging the civil rights organizations not to demonstrate until after the election. Wilkins, Young, and King spoke in favor. After a pause, Farmer and Lewis dissented, refusing to go along. Farmer argued that CORE was an activist organization. There would be no CORE without demonstrations. The rather confusing result of the meeting was that two statements were issued, one proposing a "voluntary, temporary alteration in strategy" and the other condemning "looting, vandalism and any type of criminal activity" and explicitly rejecting Communist support. What was significant for Bayard was that once again he could be seen as standing with the liberal establishment rather than radical activists.[26]

Both the Harlem riot and the controversy over demonstrations went on at the height of Freedom Summer in Mississippi, between the time that Andrew Goodman, James Chaney, and Michael Schwerner were murdered and the time when their bodies were discovered. Freedom Summer was what Horowitz, Moses, Rustin, and many others hoped and feared. It was a marvelous, horrifying, uplifting, and terrorizing few months. The MFDP held its own registration (in cardboard boxes carried around in the streets) and then organized local caucuses and a state convention. The state convention chose a delegation to Atlantic City to challenge the regular Mississippi delegates, who had been chosen by an all-white Democratic state party.

Many, perhaps most, members of the MFDP assumed that they would challenge the all-white delegation, that the challenge would be rejected, and that they would return home to form a new party in

Mississippi. Victory would be achieved if they prevented the seating of the regular Mississippi delegation. Joseph Rauh, the man who in 1941 had drafted the order ending discrimination in defense plants, now the lawyer for the United Auto Workers, had come down to Mississippi to add his legal ability to the enthusiasm of Allard Lowenstein. "No, we can seat you," said Joe Rauh to the MFDP delegation, and in fact he and Eleanor Holmes wrote a brief to the credentials committee to make the case. Thus the stakes were raised. ("Damn Joe Rauh!" said Horowitz, thinking back on it.) Victory would not now consist merely of unseating the regulars, difficult as that might be. To be considered victory the MFDP delegation would have to be seated instead.[27]

Lyndon Johnson was focused on national politics. He had to avoid a southern walkout as in 1948, he had to keep faith with the civil rights movement, and he had to get elected in November.[28] We now know that the election was a landslide, but he did not know that in August. In the middle of August, a week or so before the convention, Rustin was trying to arrange a meeting between Martin Luther King and the president, in which King could make a plea for recognition of the MFDP. The meeting was finally held on August 24, but as Rustin and Joe Rauh had feared, it was not a meeting but a monologue in which the president filled the time with telling how much he had done for the Negro revolution and insisting, in fact assuming, that the MFDP had to be stopped.[29]

Johnson might be focused on national politics, but the members of the MFDP delegation came from the depths of Mississippi brutality. Their burning concern was Mississippi. Thinking back many years later on murders of civil rights workers in the 1960s in Mississippi, Bob Moses remembered, "In 1961, when they assassinated Herbert Lee in Liberty, we were not in a position to respond . . . and the only witness to that was Lewis Allen." Then, while the Mississippi SNCC people were in the midst of debating whether they would have a Freedom Summer, during February 1964, Lewis Allen was assassinated. Bob Moses said that right then he realized that in order to make any headway in Mississippi they would have to go outside "the closed society" and find leverage from somewhere else. In talking about the oppressive and seemingly invulnerable power of the white Mississippi Democratic Party, he said, "There was a soft spot in this whole apparatus that had been set up there in Mississippi, but the power of it depended on its being credentialized by the National Democratic Party. And here we have a once in a lifetime opportunity to actually strike a blow where they had no protection. We could really penetrate to vital organs, so to speak. With that apparatus." In other words, the MFDP wanted to use the national convention for its own purposes in Mississippi. If that meant the election of Goldwater, Moses felt, at least the reason people voted for Goldwater would be clear.[30]

Johnson deputized Hubert Humphrey, senator from Minnesota, to arrange some kind of a compromise, and Humphrey in turn deputized his protégé, Minnesota attorney general Walter Mondale. The compromise Mondale and Humphrey worked out, with Johnson's approval, was presented to the MFDP not as a negotiating position but as a fair proposal—take it or leave it. The proposal was that the MFDP would get two seats at large, all convention delegates would have to sign an oath to support the party nominee, and no future convention would accept delegations elected on a discriminatory basis. The compromise also specified to whom the two seats should go: Aaron Henry, pharmacist, black, and Ed King, one of the four white members of the MFDP delegation. These two were the two most "respectable" members of the delegation. This was not a wholly unreasonable choice on the part of Humphrey and Mondale, however, for the MFDP had run that precise ticket for governor and lieutenant governor the year before. But in the meantime, Fannie Lou Hamer had emerged as the most visible and dramatic member. "They should have allowed an election," said Rauh, "which would have picked Mrs. Hamer, and if they'd had Mrs. Hamer it would have been all right. It was outrageous not to."[31]

The question was, would the MFDP accept the compromise? The country debated, the *New York Times* debated, the black press debated, and the MFDP delegation debated.[32] In the meantime, most of the regular Mississippi delegation, outraged at the loyalty oath provision of the compromise, went home, presumably to vote Republican. "We expected that," said Mondale, remembering the incident. "We put in the loyalty oath as a way of getting them to walk."[33] By that action, the MFDP had won what a few weeks earlier it would have regarded as a great victory. Now there was another issue to be decided.

A crucial meeting took place in Humphrey's hotel suite on August 25. At first, Bob Moses did not want to come, because he thought it was just a tactic of Humphrey's to get in LBJ's good graces and be chosen as the vice presidential candidate. Martin Luther King and Rustin talked to Moses, saying that whatever Humphrey's motives were, their aim was to get some MFDP members on the floor. So Moses came. Besides Moses, there were Ed King, Aaron Henry, and Fannie Lou Hamer. There were also Hubert Humphrey, a couple of aides, Martin Luther King, Andrew Young, Walter Reuther, Allard Lowenstein, and Bayard Rustin, all urging the MFDP people to regard the offer from the party as a great victory and accept it. "[Bayard] also spoke. A brilliant speech, made a great speech, a marvelous speech," recalled Ed King. "I don't think [it] persuaded many people, but they listened. Bayard's comments later became an article in *Commentary*, . . . the basis for 'From Protest to Politics.'" Bayard argued that now they were in the party, not demonstrating on the outside to get in. "It was a very good talk. It was wrong, but it was very good," said Ed King.[34]

The next morning, the MFDP and representatives of the major civil rights organizations gathered in the basement of the Union Temple Baptist Church to make the final decision on whether or not to accept the offer. It was a stormy, angry meeting. As Bayard repeated his general position, that Negroes were only 10 percent of the population and needed allies and that the MFDP was "snatching defeat from the jaws of victory," one of the SNCC members present, as James Forman recounted it, shouted, "You're a traitor, Bayard, a traitor. Sit down!" King argued that they should regard the compromise as a victory and "let this flickering flame grow into a mighty conflagration" of political change in the South.[35] "People who were working in Mississippi," said Rustin in 1969, "didn't really realize that they had come up to Atlantic City to begin an entry into the political process. They had been protesting and demonstrating to such an extent that . . . when they were offered a compromise, they couldn't accept it because they were still of the mood that their function was to protest." The decision was to reject the compromise. "We didn't come all this way for no two seats," said Mrs. Hamer. "It was nothing," said Victoria Gray.[36]

She was wrong, as Bayard was wrong in his remarks about snatching defeat from the jaws of victory. Later he in fact called the results a magnificent victory. Despite the emotional furor in the summer of 1964, it did not matter whether or not the compromise was accepted. The very offer of a compromise was a major accomplishment for a group of very poor, very oppressed political novices. Whether the compromise was accepted or not, the politics of Mississippi was changed, the politics of the Democratic Party was changed, and with the Voting Rights Act of 1965, the politics of the South was changed. Whether or not the compromise was accepted, Lyndon Johnson would be the party nominee and would be elected in November.

In Atlantic City, after Johnson and Humphrey were safely nominated, a delegation of civil rights leaders, including King, Wilkins, and Rustin, had a meeting with Johnson at which he assured them he would carry on with vigorous measures. Thus the leaders could say, in Rustin's words, "We talked to the man, and this is what he is going to do." King and Rustin traveled all over the country that fall not specifically urging blacks to vote for Johnson but pointing out the disaster a Goldwater victory would mean.[37]

Bayard Rustin's role in the civil rights movement, however, was permanently changed. No longer was he a civil rights radical of either the northern or southern parts of the movement. Now he was part of the civil rights establishment or the liberal, or even the white liberal, establishment. "I think he flip-flopped," said Bob Moses in thinking back on it. "The civil rights forces just had to move with the common people." Moses added, without anger, "And Bayard, Bayard was moving with Humphrey and the Administration." To Moses, ever afterward, Bayard was simply on the wrong side, the "conservative side." Moses and others had a vision of creating a New Society. John Lewis thought of the Atlantic City convention as a turning point. He, too, wanted to create a New Society, which he called "a beloved community." Rather than create a New Society, Bayard wanted to improve the one already in existence, not in some distant future but as soon as possible. His immediate goal was the quite practical one of reelecting the president and defeating Goldwater. He was not willing to contemplate a Goldwater victory simply to make the issue clear, as Moses was.[38]

The break was not yet complete, however. Rustin claimed that he and the MFDP disagreed only on "tactics," though some of the Mississippi people certainly considered the differences larger than tactical. Rustin continued to work for what became a unified "Loyal Democratic" Mississippi delegation to the 1968 convention, which included some MFDP members. But now the term "liberal" was becoming a pejorative in the mouths of some members of the civil rights movement. A liberal was a sunshine patriot, a person who would compromise on questions of right and wrong for political expediency, and Rustin was part of that group. Some people even began to see Martin Luther King as part of that group.[39] To Bayard Rustin, the new directions the civil rights movement was taking were both irrational and self-destructive. And so they in fact proved to be, for over the next few years SNCC and CORE went effectively out of existence.

12

From Protest

to Politics

Between late 1964 and mid-1966, the civil rights movement continued to lose clarity. Martin Luther King, against Bayard Rustin's advice, tried to expand his version of NVDA to the North, where it proved ineffective. At the same time, a younger generation of black activists, out of anger and frustration, were arguing ever more stridently for one version or another of black nationalism and separatism. While perhaps psychologically understandable, these arguments proved self-defeating. Bayard Rustin saw the futility of King's attempts and the suicidal consequences of nationalism and separatism. He insisted that a new constellation of issues, essentially economic, had to be faced. His proposed solutions may have been correct in the long run, but in 1966 reality they were doomed to be ignored.

Martin Luther King's influence was declining within the civil rights movement, but it was ever brighter in the international world. On October 15, 1964, he was awarded the Nobel Peace Prize. King so valued Bayard Rustin's counsel that whether or not Rustin was in SCLC, King wanted close communication with him. Hence Bayard was invited to accompany the new Nobel laureate to Oslo in November—it turned out to be a party of some forty people—and to help prepare his acceptance speech. King said he wanted something like William Faulkner's speech accepting the 1949 prize for literature. Faulkner, in the face of atomic terror, had proclaimed, "I decline to accept the end of man."[1] As a matter of course, it was Rustin who took care of the logistics: first in Oslo, then in Stockholm, then London, and when King returned to the United States in December, a reception at the United Nations with Ralph Bunche as host and the newly elected senator from New York, Robert Kennedy, in attendance.[2]

In Oslo, Rustin also performed duties that were not a matter of course. The parties among King's entourage the night before the awards ceremony got fairly raucous and also scandalous. There were a number of Norwegian prostitutes running in and out of various rooms, particularly A. D. King's, Martin's brother, in various stages of undress. The police were called and arrested the prostitutes in the middle of the night. Dora McDonald, King's secretary, distressed at the seemingly unavoidable scandal, woke Bayard and asked him to intervene. Bayard went downstairs in his pajamas and slippers and demanded that the police release the women. "If you arrest them," said Bayard, "I will go to the press before you can get to the press with that story, and simply say that your king was unable to protect Dr. King's party while he was a guest of the king." After consulting with their superiors, the police released the women, and there was no scandal. Bayard, with something of a secret life of his own, was forever convinced of Martin Luther King's propriety and that J. Edgar Hoover was trying to smear him with smarmy innuendo and rumor. "Not Martin," he would say to Rachelle Horowitz, "not Martin!"[3]

The King group returned to the United States in early December, and soon Rustin began to work, with Tom Kahn's aid, on what would be his most famous essay, "From Protest to Politics." It appeared in *Commentary* for February 1965 and was significant in a number of ways. First was the fact that it appeared in a Jewish liberal—for *Commentary* was still liberal—intellectual magazine. That was a milieu that he found accepting and intellectually nurturing. Second, the essay marks a turn from Bayard being an activist who was analytical to being an analyst who was sometimes active. Third, it summed up the ideas he had been expressing in various bits and pieces over the previous couple of years about the direction in which he thought the civil rights movement had to go.

The article is complex, emphasizing the interrelationship of economic, racial, regional, historical, political, and class issues. The elimination of racial barriers, he argued, which was in the process of happening and was likely to continue, was not enough. Some well-meaning liberals and some Negroes defined the goals of the civil rights movement in this limited way, but that was self-defeating. It did Negroes no good to have the right to eat at a lunch counter if they did not have the money to pay for lunch. A social and economic revolution must come in the wake of this civil rights revolution.

Some Negroes, continued Rustin, seeing the reluctance of white liberals to go beyond civil rights, concluded that only shock therapy through rhetoric of the Malcolm X variety would change white awareness. Although Malcolm had no program, wrote Rustin, his supporters hoped that whites would be frightened into doing the right thing. This assumed that what was needed was a change of heart. But Rustin posited that "it is institutions—social, political, and economic institutions—which are the ultimate molders of collective sentiments." These institutions, he wrote, not people's hearts, must be reconstructed. (One can, of course, argue precisely the reverse.)

On the other hand, "there is a strong moralistic strain in the civil rights movement which would remind us that power corrupts, forgetting that the absence of power also corrupts." To eliminate slums, to create jobs, to create good schools—all these things take money, and money from the central government. Self-help will not do, lunch counter protests will not do, local ordinances will not do, and certainly separatism in any form will not do. What is needed is many—Rustin guessed one hundred—billion dollars, which can only come from Congress and the president. These broader aims of the Negro revolution can only be obtained through national policy, which means politics, and that means the necessity for coalition. The country's twenty million black people cannot win political power alone. "We need allies." Rustin recognized that "necessarily there will be compromise," but without compromise there can be no power. "The leader who shrinks from this task reveals not his purity but his lack of political sense."

What will be the elements in this coalition? "The labor movement, despite its obvious faults, has been the largest single organized force in this country pushing for progressive social legislation," Rustin wrote in "From Protest to Politics." And to make that coalition work, the civil rights movement has to broaden its own social vision. "We need to propose alternatives to technological unemployment, urban decay and the rest. We need to be calling for public works and training, for national economic planning, for federal aid to education, for attractive public housing—all this on a sufficiently massive scale to make a difference. We need to protest the notion that our integration into American life . . . must now proceed in an atmosphere of competitive scarcity instead of in the security of abundance."

Rustin thought that Lyndon Johnson's landslide victory was a hopeful sign, but only that. The victory was more a rejection of what was perceived as right-wing extremism than any expression of the sort of "progressive" coalition he thought necessary. Significantly enough, he did not even mention the war in Vietnam, which was to destroy any hopes for the sort of coalition politics Rustin wanted.[4]

At almost the same time that his article appeared, February 1965, Malcolm X was assassinated in Harlem's Audubon Ballroom. There was some fear that his assassination might be part of a general plot to assassinate black leaders. Rustin thought that Martin Luther King was now a marked man, and he called both Coretta King and Ralph Abernathy about his fears. Concerning his own security, he told a worried caller that he "had good protection here"; there were two policemen downstairs.[5] Malcolm had for years been advocating separatism between the races. He and Rustin had debated the issue many times, for example in 1960, on radio station WBAI. Malcolm had argued again and again that white America would not let black people be full members of society and that therefore black people, by one method or another, should separate from that society. Rustin had called that solution ridiculous. Black Americans had to find their freedom within, not separate from, American society. By the time of his death, Malcolm had softened his views on white people as necessarily evil, but it was his earlier position of hostility to whites and the necessity of racial separation, not integration, that was widely popular among some young blacks, for example, Stokely Carmichael and Floyd McKissick.[6] Coalition politics became more and more difficult as SNCC and CORE became increasingly separatist, finally expelling their white members.

Rustin himself had always embodied the coalition he envisioned, with his close relationships to both organized labor and the civil rights movement. During the winter of 1964–1965, the idea began to form of an organization that Bayard Rustin would run and that would precisely act as the bridge between the civil rights and the labor movement. It could thus promote the new directions in which Bayard wanted to go. The idea was probably in several people's minds at the same time, but the first suggestion came from Max Shachtman. Shachtman had for many years known Donald Slaiman, assistant to the civil rights director of the AFL-CIO, through the Social Democratic Party. Shachtman introduced Slaiman to Bayard Rustin. Throughout 1964, the three of them talked about the idea of an organization for Bayard. A. Philip Randolph would head the organization, to be called the A. Philip Randolph Institute, but Bayard would actually run it on a day-to-day basis. The APRI would bring the best ideas of the civil rights movement to labor, and working with the AFL-CIO's political arm, the Committee on Political Education (COPE), it would get out the black vote for candidates whom organized labor supported. The money would come partly from the AFL-CIO, partly from various civil rights groups, and partly from friends of Bayard's, which meant essentially his longtime supporter from the American Friends Service Committee (AFSC), Robert Gilmore. Here was a chance for Bayard to do exactly what he had urged in "From Protest to Politics."

Shachtman asked Slaiman about getting labor support, and Slaiman thought that was possible. Slaiman wrote a memo to Lane Kirkland of the AFL-CIO, who in turn passed it on to George Meany, proposing the idea and saying it would be good for labor.[7] Slaiman did not say so in the memo, but he knew that Meany, although he had spoken out against discrimination in unions for years, had been criticized by the civil rights movement for not doing more about it and for not supporting the March on Washington.[8] Slaiman thought that Meany would be amenable to something like this proposal, which he was. At the February 1965 executive council meeting of the AFL-CIO in Miami, Meany, with Slaiman's memo in his lap under the table, proposed the establishment of the A. Philip Randolph Institute, headed by Randolph with Bayard Rustin as executive secretary. Don Slaiman, who had been invited to attend for precisely that purpose, made a presentation of the idea. "Who is this guy, Rustin?"

asked one member, who Slaiman learned later had been in touch with J. Edgar Hoover. Randolph endorsed Rustin, and with "Phil" sitting right there (Meany was one of the very few people who could call him that) the executive council endorsed the idea at a level of twenty-five thousand dollars per year.

The institute was announced on March 12, 1965, but the money did not appear. Rachelle Horowitz, who was to be the general factotum, called Slaiman and asked where the money was. Slaiman found that Meany had begun to have doubts, so Slaiman called Bayard to say there was something going on. Bayard replied that "Meany must have gotten this F.B.I. thing on me." He sent Slaiman a copy of Randolph's vigorous defense of Bayard against Strom Thurmond's attack at the time of the March on Washington. Slaiman took it into Meany's office. Meany read it and then turned to his secretary. "Send the check!" he said, and the A. Philip Randolph Institute became a reality.[9] In fact, the institute was financed from two, not three, sources: labor and Robert Gilmore. Most of the support came from the two branches of organized labor, not just the more conservative George Meany section but also the Industrial Union Department, essentially Walter Reuther. Other individual unions also made smaller contributions. In July 1965, the A. Philip Randolph Educational Fund was established as a tax-exempt arm of the APRI. This was so that Robert Gilmore and later the Mertz-Gilmore Foundation could contribute tax-exempt money for Rustin's support and where Rustin's speaking fees could go. The Educational Fund was the chief source of Bayard's income from then on. Rustin at first proposed that he get a salary of five thousand dollars per year, but his friend and financial adviser Charles Bloomstein persuaded him to take ten thousand. "No one will listen to you if you take $5000," said Bloomstein. Bayard Rustin was now assured of a permanent home base and also an income he could count on.[10] He quickly established an advisory board of the major civil rights leaders and a national board that, more or less, tried to re-create the coalition of the March on Washington including labor leaders and representatives from the major religions. The APRI was not a civil rights organization. It was Bayard Rustin with some assistants and co-workers doing what ever he decided should be done.[11]

The APRI offices were not just the focus of activism and press releases. They were also Bayard's home away from home and his office for all sorts of help to individuals. When he was at the War Resisters League, people with problems had come to him, and they continued to find his office on 125th Street. Perhaps it was a young man in search of a job or asking help finding a college scholarship. Or it might be someone in trouble with the police or parents looking for bail money. He might help a young drug addict who wanted to kick the habit find some sort of rehabilitation program. "I have been working with a small group of young men who are trying to kick the dope habit," he wrote to one correspondent. "I've found them jobs and got them some counseling." Just as at the War Resisters League, Bayard relished this role.[12]

The APRI Educational Fund was also soon the home of what was to be Bayard Rustin's largest and longest-lasting project. It started out small, and actually before the Randolph Institute was formed, and it changed fundamentally Rustin's relationship to organized labor. Up until about 1964, the relationship had been one in which a few unions, like the United Auto Workers or the Packinghouse Workers, or an important individual, like A. Philip Randolph, supported Rustin's efforts in the civil rights movement, but Rustin had not tried to exercise any influence within the labor movement itself. After 1964, Rustin was trying to work against racism within organized labor, particularly the building trades, starting in New York. Bayard asserted again and again that a person was defined by his work. Welfare, he claimed, provided no self-definition. Those jobs that had traditionally been described as Negro jobs, unskilled and unpleasant, were becoming technologically obsolete. Negroes had to force their way into skilled occupations, among them the building trades.

The building trades, those highly paid skilled workers such as plumbers, electricians, sheet metal workers, old American Federation of Labor craft unions, protected their economic strength by restricting entry into their trade. For instance, they might require aspiring apprentices to have a sponsor who was already a union member. The sheet metal workers even restricted entrance to sons of union members. This worked automatically to exclude blacks. Or the entrance examination for apprenticeship might exclude the poorly educated, which in New York City would also exclude blacks who had gone to trade schools. "They were notorious," said Rustin.[13] The building trades were not only white but divided by ethnicity. For example, masons were of Italian background, sheet rock workers of French-Canadian descent. Challenging discrimination in these trades was almost like challenging a tribal self-identity.

There was, nevertheless, a great deal of pressure on trade unions to end racial discrimination, from the Human Rights Commission of the city of New York, whose head was Rustin's friend Eleanor Holmes Norton; from the NAACP, through its labor director, Herbert Hill; from the Johnson administration. It was at the point of examinations for entrance into apprenticeship that Bayard Rustin decided to combat racial discrimination in unions, working through the Workers Defense League (WDL), on whose board he served. Little leftish reform groups in New York like the WDL, the League for Industrial Democracy (LID), the Jewish Labor Committee, various social democratic factions, and, after it came into existence, the A. Philip Randolph Institute had an informal close relationship with one another. People might be members of more than one group; they knew one another as friends, perhaps lovers, allies, drinking companions. A person might work on one project for one group and then move over to another for a different project.

In early 1964, that is, before the A. Philip Randolph Institute was born, Verna Rony, executive director of the WDL, got a call from a young man named Ernest Green, one of the original nine students to integrate Little Rock Central High school in 1957. He had just received an M.A. from Michigan State with a thesis on discrimination in the building trades and had spent the summer working with the AFL-CIO in Michigan. He was coming to New York and wanted to do something about organized labor and discrimination. With the help of a grant from the Taconic Foundations, the WDL happened to be starting a program to find young blacks and Puerto Ricans who wanted to enter apprentice programs of the building trades. Ray Murphy, an employment specialist, was to direct the program, and the WDL appointed Green as his assistant. Rustin helped Green get an apartment in the same International Ladies' Garment Workers Union complex on Eighth Avenue and Twenty-eighth Street in which he and Horowitz had apartments. Then in May 1964, Green, who soon succeeded Murphy, began operations in a storefront in Bedford Stuyvesant, Brooklyn. He tutored black applicants for the exam that would enable them to become apprentices and eventually full-fledged union members in one of the building trades. The WDL also supplied help filling out applications, loans for tools, counseling. The store-front operation was tiny and certainly not working with enough people to affect the labor situation in New York. Bayard Rustin and Albert Shanker, head of the United Federation of Teachers union, got Green together with Harry Van Ardsdale, president not only of the Brother-hood of Electrical Workers and the taxi union but, most important, the New York City Central Labor Council. Van Ardsdale was already pushing the unions to open up to Negro and Puerto Rican workers. "Talking to Van Ardsdale was kinda like talking to God," recalled Green. "I mean, here was a guy who ran the whole world. And he did all of his business under the old clock at the Commodore Hotel. He would keep a pocket full of dimes. . . . And so Shanker with Bayard's help set up a time for me to come in and sit down with Van Ardsdale and tell him what we're trying to do. . . . The relationship between Bayard and between Al and between Van Ardsdale finally began to open up the process."

Van Ardsdale helped Green get a few candidates into the appren-ticeship program of the International Brotherhood of Electrical Work-ers, which he headed. After a few months, Van Ardsdale called Don Slaiman, now director rather than assistant director of the Civil Rights Division of the AFL-CIO, as well as a board member of WDL. "You gonna get into other trades?" "How?" asked Slaiman. "I'll take care of it," said Van Ardsdale, and he set up a meeting of the New York Building Trades Council. Besides the presidents of the unions, Rustin and Green were present. Green described his project, and all the presi-dents of the unions agreed to work with him. That did not automati-cally mean compliance, certainly not at the shop level, but it was a start toward the sort of cooperation Bayard envisioned.[14]

The "Apprenticeship Program" of the Workers Defense League was not without conflict and some confrontation with the unions. In August 1964, the New York State Supreme Court ordered the Sheet Metal Workers to drop their father-son rule and to hold open entrance examinations for apprenticeship. At the first exams, no Negroes passed, although room was made for one young man—the first Negro member of that union. Ernest Green and the WDL started an intensive recruitment and tutoring program. "We decided then that most of them had never learned in school how to take a test," remembered Bayard.

> So we had to teach them. The boys had spent 20 minutes over a question they *didn't* know instead of doing everything they *did* know and then coming back; furthermore many of them were demoralized. . . . Many young Negroes go to tests feeling they are really not going to make it. . . . We took those boys into the A. Philip Randolph headquarters seven days a week for five weeks. We reduced trigonometry and algebra to arithmetic concepts; we had them playing with blocks like little children. . . . We had to assign a big brother to every one of those men—because when the time got close to the examination many of them lost hope. We had to go and dig them out. . . . We had to set up a fund and get some money for some of them, because the brightest boys didn't want to go down and take the tests because they didn't have decent clothing to wear. They couldn't go into a test feeling they didn't look right.

"Damn it," Rustin concluded, "we [know] how to break those building trades." The sheet metal workers tried a number of delaying devices, but in another examination in November 1965, most of the tutees passed. Some union spokesmen could not believe the results and insisted that the Negro applicants must have cheated, but in fact they had passed and became members of the previously all-white union. "This is a break-through," announced Rustin at a news conference held in the Workers Defense League storefront.[15] In a way it was, but still on a small scale.

By 1966, the program had expanded, and the A. Philip Randolph Educational Institute joined as co-sponsor, with the Workers Defense League, of what now became known as the Joint Apprenticeship Program (JAP). The difference was more formal than real, because the same people did the same things in either case. JAP was still small, but early in 1968 after about a year and a half of joint operation,

Rustin could report that they had placed 250 apprentices in the building trades in New York City. The program continued to grow and, renamed the Recruitment and Training Program (RTP), with grants from the United States Department of Labor, was to become the largest program of the APRI. Eventually it grew to the point where it became a separate corporation, with Rustin as chairman of the board.

Whether called JAP or RTP, the approach was the one Bayard Rustin saw as the way for the civil rights movement to move into urban industrial life. Any expansion of the number of job seekers could be, and was, perceived as a threat by the unions. But JAP quickly gained the confidence of the unions as "obviously more interested in getting Negroes and Puerto Ricans into apprenticeship programs than in embarrassing the unions," said F. Ray Marshall, a labor economist who would become secretary of labor under President Jimmy Carter. Soon JAP became, continued Marshall, "by unwritten consent . . . the chief referral channel through which virtually all minority applicants must pass if they seek entry into an apprentice program."[16] The training programs were clearly less of a threat to the unions than what became the alternative: "affirmative action," meaning hiring quotas. The term deserves quotation marks, because the apprenticeship training programs were also a form of affirmative action. With his essentially class-based view of society, Rustin believed that substituting a black worker for a white, and creating thereby an unemployed white person, would be pointless. It would also create enormous anger, which it has, and would destroy any hope of a labor-black coalition. After all, no matter what his or her racial attitudes, the white person needed the job, too.[17] Apprentices, in contrast to "affirmative action," did not directly keep anyone out of work, as quotas, however defined, might. Moreover, the RTP was a solution within the unions' own system, not against it. Unions were still the bargaining agents with management; they still maintained seniority systems. They had to stop racial discrimination, as with other institutions in the country, but otherwise they could continue with whatever power and influence they already had. Of course there would have to be continued economic growth so there would be enough jobs, and that soon became a crucial stumbling block. Whether training black teenagers for apprenticeship exams would actually work in practice to increase black membership significantly in previously discriminatory unions would not be clear for several years. It offered Bayard hope, however, of holding together the labor and civil rights movements.

While Rustin was establishing this new direction, the civil rights movement in the South continued its progress. There may have been a diffusion of clarity on other issues, but as far as voting rights went, the issue was clear. SCLC was going through its last paroxysm of mass protest, police brutality, and political triumph in Selma, Alabama, in the spring of 1965. Selma was the culmination of that voting rights campaign that had been a strong thread in the movement since at least 1957. Bayard was only there at the end, but he "was totally in support of Selma," said Andrew Young. "It was exactly what he thought we should be doing, and he was very helpful in bringing in organized labor support." This support meant not just old reliable sources like the Packinghouse Workers but also George Meany.[18]

From Selma, Martin Luther King and Andrew Young were often on the phone with Bayard. March 7 was "Bloody Sunday," when state troopers with dogs and on horseback beat terrified men, women, and children trying to march from Selma to Montgomery. On March 9, the very day the marchers planned to renew the march, federal judge Frank M. Johnson issued an injunction forbidding a Selma-to-Montgomery march. Attorney General Nicholas Katzenbach, finding he could not get through to King himself, tried to use Rustin as a go-between, asking King to obey the order and call off any march. The same day there was a particularly revealing conference call from King with Rustin, Andrew Young, Harry Wachtel, Jack Greenberg, and Clarence Jones. King started out by saying, "I am at one of the most difficult moments of my life. I have to make a terribly difficult decision. I wanted to share it with you and get your thinking." The dilemma was that King had never disobeyed a federal court order before. Federal courts had generally favored the civil rights movement, and King was tortured over the thought of defying one. Yet how could he turn back? What would he say to the hundreds of people prepared to march, and what would he say to his own sense of mission? Rustin, perhaps because of his experiences in New York, was acutely aware of the declining appeal of nonviolence. "All over Cleveland and other cities they are demonstrating," said Rustin. "Doctor King cannot allow the federal injunction to stop him from moving." King was worried about causing more violence, but Rustin said, "I don't think violence will ensue. I think he will be halted very early." Then, later on in the call, "I feel that Martin has to make a real moral and political decision. For him not to march causes incalculable harm to Martin and the non-violent movement. Roy, who is considered a conservative, has literally called for Negroes using violence if the federal government doesn't protect them."

Here Harry Wachtel interjected, "Right, self-defense."

Rustin went on, "Martin, there is only one answer to Wilkins and the people in the street. That is that the people who believe in non-violence are not now going to retreat."[19]

King did march, but not to Montgomery and thus not, he would argue, in violation of Judge Johnson's order. He turned back halfway across the Edmund Pettus Bridge leading out of Selma, thus keeping to an agreement he had worked out with federal officials but to the consternation of many of his followers. A week after Bloody Sunday, President Lyndon Johnson introduced the voting rights bill and, looking right into the TV camera, right into the eyes of every viewer, used that phrase that was the anthem of the civil rights movement, "We Shall Overcome." Bayard's enthusiasm for the speech was unbounded. "Nobody, Abraham Lincoln, Kennedy ever made a speech, as forthright a speech in defense of our movement as Johnson made tonight," he told Harry Wachtel. In *Commentary* he called it "the most radical statement ever made by a President on civil rights."[20]

Just as King was getting support from the Johnson administration, he was agonized by pressure from his own left wing. He was worried about James Forman and James Bevel calling for civil disobedience in Washington, when in fact the voting rights bill was moving forward "as fast as possible." What would the civil disobedience be for? "I've come to the conclusion," King said in a phone call to Rustin in March, "that I see no possibilities of working with SNCC. There is no hope." Bayard agreed and went further, "These people are no-win and sooner or later you are going to have to cut yourself off from them. There is nothing to be gained with a continuing relationship with SNCC in these projects. You are going to have to just draw the line." King agreed: "They confuse the press and say all these nasty things about me. . . . They do not believe in non-violence. They are violent. They worship Malcolm X. . . . They have a strong nationalistic attitude." King was reluctant to make too explicit a break, because he "had to work with these people," but the tensions within the movement were rising.[21]

Eventually Judge Johnson vacated his order; the march did take place, not only with civil rights leaders and followers but with nuns, priests, wounded veterans carrying American flags, and hundreds of white and black marchers. Bayard did not march, but he was part of the final rally when the marchers reached Montgomery.[22] Less than five months later, the voting rights bill became law, leading to enormous increases in southern black voting. It seemed like triumph, it was triumph, but Bayard had foreseen what was to come, and it was not only triumph.

What did voting rights mean to a resident of Watts, a black district in Los Angeles? Citizens of Watts could always vote if they wanted to, if they thought it would make any difference to their lives. Starting with even less provocation than Harlem, a confrontation between a white policeman and black residents on August 8, 1965, escalated into a six-day explosion put down by thousands of local policeman and National Guard troops. Dozens of people were killed, hundreds were injured, and thousands were arrested. King and Rustin were both asked by Los Angeles ministers to come there to help calm the situation, but both felt that things had deteriorated so much that they could not help. Ministers in Los Angeles had done nothing and now wanted Martin Luther King to come out and rescue them. Rustin and Roy Wilkins agreed that King should not go to Los Angeles, that he would be regarded by the black community there as "an emissary sent to quiet the rioters." But King at least had to make a statement and asked Rustin to help word it. Rustin gave what by now had become almost a routine formulation: that we deplore violence and also the conditions that lead to violence.[23]

However, after a couple of days of thinking about it, King felt the burden of his mission. He simply had to go to Los Angeles, even if there was not much he could do. He asked Bayard to go along. Rustin drew up a program for King in Los Angeles, which contained some strange features, certain to anger the protesters there. Rustin suggested that King promise to help innocent victims, to confront local government officials, to encourage long-range action by Angelenos, and to visit Negroes in jail "in an attempt to find ways in which they can help restore damage that they have done and attempt to redeem themselves." Did Rustin really believe that "redemption" was on the minds of the people in jail, or was the suggestion more to appeal to King's sense of compassion?

He was right, though, in his judgment that Martin Luther King had nothing to offer that the residents of Watts wanted. "Mr. Rustin," a young man said to them at a meeting in a school gym, "don't you and Dr. King come in here and tell us to behave ourselves. We are sick of Negro leaders telling us to behave ourselves; 'cause, Daddy, when you tell me to behave myself, you are asking me to accept this condition, and I don't accept it." King and Rustin kept hearing people refer to the "Watts Manifesto." Finally Rustin asked, "What do you mean, the manifesto? Would you mind letting me and Dr. King see a copy of it?"

The young man pulled out a match box; he pulled out a single match; he lit it. He said, "Daddy, that was our manifesto, and the slogan was Burn, Baby, Burn." And, he said, "We won." Rustin asked how had they won.

"Well, I'll tell you how we won. We were for years telling these white folks peacefully what was needed. We asked them to come and talk with us. They didn't come. We tried to get some war on poverty. It didn't come. But after our manifesto, daddy, the Mayor, the Governor, you, Dr. King, everybody came." And then, speaking sotto voce but so that everybody could hear: "And when you and Dr. King go out into the street, you better be careful, because they sent us so many damn sociologists, baby, so many economists, so many social workers, if you and King aren't careful, you will trip over them in the street."[24]

King's reaction may have been despair; Rustin's was more anger at the utter blindness that seemed to infect policy makers. For years, he had seen social change driven by his ideal, nonviolent direct action. NVDA was now going up in smoke. "If you wait until youngsters are forced to riot to listen to their grievances," he said later, "woe unto you and damn you, for you will get nothing but violence." That policy blindness was manifested for Rustin in the "McCone Report," the report of a commission that Governor Edward P. Brown appointed to find the causes and possible cures for Negro discontent. The McCone Report, said Rustin, talks about an "insensate rage of destruction," when in fact the outbreak was "a major rebellion of Negroes . . . asserting that they would no longer quietly submit to the deprivation of slum life." The report, said Rustin, placed the burden of responsibility on the Negroes, saying that they were unprepared for urban life and an industrial economy. There was not "one word about whether the cities have been willing and able to meet the demand for jobs, adequate housing, proper schools." Always the integrationist, Rustin excoriated the McCone Report for suggesting improvement in ghetto schools but "not [saying] one word about integration." The report called for fifty thousand jobs but did not have any ideas about where these jobs might come from.[25]

Bayard Rustin argued, as he had in "From Protest to Politics," that poverty was the same deadening problem for any poor person, black, white, Puerto Rican. When Lyndon Johnson in 1964 declared "unconditional war on poverty," the words were promising, but the reality was not. The War on Poverty was not what Bayard wanted and not what he would propose in the "Freedom Budget for All Americans" in 1966. Johnson's War on Poverty, thought Bayard, did not include the sort of huge jobs program that might in fact end poverty. Most of the money went to salaries for the black middle class to, as Bayard said, "keep them from revolting." Very little of the money actually reached the poor. Besides, all the programs were for training or education, that is, for youngsters. That did not address the terrible need for jobs that could support families.

In Harlem in 1964 and Watts in 1965, reality had looked Martin Luther King in the face and had said, "You are irrelevant, man, irrelevant to us." Bayard Rustin had heard. King had listened but not heard. Rustin had said that "there are no victories for him to win in the North," but King was determined to seek them. During the summer and fall, the SCLC surveyed several cities and decided that Chicago offered the most hope for some sort of victory. In the fall of

1965, soon after visiting Watts, when King decided to move into Chicago, Rustin warned, "You don't know what you are talking about. You don't know what Chicago is like. . . . You're going to get wiped out."[26] Rustin knew that the church, the basis for King's strength in the South, had neither the same function nor structure in the North. Like New York, Chicago was not simply white versus black as in Birmingham or Atlanta. There were black people on both sides of the issue and in fact black people in the political organization of Mayor Richard J. Daley. After eight months of confused and sporadic demonstrations, including one where King was hit by a stone, and endless negotiations with the Chicago Real Estate Board and the city government, King, the civil rights forces, and the authorities in Chicago signed a document in August 1966, with important-sounding promises about ending housing discrimination. The promises meant nothing. The racial patterns in Chicago remained unchanged. Joseph Lowery, the man who succeeded King as head of SCLC and had been in the organization since the beginning, acknowledged years later that Rustin had been right. King had been wiped out. "But we had to do it, we had to do it," said Lowery. Then, thinking about what he'd said, "Matter of principle."[27] In fact, neither King nor any of the forces of NVDA found a way to confront northern racial patterns. Perhaps not protest but rather politics in the service of social and economic change could provide an answer.

"The situation in Watts erupted in volcanic form, because the people there knew or felt that their deep troubles were interlaced with manifest injustice. And this eruptive potential is seething just below the surface in portions of almost every large city in the U.S.," wrote Bayard Rustin in the spring of 1966, for a draft introduction of the "Freedom Budget for All Americans."[28] He thus linked Watts to what would be the major project of the A. Philip Randolph Institute for the next couple of years. Randolph had been recommending a huge federal public works program for years, and the "Freedom Budget" was a specific plan for putting that idea into action. It was Bayard Rustin's attempt, starting only a few months after Watts, to move from protest to politics, but politically it was a fiasco.[29] It died.

This is not to say that the ideas in the "Freedom Budget for All Americans" were not well thought out and well presented. The name itself was a good idea, emphasizing that it was for all Americans, not just black Americans or even just the poor. The arguments were all sound and convincing, if one accepted the assumptions. The War on Poverty was all well and good, wrote Rustin, but "the anti-poverty program, stemming from the Office of Economic Opportunity, should be improved qualitatively and greatly augmented quantitatively." But the War on Poverty was not a jobs program. It trained people, hoping that the economy would absorb them. Its focus was on changing the poor themselves. The Freedom Budget's focus was on changing the economic system. In essence, it was a huge federal program to employ people doing what needed to be done, for instance, building and repairing schools and hospitals. It never said so, but it was the Works Progress Administration and Public Works Administration of the New Deal revived. The economics were worked out by Leon Keyserling, an old New Dealer who had been chairman of the Council of Economic Advisers under Harry Truman. For years, Keyserling had been arguing that the 1961 tax cut had been a mistake and that there should be federal spending to fight against continuing poverty. He had his own consulting firm, but it did not have the sort of mass support from organized labor that might come from the A. Philip Randolph Institute. For Randolph and the APRI, Keyserling could provide the sort of professional credibility that their mere advocacy lacked.

The idea of the Freedom Budget was to spend a sum as high as $185 billion over ten years, which would amount to about one-eighth of the *increase* in federal revenues from a growing economy. That sum would be used to ensure full employment (a verbal goal of the federal government since 1946) at a livable wage, adequate welfare, education, housing, medical care, and pure air and water. The Freedom Budget included a growth in military expenditures "consistent with recent experience." At the same time, "the Freedom Budget neither endorses nor condemns present military spending policies." Rustin and Keyserling insisted that the Freedom Budget was affordable along with current military expenditures. The APRI issued several editions of a pamphlet explicating the plan, filled with dramatic figures, dramatic rhetoric, and dramatic photographs, as well as page after page of diagrams and graphs. The second edition included an introduction by Martin Luther King saying that "the long journey ahead requires that we emphasize the needs of all America's poor, for there is no way merely to find work, or adequate housing, or quality integrated schools for Negroes alone." King thus signaled a clear shift from civil rights to an emphasis on economic change. Walter Reuther is listed as a supporter of the Freedom Budget, but George Meany is not! The pamphlet said the budget was anything but "Pie in the Sky," but that in fact is what it was, for that place at that time.

The loudest voices in the civil rights movement were going in another direction entirely. The slogan "Black Power" became nationally known on the "Meredith March against Fear" in the summer of 1966, although the white volunteers in Mississippi had heard it three years earlier. In early June 1966, James Meredith, the man who had integrated the University of Mississippi with the support of federal marshals and troops, started a solo march from Memphis, Tennessee, heading for Jackson, Mississippi, to show young blacks to be fearless in asserting their rights. Just inside the Mississippi border he was shot with birdshot—wounded but not killed. Civil rights leaders wanted to resume the march at the end of June but were uncertain about who and what doctrines would dominate. Martin Luther King decided that he had to be there, as a way of keeping the march nonviolent and integrationist. Stokely Carmichael and Floyd McKissick were there with their own agendas. King wanted Rustin to come. Stanley Levison thought that the best way to bury the idea of any sort of separatism or violence was to have King, Rustin, and some whites participate. Rustin himself was reluctant, afraid that "Stokely and McKissick and other left wingers would take advantage of [him] and that it would degenerate into a black nationalist thing." He did not go, and though King did, his forces singing "We Shall Overcome" got outshouted by "We Shall Overrun" and "Black Power." The march did become "a black nationalist thing."[30] If nonviolence and integration were obsolete in the minds of the most vocal blacks, was there any hope for coalition politics or the Freedom Budget?

The Freedom Budget, of course, evoked scorn from the conservatives. The civil rights movement should not tie itself to a general "leftward march," they argued.[31] By late 1966, Bayard's friends on the left also expressed outrage. Irving Howe and Norman Thomas did not see how the Freedom Budget could avoid condemning the

Vietnam War and could contemplate continued high military spending. Seymour Melman of Columbia University, something of a New Leftist, an advocate of decentralization and emphasis on domestic rather than military needs, wrote to Benjamin Spock, "I read with disbelief and dismay that you have fixed your name to this proposal." Keyserling and Rustin responded with the quite reasonable argument that military spending would remain high, with or without the war in Vietnam, and to condition the Freedom Budget on a lower defense budget would be to postpone it indefinitely. In this, they were quite right. The end of the war did not lead to any "peace dividend."[32]

Opposition from the Left had personal importance for Bayard, setting him further apart from some friends and allies, but it had no political significance. He remained personally friendly with most of his pacifist former allies, but there was always a bit of tension. They regarded him as morally weak. He regarded them as totally impractical. The Freedom Budget got nowhere in the forum where it really mattered: the broader electorate and Congress. The Randolph Institute sent copies to every senator and representative and also to economists, university and college presidents, social activists of all varieties. Some replied with endorsement, others with partial endorsement, still others with opposition, and many did not respond. After all, for many people, the pamphlet on the Freedom Budget was simply another bit of unsolicited mail. In October, the budget was summarized in a page-one story in the *New York Times*, but again with no apparent consequences.

Randolph and Rustin did get a chance to present the Freedom Budget at a special hearing of Senator Abraham Ribicoff's Subcommittee on Executive Reorganization in early December 1966. Rustin was at his eloquent best, arguing that though some had called the Freedom Budget a utopia, ignoring it would create an anti-utopia of "the politics of fear and frustration." This was a theme he would come back to in various articles over the years: whites fearing blacks, and blacks filled with frustration with white society. In this, before the worst of the Long Hot Summers, he was absolutely correct. "I do not happen to believe that we ought merely to damn the people who threw stones at Dr. King," he said, adding:

Except for their racial prejudice, which was permitted to come to the surface by objective economic and social conditions, the people who threw stones were, by and large, people who were buying homes that were only one-third paid for, who were saving money to send their children to college, who were sending their wives to work, and therefore needed two automobiles rather than one, and who felt that if anything happened to their husbands for a few weeks their entire economic situation would be destroyed. It was this economic fear that made it possible for their latent prejudice to come to the surface and be politically organized. . . .

If one looks into the frustration elements of the complex, then one sees that 12 years after the Supreme Court decision of 1954, Negro people are almost twice as crippled with unemployment as whites, that Negro teenagers have an unemployment rate three times that of whites (and Negro young girls four times as great), that there are now more Negro youngsters in segregated schools than there were in 1954, and that the ghettos have remained the same size but with more people, more rats, more roaches, and therefore more despair.

Rustin therefore put economics at the root of racial issues. Racial prejudice there was, and could not be denied, but if poor whites felt economically more secure, and if even poorer blacks saw prospects for economic improvement, these latent prejudices might not spur destructive political organization.

Ribicoff and Robert Kennedy, the other committee member present, asked only friendly questions. Ribicoff asked Rustin how his position contrasted with that of Stokely Carmichael. "Well," answered Rustin, "I don't think there is any basic comparison, because Mr. Carmichael has invested his time in debating a slogan [by which Rustin meant "Black Power"] which directs young Negroes away from an intelligent discussion of housing, schools, and jobs. He has not come forth with any concrete proposals. We have come forth with the Freedom Budget." Some months later he would say that the Black Power people were engaged in "frustration stupidity."

Later in his testimony, Bayard talked about a change in the civil rights movement. The major issues were no longer voting or equal accommodations. "We are now dealing with basic contradictions in American society. . . . Many people who marched on Washington for a vague dignity are not now prepared to follow through on doing something about full employment or minimum wages, and there has been a splintering. And what we have to do, it seems to me, is to rebuild the coalition." The full text of the Freedom Budget, with supporting material, was included in the Committee Report.[33]

The Freedom Budget was mentioned again in a congressional hearing on May 8, 1967, before the Subcommittee on Employment, Manpower and Poverty, by Dr. Arthur Logan, personal physician, longtime friend, and associate of Bayard Rustin and head of the Antipoverty Committee of the United Neighborhood Houses of New York City. Logan brought up the budget as something that might do what the War on Poverty was not doing. Senator Joseph S. Clark said that he had read it and that it might be a nice thing in the best of all possible worlds, "but as a matter of pragmatic politics, it seems to me utterly unrealistic." And later, "My constituents aren't ready for anything like that."[34] Thus with bits of support here and there, but with opposition from the Right, the Left, and the Center, the "Freedom Budget for All Americans" disappeared from view. Rustin and Keyserling continued to have some hope for it, but that hope was wishful thinking.

Some of Bayard's friends in looking back said that the Freedom Budget was sabotaged by the political Left with its insistence that the budget denounce the Vietnam War. But in fact it was "utterly unrealistic" to begin with. Rustin had urged a new emphasis on politics but showed no understanding of the political process and no appreciation of what was politically possible. Even with good ideas, simply presenting them in one hundred thousand copies distributed all around the country is not the way to proceed toward any political goal. Rustin ignored the War on Poverty. He was friends, from the Jewish Labor Committee, with "Bookie," that is, Hyman Bookbinder, assistant director of the Office of Economic Opportunity. Bookbinder tried again and again to convince Rustin of the very real benefits of the Office of Economic Opportunity (OEO). Rustin was unconvinced and ignored his other routes into the administration. He could have gone to Hubert Humphrey or perhaps Robert Kennedy and suggested that an element of a jobs program could be added to the War on Poverty.[35] Or he might have presented incremental ideas to a Senate committee. Instead he followed his own and Leon Keyserling's unrealistic impulses into what was quite possibly a correct analysis but one that constituted a grandiose and futile dead end.

By the end of 1966, then, frustration and confusion marked the civil rights movement. NVDA had been shown to have no future outside the South and was even of declining persuasiveness in the South. "Civil disorder," as in Watts, despite the hopes of that young black activist Bayard had spoken to in Los Angeles, provoked further repression and reaction. Racial separatism was conquering integration as a goal. Northern politics on a local level was unresponsive, even resistant in ways more intractable than in the South. The War on Poverty, with all its limitations, was being hollowed out to pay for the war in Vietnam, and there was certainly no political will for an even more ambitious antipoverty program. National politics, which had been the route to progress in the South, became more and more impenetrable at the same time that the attention of reform forces was shifting from the civil rights movement to the antiwar movement. What had seemed momentum in 1965 had turned to dust by 1967. The only bright spot for Bayard Rustin himself was the formation of the A. Philip Randolph Institute, which gave him the combination of security and independence that he had never had before.

13

Increasing

Isolation

"You don't understand power. You don't under-
stand power," said Bayard Rustin to Ralph DiGia outside the War
Resisters League offices in New York. DiGia had rebuked Bayard,
for not clearly and unequivocally opposing the Vietnam War. "You
guys," and Bayard gestured toward the WRL office, "can't deliver a
single pint of milk to the kids in Harlem, and Lyndon Johnson can."
And DiGia had to admit that Bayard was correct. They could not.
And yet pacifists regarded the war as immoral, as were all wars, and
felt it must be opposed no matter the consequences.[1]

The Vietnam War split the Democratic Party, it split the labor
movement, it split the civil rights movement, it split the country,
and it split Bayard Rustin. On the one hand, he had his long-standing
and active pacifism as well as his friends in the peace movement. He
had friends and associates on the political Left who may not have
been pacifists but who saw this particular war as increasingly abhor-
rent and Lyndon Johnson as increasingly duplicitous. On the other
hand, he had his strong anticommunism, there were major elements
in the labor movement supporting the war, and above all there was
the man in the White House who Bayard felt was doing more than
Kennedy and perhaps even more than Lincoln for Negroes. To oppose the war meant an end to any hope for a coalition with the Democratic Party of Lyndon Johnson.

Martin Luther King had been finding that out all through 1965
and 1966. He had begun speaking out against the war, in rather mild

terms, in August 1965 and in increasingly strong moral tones there-after. King was not yet calling for unilateral withdrawal but for nego-tiations with the Communist side to end America's involvement.[2] Rustin, Andrew Young, and Martin Luther King himself tried to reestablish King's primary role as a civil rights, not an antiwar, spokes-man. "I want to emphasize that my central concern is civil rights, but under no conditions will I bring an end to my speaking on the question of peace." He certainly did not, for much to Bayard Rustin's distress, King, in April 1966, persuaded SCLC's board to adopt a strong moral condemnation of the war and of the South Vietnamese regime.[3] As a result, Lyndon Johnson would no longer communicate with King.

Some of the tensions around Rustin's position can be seen in the months leading to the first sizable Washington demonstration against the war, on November 27, 1965. The chief organizing group was the Committee for a Sane Nuclear Policy (SANE), but others were also involved in the National Coordinating Committee, which was ar-ranging the march. The question was, would the demonstrations be a mass movement of uncontrolled participants, welcoming all com-ers including Trotskyites, Communists, and Communist sympathiz-ers, or would it be as carefully planned and controlled as the March on Washington? In a testy conversation with A. J. Muste, Rustin re-ferred to the Students for a Democratic Society (SDS) as "just danger-ous people." "You can't have a demonstration with a vague slogan like 'end the war,'" he said. "It's contrary to anything you ever taught me. You cannot have a vague slogan if you bring in the Du Bois Club and the Communists and Progressive Labor. . . . Mark my words, this crowd is going to do more to discredit the American Peace Move-ment than any combination of old adults. . . . I know this crowd. I know how deviously they work."[4]

Evidently Rustin convinced A. J., at least for a time. Rustin and Farmer were listed originally as among the sponsors of the demon-stration, but on April 16 they and a long list of leftist luminaries, including Muste, Norman Thomas, H. Stuart Hughes, Benjamin Spock, I. F. Stone, and others, issued a press release saying, "We wel-come the cooperation of all those groups and individuals who, like ourselves, believe in the need for an independent peace movement, not committed to any form of totalitarianism or drawing inspiration from the foreign policy of any government." This was the traditional position of the non-Communist Left: excluding Communist or Communist-dominated groups. The anti–Vietnam War campaign for a spectrum of reasons, however, increasingly discarded this exclusionary policy.[5] The most common reasoning was probably that various peace factions did not want to regard themselves as participating in what they considered cold war hysteria.

Reaction from the peace groups to Rustin's position was swift and angry. After only three days, Staughton Lynd wrote to Bayard, with a copy to *Liberation*.

> You believe in a peace movement dependent on the Johnson Administration.... We can oppose this horrible war only as house radicals, only as court jesters. And you, who should be leading us in civil disobedience, have gone along.
>
> Why, Bayard? You must know in your heart that your position betrays the essential moralism which you have taught myself [*sic*] and others over the years.

A few lines later, Lynd referred to Rustin's "apostasy on Vietnam."[6]

Talk about "apostasy" was overdrawn in 1965. Rustin's position was not that clear. Early in 1965, his had been one of several thousand signatures on a "Declaration of Conscience against the War in Vietnam" drafted jointly by the *Catholic Worker*, the Committee for Nonviolent Action, the Student Peace Union, and the War Resisters League counseling draft refusal. But that was a little-noticed effort, and over and over again he said to various callers that he did not want to make the same mistake that King had made. He was "for peace, but he [did] not want to make any enemies over Vietnam and cloud the issue." The civil rights field was too important.[7]

When the march actually took place in Washington, November 27, 1965, it was a decorous affair of perhaps twenty thousand to twenty-five thousand, with, as the *New York Times* said, "more babies than hippies," but a small group insisted on handing out Vietcong flags. Norman Thomas did attend, but no prominent civil rights leader did. Most of the marchers were white and middle class. There were also some counterdemonstrators supporting the war. In a phone call the next day, Harry Wachtel and Bayard agreed that it had been a good thing that the civil rights movement was not involved, and they were pleased to note that the newspapers had particularly mentioned that Farmer, Rustin, and John Lewis were not there.[8]

A few months later, summer 1966, Rustin was interviewed by James Finn, who was gathering the views of a variety of opponents of the war for his book *Protest: Pacifism and Politics*. The answers Rustin gave to Finn were from a generally near-pacifist position: against nuclear arms, against the national state, assuring Finn that he would never personally carry a gun, praising conscientious objectors. It was important, Rustin said, that there was a peace movement in the United States, and he agreed that the United States should get out of Vietnam. The question was, however, "*How* do we get out? And it's not enough to just keep saying 'Get out.' I think that many groups in the peace movement fail to provide a step-by-step method by which the U.S. can get out and still have any national pride. . . . I call for negotiations. I call for sitting down with everybody involved. I call for the United States taking unilateral steps, to stop the bombing in the North. Now if the nation does all that and the other side still rejects it, my next step may be to take the Muste [immediate unilateral withdrawal] position. But I am not prepared to do that yet."

Overall, Rustin's positions in that interview contained some contradictions. In answer to one question about reform in general, he advocated working not "for that which is now feasible" but rather for "that which is essential, relevant and necessary." And yet he in fact was arguing for a pragmatic adjustment to what was feasible. In addition, he said the nation-state was obsolete, and yet he wanted to preserve national pride as the United States disengaged from Vietnam. What he meant by "negotiations" was also unclear. In one meaning of the term, the Johnson administration, too, wanted to negotiate an exit from Vietnam.[9]

"Because I take this position," he said later in the Finn interview, "some people have called me a 'forerunner of the Marines' and 'social fascist,' and one thing and another. I want you to take notice, I have not made any moral judgement on them because they differ with me." Staughton Lynd may have been the most vocal of these critics, but others like Ralph DiGia, Dave Dellinger, James Peck, and

Dave McReynolds were equally distressed at what they felt was happening to their old comrade without arms. Julian Bond said that he had lost all respect for Rustin. "He seems to have sold his soul completely to the Democratic party."[10]

Rustin felt he had to resign from the executive committee of the War Resisters League and the co-editorship of *Liberation*. He remained a member of the WRL but began moving in a different circle of friends after about 1965 or 1966 and only saw his pacifist friends on occasion. Once, some years later, he came a little late and a little drunk to a birthday party that the WRL was having for Ralph DiGia. As he entered the room, Jim Peck confronted him, almost shouting. "I have just one question for you. How can you live with yourself?" The others in the room tried to calm Peck, but Bayard said, "No, no, let him speak! He's paid his dues." And replied to Peck in a somewhat exaggerated English accent, perhaps indicating discomfiture, "Quite well, thank you, quite well." Bayard retained a soft spot for the WRL right up to his death, even while disagreeing with the organization, and actually helped raise money for it in the eighties.[11] But Rustin was now no longer part of that peace movement with which he had grown up, for which he had gone to prison twenty years earlier.

Rustin tried to make his position clear in two articles in the *Amsterdam News* in March and May 1967. In the first of these, "Vietnam: Where I Stand," he reiterated his position on negotiations and said, "Nor can I go along with those who favor immediate U.S. withdrawal, or who absolve Hanoi and the Vietcong from all guilt. A military takeover by those forces would impose a totalitarian regime on South Vietnam and there is no doubt in my mind that the regime would wipe out independent democratic elements in the country. Of these there may be not many, but they deserve our support." In "Dr. King's Painful Dilemma," Rustin recognized that King felt a duty to oppose the war, both because Negroes were dying in Vietnam disproportionate to their percentage of the American population and because King was a winner of the Nobel Peace Prize. Rustin argued vigorously that any Negro had a right and civic duty to take whatever position on public issues seemed best to him or her, but he gently chided King and SCLC when he said, "I would consider the involvement of the civil rights organizations as such in peace activities as unprofitable and perhaps even suicidal."[12] Once having articulated his somewhat unclear positions, Rustin tried to stay away from the issue as much as possible.

Various people, particularly white liberals and pacifists, have explained Rustin's ambivalence simply as selling out. He was close to power, this argument runs, and bewitched by power; he did not want to return to the wilderness of radicalism. This is far too one-dimensional. In the first place, he was not that close to power, even with Hubert Humphrey, whom he supported for vice president and then president. Other factors have to be taken into account. First is that by 1965 Rustin was no longer a pacifist. Second, he was strongly anti-Communist, with at least some of the fervor of a former Communist. In looking back at Bayard's life after about 1966, George Houser said, "Bayard was playing the cold war game, he was playing the cold war game." But for Rustin it was no game. Third, whatever his distance from national power, he was now virtually a part of organized labor, and many union members supported the war and regarded the peace movement as traitorous. Fourth, he was now so devoted to domestic issues that he regarded the war as a secondary matter. He did not want Martin Luther King to speak strongly against the war, because King, in the popular mind, *was* the civil rights movement, and Rustin did not want to add opposition to the peace movement to opposition to civil rights by linking the two. Fifth was the man in the White House, who had done more for the Negro than any other president, perhaps even Lincoln. Rustin desperately wanted to preserve as close a relationship as possible to the administration even if it was, to a degree, as Staughton Lynd said in *Liberation*, a "coalition with the marines."[13]

For white liberals, opposing the war was an absolutely required test of good faith. It was not so for black liberals. For example, James Farmer, pacifist, opposed a resolution at CORE's 1966 annual convention calling for an immediate pullout. "I felt then at that time that these were separate issues."[14] Besides King and John Lewis, Bob Moses, also a pacifist, was one of the few black prominent civil rights figures to join the antiwar movement unequivocally. He, too, disagreed with Rustin but was sure the motivation was an effort to preserve the civil rights movement, not because Bayard had become a "social fascist."[15] In photographs of demonstrations against the war there are a few, but only a few, black faces. These crowds were more white than the March on Washington had been black.

Disputes over the war and over the direction of the civil rights movement were put aside when, in the fall of 1966, the House of Representatives, led by southern congressmen, moved to expel Representative Adam Clayton Powell of Harlem from his seat. Randolph, Rustin, the A. Philip Randolph Institute (APRI), and other black leaders gathered in Powell's support. The case against Powell was intricate in detail, but perhaps more than anything else it was because Powell flaunted his independence from House customs. In January 1967, Rustin prepared a statement: "Without condoning the actions of Mr. Powell, the civil rights movement . . . strongly object to the unseating of Powell. Powell has been denied due process [and] his constituents have been unduly deprived of representation in congress." Later that month, King, Randolph, Rustin, Wilkins, and Whitney Young issued a press release in support of Powell. When the House voted to exclude him on March 1, 1967, Rustin's column in the *Amsterdam News* was called "The Trouble with Adam." The trouble was "that he makes it difficult to support him, but not in this case. The decision to bar him from his duly elected seat is a violation of his rights." Eleanor Holmes Norton wrote a note to Rachelle Horowitz: "No matter how you feel about ole ACP, he's got a damn good constitutional argument going for him (Too bad that's *all* he's got going for him.)." Norton was right, because after considerable furor, Powell got his seat back by court order. For a moment, the civil rights movement seemed united, but it was only for a moment.[16]

Powell's exclusion was one sign of growing white backlash, and the Long Hot Summers of 1966 and 1967 made things worse. Not only did black frustration, as in Harlem and Watts, boil over into violence, but the violence was put down with the sort of brutality that can only be explained as an extension of America's racial attitudes. In July 1967 President Johnson appointed the National Advisory Commission on Civil Disorders (known as the Kerner Commission, after its chairman, Otto Kerner, governor of Illinois), which issued its report in March of the following year. The report was a thorough examination of eight "civil disorders" and ended with a summation of the recommendations. The first of these was employment, and the language sounded very much like that of the Freedom Budget. "We propose," said the report, "a comprehensive national manpower policy" that would include "large-scale development of new jobs in the public and private sector." Whereas Rustin had been very critical of the McCone Report on the outbreak in Watts, he praised the methods and conclusion of the Kerner Commission. He had only one "minor disagreement." The report states that it is racism that causes riots, not poverty or frustration. "I would put it somewhat differently. It is poverty and frustration that cause riots, but it is racism that causes poverty and frustration." Rustin argued that the Kerner Commission report strengthened and underlined the conclusion of the Freedom Budget, which it did. The budget and the report, however, had exactly the same influence on public policy.[17]

The growing strength not only of racial but also of economic conservatism was illustrated by the aggressiveness of the National Right to Work Committee. In February 1967 there was a major push for a "right to work" law in California. Such laws would prohibit management and labor from agreeing that workers in that firm must join the union. This would allow workers to have all the benefits won by unions, without joining the union or paying dues. "Right to work" was regarded by the labor movement as essentially a union-busting device. Rustin went to California, where he spoke and participated in round tables opposing "right to work." He was eloquent, as usual. "When the racists, bigots and monopolists were not shedding our blood, they were blocking our way with all kinds of stratagems. We have heard them all—'Property Rights,' 'States Rights,' 'Right to Work.' All of these slogans . . . plead for nothing else but the perpetuation of their own special, exploitative interests." At a round table in San Francisco on February 18 of the California Negro Leadership Conference, he heaped scorn on "right to work" but also tried to deal with black skepticism about unions. He knew unions had a history of discrimination, but Negroes, he argued, would lose only if the labor movement was weakened. "What we need to do is vigorously press the trade union movement to open up. God knows I hate to say to any Negro audience 'Take on another burden.' But we've got to take on the burden. . . . We've got to scream and pull our hair about the union. . . . In addition to fighting the trade unions we've got to face something else: trade unions do not *make* jobs, they put people in them. We have got to insist that this government come out with public works and full employment. That's the major job, and don't ever lose sight of that."

The APRI also prepared a pamphlet against "right to work" for unions and other workers to distribute. Rustin got NAACP and Urban League endorsement, and the APRI issued a Spanish-language translation of the pamphlet in cooperation with Cesar Chavez and the Farm Workers' Union. "Right to work" faced great opposition in California and did not win there. Its successes were confined to southern and Sunbelt states where organized labor was weakest.[18] This was not a victory for either the labor or the civil rights movement, but at least the defeat of "right to work" staved off a growing conservatism. Worse was to follow.

Between the time when the Kerner Commission was formed in mid-1967 and the election in November 1968, the civil rights movement suffered three disasters in which Bayard Rustin was closely entwined: the Memphis garbagemen's strike at which Martin Luther King was murdered; the failure of the Poor People's Campaign; and the conflict over the public schools in New York. The combination virtually ended the civil rights movement for Rustin, and perhaps for the country.

When Martin Luther King wrote an introduction for the Freedom Budget, he signaled a change of emphasis from purely civil rights to economic distress for poor blacks and whites. It was a transition he had been slowly making for some time in a "Rustinian" direction. Rustin was, of course, not the only one thinking along these lines. Whitney Young had called for a "domestic Marshall plan" in 1963, but it was Rustin and Keyserling who had spelled out details. Beginning in 1967, King searched for a way SCLC could highlight the economic plight of poor blacks—and poor whites—in the United States. He finally came up with the idea of a "Poor People's Campaign." Poor people, black and white, would come to Washington, perhaps some in mule-drawn carts, and camp there for some time to demonstrate the extent of poverty in prosperous America.

Early in 1968, Bayard wrote a memo to Martin Luther King saying that the aims of any Poor People's Campaign have to be clearly spelled out. "We are not now in the period we were in 1963," Rustin wrote, "at the time of Selma, Birmingham and the March on Washington, when there was absolute clarity in everyone's mind as to objectives. The confusion today around economic questions and the splintering of the movement, I am convinced, requires a clear statement as to objectives, strategy and tactics."[19]

By March, he felt the objectives, strategy, and tactics had not been spelled out. "At the present time," Rustin said in March, "I am not working with him [King] on it, though I wish him well. The reason I am not working on it is I was never able to get out of Dr. King and his lieutenants the answers to three questions—What are your objectives? I don't think they really worked them out yet clearly. What are your tactics going to be? Are you going to disrupt government buildings and hospitals and other areas? Or are you going to have a peaceful demonstration, picketing that is within the law, or are you going to use something extra? They told me they don't know." During his years of running demonstrations, Rustin had said over and over to his friends that a demonstration must have three groups of objectives: one, attainable, because most people will not participate if there is no victory at all in sight; two, some possibly obtainable objectives, if luck, politics, or leadership works out well; three, objectives that push the movement forward, perhaps in ways that have not really caught on yet. In Bayard's eyes, the Poor People's Campaign had none of these three.

Bayard was also always the practical reformer. "When it comes to the strategy of how they are going to keep 3000 people in tents, I was not able to get any answer, even though I had drawn up several pages showing the millions of dollars it would take to keep 3000 people in tents in Washington. By the time you run electricity in, by the time you buy your tents, by the time you rent your toilets—mobile toilets which are up to $80 a day for four-seaters, and $40 a day for two seaters—by the time you bring in portable showers and do the plumbing at Union rates for installing those showers, the price was astronomical."[20]

King and SCLC nevertheless pushed ahead with the plans, no matter how vague. In March 1968 King interrupted his work on the

Poor People's Campaign and went to Memphis to support a strike of garbage workers, mostly black, asking for higher pay and union recognition. Bayard and Roy Wilkins flew to Memphis on March 13 to speak at a mass meeting supporting the strike, and King came the next day. Norman Hill, Bayard's assistant at the A. Philip Randolph Institute, and Rustin organized the Committee on the Move to Equality (COME) in support of the strikers. King led what he had planned as a peaceful protest march on March 28, but it turned violent as some youthful protesters broke store windows, looted, and set fires. Police responded with tear gas and bullets, and King, sorely depressed, returned to Atlanta to continue work on the Poor People's Campaign. Norman Hill went to Memphis on April 2 to try to bring order back for a second march. In preparation for that march, King came back to Memphis on April 3 for what he hoped would be a nonviolent demonstration.

When King was assassinated the next evening, the mood changed. In other cities, black anger again set fires burning, but in Memphis, wrote Rustin, "these same young people [who had been violent] were deeply moved by the death of Martin Luther King. . . . It was my hope that their energies could be put to constructive use." Rustin spoke on Channel 13, the educational TV station in New York, raising money for the effort in Memphis. He could not hold back the tears, even when he was on camera. Then he flew to Memphis the day after King's murder to organize a nonviolent demonstration. He had to change planes in Washington, and a presidential message reached him there, asking him to come to the White House. A broad spectrum of Negro opinion was there, but deliberately not Stokely Carmichael. After the White House meeting, the group drove to the Washington Cathedral for a service honoring King; then Bayard resumed his journey to Memphis.[21] He and Norman Hill organized another march for April 8, partly in support of the garbage workers, partly as a memorial to King. They asked the young people, "the ruffians," who had rioted a week earlier and were now, Rustin thought, feeling very guilty, to act as marshals for an April 8 march.[22] Bayard tried to get as many civil rights spokespeople as possible to join the march, and many came: Ralph Abernathy and Coretta Scott King, of course, but also Benjamin Spock and Don Slaiman.

The demonstrators first marched to City Hall Plaza for a rally. Ralph Abernathy was the first speaker. In the middle of his speech, the microphone went dead, and Rustin rushed around backstage to find a bullhorn so Abernathy could continue. At the end of Abernathy's speech, Rustin led spirited singing of a church hymn that everyone knew, "A-amen, A-amen," and the crowd came alive. After a few more speakers, Rustin himself spoke. "I have a two-minute speech," he said, "and I don't want you to interrupt." He did speak for about two minutes, the shortest speech that day. He told the crowd that he'd had counters and they had come up with forty-two hundred people at the march. Then he went on, "King did not know hate. He took hatred out of himself." Rustin insisted that "nothing that is wrong with us can be cured by hatred." King knew no racism. "At the moment he was shot down . . . he didn't say 'feed my black brothers' he said 'feed my flock.'" After some more speeches, the march resumed, again in perfect order. As City Hall Plaza emptied out, Bayard Rustin, still in suit and tie, went around gathering loose papers, putting them in trash barrels and moving trash barrels so city sanitation workers could more easily clean up.[23]

There had been a confusion of aims and methods in the Poor People's Campaign while King was alive, and it grew worse after his death. Abernathy was King's designated successor, but since he did not have King's hold on other SCLC members, confusion and competition, always present in SCLC, increased.[24] The demonstrations in Washington did, however, go ahead. Poor people, some in mule carts, came to Washington in May to create "Resurrection City" on the Mall, but neither Congress nor the administration paid much attention. The summer turned out to be unusually rainy, so rain and mud made life miserable. On May 24, SCLC enlisted Bayard Rustin to try to rescue a desperate situation by organizing a "day of conscience" demonstration on June 19. It was to be a "Mobilization in Support of the Poor People's Campaign," with individuals and groups from all over the country converging on Washington. Aware of the confusion within SCLC, and skeptical of the whole Poor People's Campaign, Rustin first got Ralph Abernathy to agree on some attainable objectives. Then he talked to Attorney General Ramsey Clark, who made some encouraging noises about the administration being prepared to respond. Then Rustin agreed to head the Mobilization.[25] But the joint news conference at which Abernathy announced Rustin's appointment revealed the tensions between the two. Abernathy refused to specify goals of the Poor People's Campaign. "When it comes to specific legislation, that is not our job," he said. "If the leaders of this country have enough sense to put a man on the moon, they have enough sense to put an end to poverty in this country." Rustin said that specific demands would be formulated, including a guaranteed national income, job creation, and repeal of "restrictive amendments to the social security act."[26]

Immediately Rustin sprang into action. Here was an opportunity to use the techniques he had developed to such a high level for the March on Washington, but this time in pursuit of the goals that had been ignored in the Freedom Budget. Headquarters were in New York, but only for the one-day Mobilization. The Poor People's Campaign headquarters were still the SCLC office in Atlanta, and Ralph Abernathy was in charge. Rustin immediately set up an organization similar to the system he used in 1963. He began contacting people, particularly in the labor movement and the churches. Walter Reuther's United Auto Workers quickly donated twenty-five thousand dollars, and letters of support came from many other organizations. Rustin planned a massive demonstration of blacks, whites, Jews, Catholics, Protestants, trade unionists, intellectuals, perhaps even as big as the 1963 march. He formulated specific objectives, starting with the creation of one million jobs and a minimum wage of two dollars per hour—like the Freedom Budget.[27]

In fact, he lasted less than two weeks in the job, resigning June 7. Abernathy's version was that Rustin "was causing more problems than he was solving, and finally he resigned when he could not have his way on all important matters."[28] Rustin simply would not, could not, work with Abernathy and the power and ego struggles within SCLC. Abernathy assured people that the demonstration would not involve civil disobedience, but he would not formulate goals. He at first accepted but then repudiated a fourteen-point agreement he and Rustin had drawn up spelling out Rustin's absolute authority in running the Mobilization. Then he did not return several phone calls from Rustin. James Bevel, whom Bayard described as "both a genius

and a kook," denounced Rustin. Hosea Williams made angry statements. "The picnic is over. . . . The police want to use their billies.
Well, we're going to give them a chance." He called Rustin's specific
demands a "bunch of foolishness."[29] When Rustin resigned, his friends
were furious at Abernathy. Arthur Logan telegrammed Abernathy
that he must support Bayard. "Your functional survival as head of a
significant civil rights organization hinges totally on your immediate forthright statement and performance."[30] But Rustin was permanently out.

Even without his support during the last two weeks before June
19, the Mobilization was reasonably successful. About fifty thousand people showed up, half white, half black, and listened, rather
casually, to speeches by Abernathy, Roy Wilkins, and Whitney Young,
among others. In contrast to the 1963 march, however, there were
some eighty arrests, some civil disobedience demonstrations at the
Department of Agriculture and Department of Justice offices, some
cries of "soul power, soul power." Jesse Jackson was afraid things
were getting a little out of hand and called for more discipline. "We
must not become a mob. We must remain a movement."[31] Marian
Logan, close friend of Bayard's and a board member of SCLC, complained to Stanley Levison that "the staff of SCLC is living at the
Pitts Motel while the poor people are up to their ass in mud." Rustin
finally concluded that SCLC was "designed as an extension of the
most dynamic personality of the century," and without that one person, the organization would likely fall apart.[32] The campaign and
Resurrection City gradually fizzled. Eventually the last holdouts at
Resurrection City were removed by the police.

At the same time, the Ocean Hill–Brownsville furor in New York
drove further apart elements of what Rustin hoped would be coalition partners as they had been: blacks, labor unions, and Jews. It was
this bitter issue that led to Rustin's being, in the words of Eleanor
Holmes Norton, "read out of the civil rights movement."[33] Rustin
was always an integrationist, both in his personal life and as a social
philosophy. But integration did not seem to be progressing in the
North. Quite the reverse. As Rustin himself repeatedly pointed out,
there were more children in segregated schools in the North in 1964
than in 1954. And clearly, many of the black students in these segregated

schools were getting an inferior education. Mechanisms were suggested to integrate schools in northern cities, but in only a few places were they implemented. Black activists, supported by many white reformers, concluded that the schools where black children actually found themselves must be improved, whether or not they were integrated. Yet the school boards in city after city seemed as indifferent or hostile toward improving predominantly black schools as they had been toward promoting genuine integration. A logical conclusion supported by McGeorge Bundy, now at the Ford Foundation, and Mayor John Lindsay was to have the neighborhood, the black neighborhood, the parents of the black neighborhood, control the schools instead of a citywide school board that had simply not been doing its job. That is, there should be decentralization. But exactly what did that mean? Was the local board going to control the budget, hiring, firing, curriculum? The United Federation of Teachers (UFT, the teachers' union) insisted that it favored "decentralization" but not "community control." To the union, this distinction might have been clear, but for the public, since both terms were ill defined, the distinction created more rather than less confusion. The *Amsterdam News*, for example, used the two terms interchangeably.

In 1967, with support from the UFT and the Ford Foundation, Ocean Hill–Brownsville, a school district in Brooklyn, was designated as an experimental decentralized district, with a good deal of somewhat undefined power. Much money was poured into the district, mostly from the Ford Foundation, to finance smaller classes and teacher aides. The UFT saw this "More Effective Schools" (MES) program as working, or at least promising. The district was busy organizing an election for the newly constituted local school board and appointing an administrator, Rhody McCoy. It was not really in operation until spring 1968.

On May 8, 1968, the district fired (or "reassigned") thirteen teachers (and six administrators, not covered by the UFT contract) whom they deemed unsatisfactory. This was only a small portion of the total teaching body in the district, but the contract between the board of education and the UFT specified that teachers were entitled to "due process," including a hearing and chance to defend themselves, before being reassigned out of their district. Bayard went to talk to

Randolph and was surprised that the older man saw the issue as a simple trade union question. A union contract had been violated. Randolph asked Rustin to help out Albert Shanker, head of the UFT, because, said Randolph, as Rustin recalled it, "if Rhody McCoy can get away with firing teachers without giving them due process, without seniority lines, and there is ever established a precedent for this, the ones who are going to suffer most under this will be blacks." The union should try to find a solution, thought Randolph and Rustin, and if there was none, the union should consider a strike to have the rules followed.[34]

The issue seemed straightforward, but it was not. Soon the controversies spiraled way beyond what people like the human rights commissioner of New York, Eleanor Holmes Norton, or people in the teachers' union like Sandra Feldman had foreseen. The fired teachers were white, mostly Jewish. The head of the UFT, Albert Shanker, was white and Jewish. The Ocean Hill–Brownsville school board was almost all black; its administrator, Rhody McCoy, was black. The schoolchildren were black and Puerto Rican. Defending teachers seemed the same as defending a system that had been systematically destroying black children for generations.[35] The details of due process rules seemed to black spokespeople and others to be quibbling about defending people who had been doing palpable harm. Milton Galamison became one of the self-appointed spokespeople for the district, issuing one belligerent statement after another. "Local control" or "community control" in Ocean Hill–Brownsville moved the phrase "Black Power" from rhetoric to reality. The president of the New York City Board of Education said the district did not have the power to fire the teachers. Now defending the teachers seemed like agreeing with the hated "110 Livingston Street," the office of the city board of education. The New York Civil Liberties Union and the New York NAACP defended Ocean Hill–Brownsville, citing the long failure of the New York schools to educate poor black children. These liberal organizations and the presumably liberal UFT issued fervent pamphlets denouncing one another.[36]

Bayard Rustin thought his civil rights credentials were unassailable. He had shown over and over again that he was as aware as anyone of the failure of the schools. He had specifically protested against inadequate education in New York for black children with two Youth Marches for Integrated Schools and a school boycott, working with Milton Galamison. Yet he was also an outspoken opponent of any sort of separatism, nationalism, or "Black Power." He was a strong defender of unions in general and of the United Federation of Teachers in particular. He had known Albert Shanker for years and had supported the idea of trade unionism and collective bargaining for many more.

Rustin also saw the dangers inherent in "community control." "Stripped of the rhetoric which so often camouflages its true significance," he wrote, "community control is revealed as a concept of social organization incompatible with a political program committed to social and racial justice. . . . [It] is the spiritual descendant of states' rights, so often invoked to sanctify the denial to blacks of their basic rights. . . . In Forest Hills right now the most vociferous and outspoken opponents of the controversial scatter site [housing] projects justify what, for some, is an effort to insulate a neighborhood against the encroachment of minorities and the poor, on the grounds that they have the right to control their community." Rustin also saw the whole idea as a dangerous form of segregation. "Separatism, no matter what form it takes or how slickly it is packaged, has always worked to the detriment of the black man." Conservatives, he argued, saw this reality more clearly than liberals. Conservatives were against equality and favored the local control that would perpetuate inequality. Liberals talked in favor of "community control" but also favored racial justice, which historically had only come from the central government.[37]

Negotiations between the union and the Ocean Hill–Brownsville board got nowhere, so in September 1968, the UFT struck the New York City school system, the first of three strikes that fall. On September 19, the A. Philip Randolph Institute, that is, Bayard Rustin, took out an advertisement in the *New York Times*, the *New York Post*, and the *Daily News* defending the teachers. The ad denied that the conflict was a racial issue or one of decentralization. The issue was, as the UFT had always maintained, the right of due process. "It is the right of every worker to be judged on his merits—not his color or creed." This is a right, said the ad, "that black workers have struggled and sacrificed to win for generations." But the APRI made clear that it knew larger issues were involved. "In this context we must ask: Will decentralization lead to *apartheid* education or the maximum feasible integration? Will our schools be dominated by a small minority that does not represent the majority but seeks to impose its will upon the community, or will genuine parent and community groups have a voice in the education of the children?"

By far the majority of the letters that Rustin received in response to the ad simply endorsed it. Yet as the only prominent black person other than Randolph to back the union, he aroused such a chorus of denunciation, of anger, of vituperation and hate mail, that it amounted to his virtually being rejected by the movement of which he had been a major part for decades.

One of the most poignant letters came from a writer who did not sign his name but identified himself as a black student at Cornell.

> Have you ever passed the N.Y.S. Regents exam in Trigonometry, Intermediate and Elementary Algebra and gone to a school and try to pass calculus 1st semester? . . . Have you ever tried to compete with kids who have 3 and 4 years of intensive language study as preparation for the second term Elementary Spanish course? . . .
>
> I compete with kids who have been educated in the N.Y.C. public school system. The only difference being they were educated in white areas whereas I was educated in the ghetto.

Many of the letters were simply angry. "Unionists: To try to make the Black people think the UFT teachers strike is not racial is a damn lie. It is part of that white power structure that has been keeping the Black community from self-determination. If your group regards your selves as friends of the Black Community then we don't need any enemies."

Or,

"Mr. Rustin, I strongly suggest that you reappraise the record and stop being a 'house Nigger.'"

Or,

"Tell me why: Why should I support the teachers. Why should Parents support the U.F.T. Why must we get behind them?

"Mr. Rustin, they did not raise the issue of the failures of the schools. Parents did. You know that."

Or,

"WAKE UP BROTHER—WAKE UP!"[38]

The *Amsterdam News*, which had expressed merely distress with the "chaos in our schools" at the beginning of 1968 without taking a clear position on the specifics, became by October clearly and angrily in favor of Rhody McCoy and the Ocean Hill–Brownsville district. "Stick to your guns, Rhody McCoy. We're behind you," the newspaper editorialized. Yet all throughout this bitter period, the *Amsterdam News* continued to run Rustin's regular column, along with regular columns by people with other points of view. Floyd McKissick repeatedly argued that black people "must have absolute power over the institutions in their communities." Roy Wilkins regularly assailed the emptiness of the Black Power slogans and leadership. Rustin's columns, except for one, were about subjects that only indirectly touched on the specifics of the New York school battle. On October 5, however, he repeated the argument that due process was a necessity for black progress. Further, he insisted that black people must be able to debate the issues "without rancor or animus." If not, the rancor and animus "will lead ultimately to giving a small but militant minority veto power over the majority because the center . . . will become fearful of raising pertinent questions." Always the rational man, he wanted to maintain an atmosphere that was "conducive to clear thinking." He concluded by saying that he and Randolph might be wrong, "and if wrong we stand ready to be convinced—but convinced by intelligent argument."

He enclosed that article in a letter to a friend in Newark. "My position on the UFT strike has not been popular to say the least," he admitted in that letter.

We are in a very difficult political period, and often problems of psychology and self-image are as important as political program. But I sense that a giant hoax is being perpetuated [*sic*, he meant perpetrated] on black people. . . . I am not fooled into thinking that giving a local board control of a system will by itself substantially effect [*sic*] the educational system. . . . For years Negro children in the South had only Negro teachers. Standards for Negro teachers and pupils were lower than in the white schools. . . . I still believe that the Negroes's [*sic*] best hope is an integrated society.

Eleanor Holmes Norton thought Rustin might have acted as a mediator between the UFT and the black community, but he probably could not have. He had made clear for years his opposition to Black Power, separatism, and his support of integration. On a personal level, Rustin and Galamison were now scorning each other. Rustin simply did not have entrée or credibility in the world of black militancy in 1968.[39]

This was not a time for promoting integration or clear thinking, however; it was a time of high emotions. Tommie Smith and John Carlos gave the Black Power raised-fist salute from the winners' platform at the Mexico City Olympics. Adam Clayton Powell was seeking reelection to his old seat, and the Black Panthers were making constant headlines. All this was taking place in the midst of a national crisis. The antiwar movement was growing in numbers and in anger. Students at universities across the country were taking over buildings and being forcibly ejected. Robert Kennedy's assassination created despair, Martin Luther King's fury. The Long Hot Summers were heated up again by King's assassination, and the rhetoric of Black Power was growing hotter. The Democratic convention in Chicago was the occasion for virtual war in the streets.

As if emotions were not already high enough, in mid-November 1968, a mimeographed letter signed by Ralph Poynter of a parents' committee appeared in teachers' mailboxes saying that all black children should be taught by black teachers rather than "the middle east murderers of colored children." The UFT gave the letter to the Anti-Defamation League, which, always alert to any sort of anti-Semitism, publicized it and condemned the Ocean Hill–Brownsville board for fostering race hate. It soon turned out that Poynter's committee was a sham, and he was speaking only for himself. Of course, there was also some antiblack expression among Jews. Anyone growing up Jewish in New York was familiar with the term *schwartzim*, Yiddish for "blacks," spoken in a tone of contempt. However, even before the

"Poynter letter," as it came to be called, there was already some anti-Jewish element in the Ocean Hill–Brownsville rhetoric. For example, one correspondent wrote to A. Philip Randolph, "It is regrettable that you must spend the last and now lamentable years of your life parroting the filthy deceptions of zionist racism."[40] So Jewish emotions were on edge and easy to arouse. A new inflammatory issue was now added, with the ADL condemning anti-Semitism and a number of Jewish liberals denouncing the ADL for exaggerating. At the same time, the Jewish Labor Committee and the League for Industrial Democracy defended the teachers.[41] At just this time, the A. Philip Randolph Institute moved from Harlem into space rented from the UFT at the union's headquarters, 260 Park Avenue South. The institute had to move somewhere, because the building it was in was being torn down. Bayard was a bit worried about how the move might look, but all the black members of the staff (Rachelle Horowitz was the only white member) favored the move downtown.[42] The move was front-page news in Harlem, with the headline "Backs UFT Then Rent Office Space." Norman Hill tried to explain that the APRI would have preferred to stay in Harlem but could not find the needed space at a good price. To the *Amsterdam News*, the explanation sounded lame.[43]

Eventually, after three strikes and some ugly street confrontations during the fall of 1968, the issue between the union and the Ocean Hill–Brownsville board was settled in court with what was mostly a victory for the union. The Ocean Hill–Brownsville board was dissolved and only reconstituted with diminished power. The union won the right to protect its teachers with due process. Albert Shanker in victory was denounced by the losers as a racist tool of the city board of education. Yet when the "paraprofessionals," that is, the almost all-black teachers' aides, hall monitors, and the like, chose a union, they chose Albert Shanker's United Federation of Teachers. His strongest support among the "paras" came from those in Ocean Hill–Brownsville.[44]

Decentralization also, in the long run, turned out to be a failure. Educationally there seemed to have been some improvement in things like reading scores over the next decade, but relating that to decentralization is difficult. The ideal picture of parents' influence in choosing who should teach their children dissolved. In the 1980s and 1990s, voting in school board elections diminished to the point where incumbents more interested in the job than in education could keep themselves in office indefinitely. Recent school chancellors of the city, all of whom were black or hispanic, have spent much of their efforts doing away with incompetent or corrupt local boards and establishing what Sandra Feldman, now head of the national American Federation of Teachers, said the UFT had wanted all along, "decentralization not local control." Bayard Rustin was essentially proved right. Local control was a bad idea. As Rebecca Simonson in defending the UFT had said, "Depressed people have little time or energy to give educational guidance."[45]

The civil rights movement had gone in a direction Rustin could not follow, and it had driven him out. He had taken himself out of the pacifist movement. With Humphrey's defeat, Robert Kennedy's murder, Wallace's strength, and Nixon's election, any hope for the sort of extension of liberalism that Rustin wanted disappeared. "White backlash" was now in control of race relations. The coalition with white liberals in general and liberal Jews in particular had come apart over the issue of the war and the increasingly overt anti-Semitism of northern black spokespeople. SCLC had died as an effective organization on the balcony of the Lorraine Motel and in the mud of Resurrection City. What Bayard considered the "frustration stupidity" of Black Power advocates and nationalists had taken over and was killing CORE, SNCC, and the northern movement.[46]

In February 1969, Thomas R. Brooks, a board member of the League for Industrial Democracy, published an article about Rustin in the *New York Times Magazine* called "A Strategist without a Movement." That was almost correct.[47]

14

The 1970s

No Place Left
to Stand

The movement Bayard Rustin had remaining was the labor movement and the A. Philip Randolph Institute. At election times, the APRI would help with voter registration and get-out-the-vote drives, but that was not a continuous effort.[1] One continuous program was for the APRI to be a bully pulpit for Bayard Rustin. From this platform he issued regular columns every two weeks. These discussed specific issues like President Nixon's proposal for black capitalism, or more general questions like separatism and Black Power. They appeared in the *Amsterdam News* from 1967 until 1970 and were syndicated to some thirty other black newspapers.[2] They appeared frequently in Albert Shanker's regular column, a paid advertisement in the *New York Times* each Sunday. They were often in the *American Federationist* and the *AFL-CIO News*. As the APRI and the Recruitment and Training Program expanded into more and more cities, the columns were regularly in newsletters of the centers.

As with his writing, Rustin's speaking also increased after he had the permanent platform of the APRI. Most particularly he was in constant demand to speak at annual conventions of various unions. To take only one six-month period, spring and summer 1970, he spoke to the United Furniture Workers, the Retail Wholesale and Department Store Union, the Textile Workers of America, the Mississippi AFL-CIO, the Illinois AFL-CIO, and the California AFL-CIO. He frequently spoke at annual meetings of the national AFL-CIO. Sometimes his speeches might be in support of particular candidates for public office or on the necessity for economic growth, or he might denounce a particular public policy of the Nixon administration. But his major theme, one that came up again and again in various forms, was the necessity for maintaining and strengthening the Negro-labor alliance. He was surely aware of the long history during which blacks had been used as strikebreakers, and he spoke frequently in opposition to the racial exclusiveness of unions, but he emphasized not past conflict but present necessities.

He could be counted on to give a marvelous speech—sometimes beginning or ending with his singing. His speaking at union meetings was simply part of his duties as head of the APRI, without extra pay, but he earned a good portion of his income from speaking fees at colleges and universities. The enthusiasm was not only for his ideas but also for his dramatic and convincing platform style. He was capable of wry humor about style. Sometimes when speaking in or near New York he would grab Rachelle Horowitz and bring her with him. "I am so eloquent I can convince myself of anything," he might say. "Come along and tell me what *you* think!"

In a major speech called "Conflict or Coalition," which Tom Kahn had drafted and Rustin delivered to the AFL-CIO convention in 1969, Bayard made the point that blacks and labor unions needed each other. "Whatever differences we have among ourselves, we have a lot more in common. For one thing, we have enemies in common." This was a part of an address summing up many ideas that recurred often in his articles and speeches. He spoke first of the twins of black rage and white fear. Blacks had certainly made progress during the previous ten years, Rustin said, but there were still millions of black people who could not get a decent job, a decent house, or a decent education for their children. On the other hand, there were millions of white people, poor or just barely able to hang on, whose jobs and homes meant everything. "And because their positions are so precarious, they feel threatened by black demands." Each group had to understand the other. "We can either spend the rest of this century denouncing these people as racist and being denounced by them in turn. Or we can attack the root causes of their fear. . . . We can eradicate white fear and black rage by satisfying the real needs of all our people. Let us build."

Then Rustin turned to the complex problem of minorities in the building trades, the focal point for racism within organized labor. This was the issue on which the APRI had expended major effort for the last five years and for which Rustin had major hope. He argued that business and conservative interests attacked the building trade unions as racist to get more workers in the trades and lower wages. "And so I say to my fellow freedom-fighters in the civil rights movement: we must continue to press vigorously for greater minority participation in the building trades. But we will not let ourselves become stooges for those powerful economic interests that would use our struggle to depress wages and standards or to cripple the unions that won them."

To the building trades unions themselves, he said he knew that they had recently passed resolutions in favor of greater minority membership. At the same time there had been resistance and foot dragging. "Statements in themselves . . . are not enough. There must be forthright action. Now there must be visible results." He knew, he said, that the unions had made progress, but this progress simply proved that more was possible.

The Nixon administration, he continued, had a two-pronged strategy for building a permanent conservative coalition. It was to go slow on civil rights and at the same time to try to divide black and white workers by going after the building trades. Rustin argued, too optimistically as it turned out, that "the Negro-labor alliance cannot be broken apart so easily. . . . We must strengthen that alliance." He concluded with, "And that is why, in the words of the old song, 'I'm sticking with the union.'"

Don Slaiman remembered that there was thunderous applause when Bayard sat down. Union leader after union leader came up to Slaiman saying that the speech had not simply moved them emotionally but moved them to action.[3] The question was, how much action actually took place?

Bayard's way of "sticking to the union," while trying to break the unions' racism, was through the Recruitment and Training Program (RTP), which started in a storefront in Brooklyn. As he wrote to Walter Reuther in January 1968, the program "has now expanded to Cleveland, Buffalo, New Rochelle and Newark. We have so far achieved remarkable breakthroughs in the first four cities—placing the first Negro steam fitters, ironworkers and sheet metal workers. . . . We are hoping to expand further into southern cities, beginning with Little Rock (the home of the Apprenticeship Program's Director, Ernest Green) and possibly Houston."[4] By 1969, the program was operating in nine cities and had placed eight hundred young men in unions that had been virtually all-white, at a cost of about five hundred dollars per apprentice.[5] Rustin developed great confidence in Green, and essentially it was the latter who ran the program on a day-to-day basis.

In the midst of a developing RTP, Rustin suffered a heart attack. He was visiting Robert Gilmore and his wife, Joyce Mertz Gilmore, in the fall of 1971 in upper New York State. On October 31, 1971, he collapsed and was rushed to a hospital in nearby Sharon, Connecticut. Bayard had hardly ever been sick. He had been able to stay up late at night, to drink more than a little, and to work prodigious hours. Being a patient ran athwart his vigorous and commanding personality. He was a terrible patient, demanding to be let out as soon as possible. After leaving the hospital he convalesced in the Virgin Islands and then at the apartment of a friend in Greenwich Village. After a few months he was more active than he had been before. Arthur Logan, his doctor, told Rachelle Horowitz that some people after a heart attack are so cautious that they become slothful. Others become even more active, and that the second type tends to live longer.[6]

In 1972, the RTP became an independent corporate entity, with Bayard Rustin as chairman of the board of directors. His contact with the program was somewhat more sporadic and distant.[7] It was still his program, however, and he supported it vigorously. At the national convention of the A. Philip Randolph Institute in 1973, he said with pride that 15 percent of the building trades apprentices in New York were now minority, and that was starting from a base of zero. By 1975 the RTP had placed 5,239 men in construction trade apprentice programs.[8]

The Recruitment and Training Program began to get public support with a grant from the Department of Labor in 1967. Financing from the federal government continued and actually increased during the Nixon years. When Jimmy Carter was elected president in 1976, F. Ray Marshall was appointed secretary of labor and Ernest Green became assistant secretary for employment and training, both to Rustin's great enthusiasm.[9] During the Carter years, the RTP received up to eight million dollars per year from the Department of Labor, running some thirty-one centers. When the Reagan administration took office, the programs were terminated. Between the first federal grant in 1967 and 1980, the RTP, according to its own figures, placed 14,227 apprentices, 4,905 journeymen, and 10,613 people in "other skilled occupations," that is, something like 8 percent of the total apprentices in the building trades. Starting in 1972, the RTP ran a special program for placing minority women in skilled trades and managerial positions in corporations. This part of the program placed almost 2,000 women and was run by Alexis Herman, who was to become secretary of labor in 1997.[10]

The unions at the leadership level might agree to open up to more minority members, but union members at the job level invented all sorts of devices to maintain as much segregation as possible—just as school districts have found devices to maintain segregated schools. The unions might keep black members in lower-paying jobs or create special divisions that ended up being all black and lower paid, or the unions simply might fail to find jobs for blacks who had completed their apprenticeship.[11]

Thus in the view of some black activists, the RTP was simply a cover for maintaining the status quo. These critics argued that the RTP did not train enough black young men to make a significant difference. In November 1968 the *Bay State Banner*, the Boston black newspaper, accused Rustin: "You have been USED as an unwitting tool to flout all existing laws regarding compliance on federally sponsored construction. . . . You have supplied the enemy with an 'out.'" The unions could now refuse to hire more blacks by claiming that they are "involved in an affirmative action program: the Workers Defense League." The following fall, the NAACP staged a "Black Monday," protesting continual discrimination in the building trades unions.[12]

The most serious and sustained attack on the apprenticeship training program came from Herbert Hill, the national labor director of the NAACP, in a series of publications well summed up in his *Labor Union Control of Job Training: A Critical Analysis of Apprentice Outreach Programs and the Hometown Plans* in 1974. He argued that most workers in the unions did not come through apprenticeship programs anyway and that the only way black workers could enter or had entered the building trades in significant numbers was through direct vigorous enforcement of nondiscrimination laws, through court orders and fines, and through minority set-asides like the "Philadelphia Plan." The Philadelphia Plan, and similar set-asides in other cities, set specific quotas of minority workers that construction projects had to meet in order to get federal contracts. Apprenticeship training programs were frauds, Hill argued, which vastly inflated their successes. "Fundamentally, Outreach [which meant apprenticeship] programs are a device used by the building trades unions to maintain their control of training and jobs." Then later in the study, "Apprenticeship Outreach programs after ten years of operation have failed to eliminate the discriminatory racial pattern in the building trades; they have served the interests of restrictive labor unions, but not the interests of Blacks."[13]

Rustin and Herbert Hill had run-ins for years. Rustin confided to one supporter, "Herbert Hill isn't one of my favorite people. He does snort and spit a lot." In 1973 Hill, in a speech at the NAACP national convention in Indianapolis, criticized Rustin's praise of the building trades unions for their progress toward ending discrimination. They did so, claimed Hill, only after suits and court orders. A few days later Roy Wilkins, in a letter of apology to Rustin, agreed that Hill should not have publicly criticized Rustin at a national convention and called Herbert Hill "the problem child of the NAACP."[14]

Bayard Rustin's most compact expression of opposition to the sort of affirmative action that Herbert Hill (of the NAACP) favored was in testimony that Rustin and Norman Hill (of the APRI) gave to the House Subcommittee on Education in September 1974. Quotas, Bayard Rustin and Norman Hill argued, had failed "and produced furor between racial groups." Quotas perpetuated the stereotype of black inferiority and would weaken the merit system, qualifications, and standards. They favored affirmative action of the broader sort, represented by apprentice outreach. But there had to be an expanding economy. "An affirmative action program cannot achieve its objective peacefully and democratically if it must function within the context of scarcity."[15]

To the unions, Herbert Hill's advocacy of forcing the unions, through court orders or fines, to hire people whether or not they were union members amounted to "right to work" laws under another name and was an attempt to destroy labor unions.[16] "You couldn't avoid the unions," said Ernest Green, looking back, and he meant that you shouldn't. As racist as they might be, they were changing, thought Rustin and Green. The racist patterns should be weakened and destroyed, but not the unions themselves.[17]

For Herbert Hill and the *Bay State Banner*, unions' insistence that workers come through the union amounted to an illegal closed shop. Unions were the enemy to be conquered or swept aside. For Bayard Rustin, unions, despite racism, nevertheless constituted the most important mass movement for potentially progressive measures in all sorts of spheres, many of which would help black people. Herbert Hill looked at American society only as racist, and nothing else mattered. Rustin assumed that class mattered and that within that, black and white working-class members should not be enemies but find ways they could be allies. Despite Rustin's hopes, as has almost always been the case in the United States, class solidarity proved weaker than racial division. This was more true in AFL craft unions but has even been the case in many CIO industrial unions.

Even with union resistance, there was some progress. Unemployment in the building trades was high throughout the seventies, sometimes as much as 18 percent, or more than three times the national unemployment rate. Unions could not find jobs for all their existing members. Forcing them to accept nonmembers into an already overfull pool was particularly difficult. In a study of the years 1972–1976, the General Accounting Office concluded that the Apprenticeship Outreach Programs (AOP) "had little effect." Yet the statistics of that very study can be read in a number of ways. The GAO concluded that minority (meaning black and Puerto Rican) members of the building trades increased only a little more than 1 percent, from 7.2 percent of the members to 8.4 percent. Yet looked at another way, that is an 18 percent increase in four years (from all causes, not just apprenticeship outreach programs), and four years when unemployment in those trades was high.[18]

At the same time that the RTP was being resisted, direct attacks through courts or government agencies were furiously resented and also skirted by various subterfuges. Over the long run, there was also a sharp reaction against what was often termed "reverse discrimination." Onetime liberals like Nathan Glazer attacked "affirmative discrimination" in 1975. Although organized labor's leadership continued to support liberal causes, white union members have been steadily moving into the Republican column in national elections, and as Thomas and Mary Edsall argue in *Chain Reaction*, the driving force has been racial resentment. The result has been that rank-and-file labor, which had been consistently on the liberal side of issues, and for several unions that included even racial questions, moved to the right and constituted a significant portion of "Reagan Democrats" in 1980. In 1998, California outlawed "racial preferences" by referendum.[19] In the final reckoning, perhaps the worth of the RTP might not be percentages of people placed in the building trades but as an idea that forms of "affirmative action" might be invented that would arouse less opposition than what the phrase has come to mean.

Another conclusion is that racial prejudices run so deep in American society that both direct attacks, like court orders and quotas, and more cooperative approaches, like apprenticeship training, make only slow and much contested progress. On this issue as well, Bayard Rustin's attempt to hold together or strengthen a coalition ultimately failed. During and after the 1970s, a liberal black-labor alliance did not develop.

Many Jews and Jewish groups also opposed "affirmative action" (if that meant numerical goals or quotas), much to the distress of the NAACP, but this was not the issue on which Bayard Rustin confronted the stresses of the black-Jewish alliance.[20] Rustin was worried by the increasingly overt anti-Semitism of some, particularly northern, more militant, black activists. In April 1967, before the Ocean Hill–Brownsville conflict, he was condemning "The Premise of the Stereotype" in the *Amsterdam News*. Stereotypes, he wrote, have been used against both Negroes and Jews. "One of the more unprofitable strategies we could ever adopt is now to join in history's oldest and most shameful witch hunt, anti-Semitism."[21] He frequently said that if he had known about the Holocaust he might not have been a conscientious objector during World War II. He would not have fought but might have served in some noncombat role.

Rustin always wrote and spoke against anti-Semitism. In the summer of 1967, the *SNCC Newsletter* published a pro–Palestine Liberation Organization (PLO), anti-Israel article, which Rustin was quick to denounce.[22] Yet Rustin's opposition to black anti-Semitism became more open during and after Ocean Hill–Brownsville. His efforts were directed not so much at denouncing bigoted blacks—he was too much of an outsider in that world—-as in trying to explain, not excuse, black anti-Semitism to Jews. He started an address to the 1968 annual meeting of the Anti-Defamation League by acknowledging and condemning black anti-Semitism. "It is here," he said, "it is dangerous, it must be rooted out." Yet he went on to explain it as a product of frustration. "If you happen to be an uneducated, poorly trained Negro living in the ghetto . . . then you see only four kinds of white people. One is the policeman, the second is the businessman, the third is the teacher and the fourth is the welfare worker. In many cities, three of those four are predominantly Jewish." So of course these Negroes tend to lash out at Jews. It is not, he said, that these Jewish teachers, social workers, and shop owners are particularly racist but that the institutions of the country, both local and national, are racist. A change of heart would help, he acknowledged, but a change in institutions was much more important. For example, people talked about the "urban crisis," but national agricultural policy forced thousands of southern rural blacks off the land to migrate to Chicago, St. Louis, New York.[23]

Rustin was a strong supporter of Israel. As in the *SNCC Newsletter*, black anti-Semitism often took the form of opposing Israel and supporting the PLO as representing victims of imperialistic "Zionism." Rustin, in contrast, saw the Jewish state as a social democratic island surrounded by theocratic dictatorships. In supporting Israel, he was supporting a cause important to most Jews and, by implication, showing that the much publicized anti-Semitic statements of black militants did not represent a broad black viewpoint. In June 1970, the A. Philip Randolph Institute ran a full-page ad in the *New York Times*, "An Appeal by Black Americans for United States Support to Israel." The ad expressed support for "the most democratic country in the Middle East." It was sympathetic to the plight of Arab refugees but argued that continued conflict did them more harm than good. In its last line, the text urged that the United States provide Israel "with the full number of jet aircraft it has requested."

This was an astonishing statement for someone who had once been a pacifist. When Rustin argued that the Vietnam War should not be tied to civil rights, that was one thing. When he contemplated, as simple realism, a budget with high military expenditures, that was one thing. Actually promoting arms sales was quite another. Bayard's friends tried to get him to leave that sentence out of the ad, but he insisted. Later he said he had made a mistake, but at the time, the sentence stayed. Rustin went around to his friends in the civil rights movement saying, "You've gotta sign this, you've gotta sign." Many did, some almost without reading it simply because it was Bayard who asked. A number of black New York politicians refused. Those who signed included, besides Rustin's associates from the APRI like Randolph himself, Norman Hill, and Ernest Green, mostly people who represented what was thought of by 1970 as the more conservative end of the movement: Roy Wilkins, Whitney Young, Dorothy Height, Vernon Jordan.[24]

Bayard's old friends were appalled. Igal Roodenko, his traveling companion on the Journey of Reconciliation of twenty-three years earlier, now head of the War Resisters League, argued that Rustin should not support one side in the Arab-Israeli conflict but be against the conflict itself. Ann Morrissett Davidon, a friend since the early days of CORE in Chicago, a participant in the Sahara Project, wrote him bitterly, "In the circles in which you now apparently move, jets and weapons for Israel no doubt seem the logical solution. Advocating this course costs your friends no lives, and is probably good business for the APR Institute. . . . I know you won't like this letter, . . . but I hope it hits a little piece of conscience buried down inside the flab. That's the part of the old Bayard I still have fond memories of." That the ad was a way for the APRI to gain Jewish money was repeated by M. T. Mehdi of the Action Committee on American-Arab Relations.

"You support the aggressor Jewish state," wrote Mehdi. "This is to gain the response of the Zionist Jews and their financial support for the Institute." There is no record of a response to Ann Morrissett Davidon, but Rustin was curt with Mehdi. "I see no point now in corresponding beyond this note."[25]

During the 1970s, Rustin concentrated his fire on condemning the Palestine Liberation Organization and still more on the black "fringe thinkers" who supported it. He insisted over and over again that members of the PLO were not freedom fighters but terrorists and certainly not democrats.[26] In 1975, the Arab countries in the UN General Assembly introduced a resolution identifying Zionism with racism. Partly in response, Rustin organized the Black Americans to Support Israel Committee (BASIC), with Randolph nominally as chairman and Lionel Hampton as treasurer. BASIC ran another full-page ad in the *New York Times* on November 23. "Zionism is not racism," declared the ad, "but the legitimate expression of the Jewish people's self-determination." Again, there was sympathy for the Arab refugees, "but who can avoid asking why so many of these people continue to live in poverty in the midst of Arab oil wealth?" The major message was that "blacks and Jews have a common interest in democracy and justice" and that democratic Israel had a right to exist. BASIC did not last, however. Bayard intended it to be a permanent organization, but the Internal Revenue Service denied it tax-exempt status, and so it continued only as a sporadic organization whose main activity was to finance Bayard's trips to Israel.[27]

From the late 1960s, Bayard was a frequent speaker at meetings of Jewish groups, at Temple Emanu-El, center of New York's Reform, assimilated, well-to-do, mostly German Jews, and also often at sessions of the Jewish Labor Committee, more East European and social democratic. Before the JLC he was vigorous in his condemnation of the Soviet Union for its treatment of Jews. For decades, he had been anti-Soviet because it was a repressive dictatorship, but after about 1967, repression of Jews became a subject of specific anger. It was natural, therefore, that President Jimmy Carter should appoint Rustin a member of the United States Holocaust Memorial Commission in 1978, as chair of its "Committee on Conscience." Rustin insisted all the rest of his life that the memorial museum was not just for Jews but was to be a constant reminder of the evils of "theories of racial superiority," whatever race was the victim.[28]

Bayard Rustin's intensity about Jewish causes like support for Israel and the plight of Soviet Jews cannot be explained merely strategically. Jewish support was indeed crucial for civil rights organizations. Blacks did indeed need allies in those liberal causes that many Jews supported, but it was more than that. A student at a college once asked him, "You're a socialist, you're a conscientious objector, you're gay, you're Black, how many jeopardies can you afford?"[29] He could have answered, "At least I'm not Jewish," but he was in fact close to the secular, liberal New York Jewish world. He could honestly assert that "some of my best friends are Jews." In fact, almost all of his best friends were. In a secular sense, he had found a milieu, an atmosphere, an informal way of being that had become comfortable for him. He was always a black person—in his own way and not fitting into anyone's stereotype of what that might mean—but at home in the New York Jewish world of Albert Shanker, Rachelle Horowitz, Sandra Feldman, and of course Max Shachtman. Some of his friends were sure that there also might be a sense of obligation because he had stood aside during the years of Hitler's slaughter machines—not guilt exactly, but a sense of obligation.

From the black perspective, the final straw in breaking the potential and past alliance between active Jews and active blacks was the firing of Andrew Young from his position as United States ambassador to the United Nations. From the Jewish perspective, the final straw was the embrace, pictured in virtually all national newspapers, of Jesse Jackson and Yasir Arafat. Both occurred in 1979, and both were based at least partly on misperception.

In July 1979 Ambassador Young held an unauthorized meeting with the Palestinian "observer" at the United Nations, was less than candid in describing it as a mere social encounter, and, in the ensuing furor, resigned on August 15. Black spokespeople were convinced that this black man had been fired from his high position at the behest of Jews. Rustin argued vigorously that Young's race had nothing to do with it. Young had simply violated his duty to follow national policy, and when he could not agree with that policy, had honorably resigned. Jews were outraged at what Young had done, blacks at his firing.[30]

"Amid the heated controversy following Andrew Young's resignation," wrote Rustin two weeks later in the *New York Times*, "some black people have suddenly embraced the Palestine Liberation Organization . . . an organization committed to the bloody destruction of Israel—indeed of the Jewish people." One of these black leaders to travel to the Middle East in the fall of 1979 was Jesse Jackson, who did literally embrace Arafat. But Jackson also told the PLO leader that he had to recognize Israel's right to exist and that he had to stop trying to drive Israel into the sea. Yet that photographed embrace was a powerful symbol for all that Jews feared from blacks, from Malcolm X to Stokely Carmichael, and of course from the PLO.[31]

By the end of the 1970s, then, another of the constituencies that Rustin hoped to combine to create a liberal coalition had been split off. Rustin might argue, as he did in *Newsday* in October 1979, that "Blacks and Jews Still Need Each Other," but neither group seemed to agree.[32]

Nor was there much to hope for from the Democratic Party, which had seemed so forceful in 1965. The Humphrey candidacy in 1968 was the last time Rustin was enthusiastic about a Democratic candidate. With Humphrey's defeat, Democratic politics were no longer very important for him. That mechanism was no longer effective. He endorsed no one in 1972 and was distressed by the capture of the party by people he considered politically suicidal. This judgment was proved by the election results. In 1976 he worked a little for the primary candidacy of Henry Jackson, senator from Washington (known informally as the senator from Boeing). Jackson had a good record on civil rights and economic policy but could not meet the anti-Washington challenge from Jimmy Carter of Georgia. Carter might have had some of the right impulses, but he was overwhelmed by the rising tide of conservatism. Julian Bond said in 1968 that Rustin had sold his soul to the Democratic Party. A decade later it was clear that the party did not want it anymore. The Democratic Party of Lyndon Johnson was no more.

By the end of the seventies, then, the island on which Bayard Rustin had stood had become smaller and smaller, drowned from left and right. By 1979, perhaps earlier, he had nowhere left to stand.

15

Grand Old

Man—and a

New Civil Right

In 1982, when Bayard Rustin was in Bangkok for the International Rescue Committee, the Foreign Correspondents Club of Thailand invited him to speak. The invitation identified him as "one of the grand old men of the civil rights movement in America." Meant as a compliment, the phrase contained an unintended bitter taste. During the last ten years of his life, Rustin was more honored for what he had been than for what he was. The invitation did not describe him as "one of the most important fighters for the welfare of Indochinese displaced people," which he was, but essentially for something he had done many years ago. He was someone humanitarian groups wanted on their letterhead, someone who would be a member of a delegation, but not the person who framed the question or organized the group in the first place. For example, at a huge rally in New York in 1977 protesting Soviet treatment of Jews, many people made speeches. Way down in the story in the *New York Times*, among those "who also spoke," was Bayard Rustin's name.[1] In any listing of members of the United States Commission on the Holocaust, there was Bayard's name as "also a member."

But Bangkok? What was this "grand old man of the civil rights movement" doing in Bangkok? He had almost nowhere left to stand in the United States, and he turned in the late seventies once again to the international world, this time not as a pacifist but as a humanitarian. And, truth to tell, it was also a way to spend more time having a good time.

One way of having a good time was travel, which he loved. He loved meeting new people, seeing new sights, shopping. He had always traveled a great deal: to India, Africa, Europe, especially England, but in the last decade of his life, he was on the go more often and to more places than ever. In 1983 and 1984, his most active travel years, he was out of the country on eighteen separate trips, some involving more than one destination. He was frequently in far-off places as a representative of the International Rescue Committee (IRC), visiting refugee camps in Thailand, Somalia, Pakistan, Puerto Rico. A notable exception was the Arab refugee camps on the West Bank, which he did not visit. He was often an election observer under the auspices of Freedom House: in El Salvador, Grenada, Barbados, Zimbabwe. He frequently went to meetings of the Socialist International. Once in the early stages of the creation of Solidarity in Poland, he acted as an unofficial emissary from the AFL-CIO. Some of his trips were simply vacations in the Caribbean with his new companion, Walter Naegle.

Naegle and Rustin met by chance in 1977. Naegle recalled that as a white teenager in New Jersey at the time of the 1963 march, he had heard the name Bayard Rustin as one of the giants in the civil rights movement. As a young college student resisting the Vietnam draft, he had received material from the Fellowship of Reconciliation and the War Resisters League, in which Rustin's name was frequently mentioned. When they met, Naegle was at first a little overwhelmed, but he soon found Rustin entirely relaxed, a person who had no sense of self-importance, and a person who loved having young folks around him. Soon they became partners, in effect, married. Naegle brought a bit of stability to Rustin's private life—Bayard went out drinking less often—and in 1982 Rustin formally adopted him, as this was the only legal sort of connection open to them. Naegle went on some, but not all, of Rustin's trips. He also acted as Rustin's archivist.

For the founder of Black Americans to Support Israel Committee (BASIC), travel to Israel was a natural. In 1976 and again in the fall of

1979, Rustin was a member of a delegation of blacks and labor leaders to the Jewish state. They were guests in Israel of Histadrut, the Israeli labor federation. Rustin said just what their hosts wanted to hear. "To give credence or respectability to one terrorist organization gives it to all, and to make the P.L.O. in any way respectable is to make the Ku Klux Klan equally respectable." He insisted, actually in the face of considerable evidence, that the black-Jewish coalition in the United States remained strong.[2]

Two years later, in 1981, he was back in Israel to investigate the situation of a group of Americans who declared themselves the "Original Hebrew Israelite Nation" and sought citizenship under the right of return. Careful not to engage the question of who was a Jew, the Americans simply asked for humane treatment of the "black Hebrews." Rustin also sought to aid a people who were acknowledged by Israel as Jews, the "Falashas" of Ethiopia, but who were forbidden to emigrate by the Ethiopian government. He made plans to travel to Ethiopia but in the end did not go. The Ethiopian government was relenting, and eventually most of the Falashas did get to Israel—and there they ran into some serious racial prejudice because of their darker skin.

Bayard was back in Israel and Lebanon with Charles Bloomstein, secretary of the A. Philip Randolph Institute, and five others after Israel's "incursion," as the Israelis called it, into Lebanon in 1982. The report on his trip was basically a defense of the Jewish state, saying that the incursion was a legitimate act of self-defense, not in violation of international law, and, as such things go, not terribly destructive. Rustin condemned the Palestine Liberation Organization and said that peace would only come when the Arab states decided to accept the existence of Israel, but he also insisted that the Begin government should be more flexible.[3]

He often was at meetings of the Socialist International, whether in the United States, Europe, or South America. Bayard had been a longtime friend of the aging scion of the American Socialist Party Norman Thomas right up to Thomas's death in 1968, even though they disagreed over the Vietnam War. The American Socialist Party had various splits and recombinations that were important for the people involved but hardly noticed by other Americans. Michael

Harrington was the closest thing to an heir of Thomas, and he and Bayard were, for a while, co-chairs of what Socialist Party remained after 1968. The various subsequent permutations left Bayard as chairman of a faction calling itself Social Democrats, U.S.A., close to the Democratic Party and particularly concerned with international affairs. His job was as head of the A. Philip Randolph Institute, but this was a freewheeling position and allowed him to be on a great variety of boards and committees. Although nominally head of Social Democrats, U.S.A. he was not very active in the cause. He attended conventions, if they were in convenient places, made an opening address, but not much more. The Social Democrats might be below the horizon in the United States, but the Labour Party in Britain, the Socialists in France, the Social Democrats in Germany, and the Labor Party in Israel were all either the government or the chief opposition party. Thus the Social Democrats International was not a conference of splinter groups but a meeting of significant political forces. Rustin frequently was at meetings of the Socialist International. Besides, it was such fun going to Brussels or Lima!

The 1980s were also the years of receiving Ivy League honorary degrees. He had received many awards before then, both from universities and from private groups. There were dinners in his honor and many testimonials, often as ways to raise money for the Randolph Institute. He had honorary degrees from the New School for Social Research (1968), the University of the Virgin Islands (1969), Cheney State College (1971), and the University of Hartford (1979). Degrees from elite universities, however, did not come until the 1980s. Harvard honored him in 1980 and Yale in 1984. Both cited his long years of work for nonviolent social change and in the civil rights movement. There were references to specifics of his life, but nothing more recent than 1964. As far as perceptions of Bayard Rustin within the United States, he was the grand old man. As if to insist that he was still active and should not be counted out, in the October after receiving his Yale degree, he traveled to New Haven to join the picket line of Yale's clerical and technical workers, on strike to form a union. He was arrested in New Haven, for the last time in his life, on October 26, 1984.[4]

But Bayard Rustin was not just a grand old man, making ceremonial visits and enjoying travels around the world. He was an active, even a leading, member of two American international organizations: Freedom House and the International Rescue Committee. The two organizations were formally unrelated, but there was much overlap in membership and leadership. Rustin, for example, was on the board of both.

The IRC had been founded in 1933 as an organization to help intellectuals escape Nazi Germany and then in other parts of conquered Europe. After World War II, it continued to work on behalf of refugees wherever there was a need. A good deal of its budget came from government sources, particularly the Agency for International Development and the State Department's Bureau for Refugees Programs.[5] The observation of elections was under the auspices of Freedom House, a private nonprofit organization founded in the 1940s, which measured freedom, political, religious, and economic, around the world and issued periodic reports. It was sponsored by individuals and foundations and took no direct government money. Both the IRC and Freedom House were firmly anti-Soviet, as well as against any expansion of Soviet influence. The IRC, however, was essentially a humanitarian organization, and Freedom House was more political. The Freedom House view of the world was that even in repressive societies there were often interstices where democratic possibilities could be found and encouraged: perhaps a labor organization, a church group, a charitable foundation, a school. Within the totalitarianism of Communist regimes, no such openings could exist. The logical conclusion was that no matter what the alternative was, Soviet domination would be worse.[6] This argument could be, and was, used by American administrations of both parties to justify support for any regime, no matter how undemocratic, that was anti-Soviet and to oppose any regime, quite regardless of the wishes of the populace, that was not anti-Soviet. Rustin was not only on the board of Freedom House in the 1970s and 1980s but, between January 1983 and his death, chairman of its executive committee. The IRC was less absolute in its views but also anti-Communist. To some of his old pacifist friends, Bayard's outspoken pro-Western, anti-Soviet arguments seemed to make him part of that international power system that he had and they still deplored.

Rustin's longest overseas project was the continuing International Rescue Committee efforts on behalf of Indochinese refugees. The refugees from Vietnam and Laos were housed in camps in the border regions of Thailand, approved and guarded by the Thai government but run by the United Nations High Commission on Refugees (UNHCR) and organizations like the IRC and other relief agencies. Was Rustin's work on behalf of the Laotians and Vietnamese, parallel with his support for Israel, out of some sense of obligation from a person who had not more vigorously opposed the terrible cruelties that his country had inflicted on Southeast Asia?

Between 1978 and 1987, Rustin made five trips to Thailand with the IRC. The first was from February 8 to 17, 1978, and formed the impetus for all subsequent visits. He had been invited to join the "Citizens Commission on Indochinese Refugees" by Leo Cherne, president of the IRC. Cherne saw Bayard as a person with longtime international experience in India, Africa, Europe. He was a link to organized labor, Democratic Party liberals, and, Cherne thought, the black community. The "Citizens Commission" group of the IRC that traveled to Thailand in 1978 included, among others, Cherne; William Casey, later head of the CIA, who was a boyhood friend of Cherne's; Robert DeVecchi, future head of the IRC; James Michener; Rabbi Marc Tanenbaum; Albert Shanker; and Bayard Rustin. At Nong Khai, on the Laotian border, the delegation was met by an American official, a stickler for protocol and also proud of his ability to speak Thai. The official advised the delegation that before going to the refugee camps, they should make a courtesy visit to the governor of the province and that, furthermore, crossing the legs was bad form in Thailand. During the audience, they should sit straight in their chairs, feet on the ground, hands on their knees. In the governor's office, they did as they were told, all sitting straight and very dignified. The American official went around the room introducing each person with the Thai word for "mister," which was *khun*: Khun Cherne, Khun Tanenbaum, and so on. Bayard, who was sitting next to Bob DeVecchi, elbowed him in the ribs. DeVecchi knew that Bayard was planning some devilment and whispered, "Cool it, Bayard." Bayard replied in a loud stage whisper, "If that son-of-a-bitch calls me coon Rustin, I'm going to kick ass!" With that the dignity, perhaps pomposity, of the occasion was destroyed, Rabbi Tanenbaum cracked up with laughter, and presumably the American official was mortified.

In visits to the camps, Bayard often went his own way. He did not want to be briefed but would wander among the refugees, find someone who spoke some English, and get to know a particular family or a few families. Then he would rejoin the group, sometimes with his new friends, and have not statistics or generalizations but specifics about individuals to give detail to the more general picture. Often he would stay up late with the young aid workers, encouraging them, telling them tales of the civil rights movement. No matter how late these sessions lasted, he would emerge on time the next morning, elegant, rested, ready to go. "How are you," he might say, "I hope we all slept well," and on to the next stop on the journey.

Toward the end of the IRC visit, there was a ceremony of friendship between the Hmong people and the IRC representatives in a large hall crowded with refugees. The Hmong tied a ceremonial cord around each wrist of the visitors, as a token of honor and friendship. Leo Cherne made a few suitable remarks. Then, quite spontaneously, Bayard stood and said through an interpreter, "You have greatly honored us with these cords. I shall treasure mine forever. I want to respond in the only way I know how." With that he raised his arms and, keeping them high, went into a moving performance of "Oh Freedom."

> Freedom, Oh Freedom,
> Freedom over me,
> Before I'll be a slave,
> I'll be buried in my grave
> And go home to my Lord
> And be free.

Most of the listeners could not understand English. Some joined in on the melody, but the emotional thrust was clear to everyone.

At the conclusion of the 1978 mission, Rustin flew halfway around the world to New York. Nonstop flights did not exist at that point, so he had intermediate changes in Hong Kong, Tokyo, Seattle, and perhaps other places. He stopped in New York only long enough to get some clean clothes and then flew directly to Miami, where the

AFL-CIO executive committee was meeting. The IRC was going to recommend that the United States admit more Indochinese refugees, and Rustin knew that one objection might be that the refugees would increase unemployment. Rustin, joined the next day by Leo Cherne, made their argument to George Meany and the executive committee, which, on February 24, endorsed their recommendations. The next month, Bayard organized a full-page ad in the *New York Times* in which black leaders, recognizing that admitting more refugees might make black unemployment a little worse, nevertheless urged "President Carter and the United States Congress to facilitate the entrance of these refugees into the United States in the same spirit that we have urged our country to accept the victims of South Africa's apartheid." In this way Rustin hoped that two groups that might object would instead decide in favor of refugee admissions.

There were many pressures on Carter beside the IRC. On March 29, 1978, the president inaugurated a program admitting more refugees about as the IRC had proposed. This did not solve the problem, however. Thousands of refugees remained in the camps. Those who tried to escape by boat were often attacked by pirates, drowned in storms, ran out of fuel, or landed on hostile shores. The IRC asked that the United States provide greater protection for the "boat people." In July 1979 Rustin and Joan Baez organized a demonstration on the steps of the Lincoln Memorial. Chip Carter, the president's son, was among the crowd of some ten thousand. As dusk approached, perhaps a thousand people from the group moved toward the White House in a candlelight parade. In front of the fence, they sang a few more songs and then Rustin and Baez hurried back to the hotel to see if they had made the ten o'clock news. Several dozen people were still milling about outside the front of the White House when the front door opened and President Carter in his shirt sleeves, followed by presumably distraught Secret Service men, walked down to the fence. He climbed up on it a bit. Carter told the delighted crowd that he'd heard the singing and knew about the demonstration from Chip. He had already decided to order the fleet to seek and rescue the boat people. Bob DeVecchi, who had lingered behind, rushed panting to the hotel room to tell Rustin and Baez what had just happened. "I couldn't believe what I was seeing," recalled DeVecchi.[7]

The International Rescue Committee also tried to improve conditions in the camps, mostly by sponsoring doctors and medical care. In February 1980, an international delegation including Rustin, Leo Cherne, Liv Ullman, Elie Wiesel, and Joan Baez staged a "March for Survival," trying to bring supplies from Thailand into Cambodia. That country, now under the Pol Pot regime, would of course not admit them, and that was in fact the point of the demonstration.[8] Rustin was in Thailand again in 1982 and finally in late May and early June 1987, just a few weeks before his death.

Bayard Rustin's work for the International Rescue Committee might be seen as a continuation of his fight against poverty in the United States. Similarly, election observance might be considered an extension of his voting rights and registration drives in his home country. But there was a difference. His work for Freedom House seemed animated more by his anti-Communism. He essentially argued the position that there was no worse outcome than the extension of Soviet power.

It is here that his views and those of the "neo-conservatives" overlapped. "Neo-cons" like his longtime supporters at *Commentary*, Norman Podhoretz and Midge Decter, like Jeane Kirkpatrick, after 1981 at the United Nations, and led by the symbol of anti-Soviet conservatism, Ronald Reagan, blamed virtually all evil in the world on the Soviets and were willing to support any group opposing Soviet power or what might become Soviet power. Rustin was as firmly anti-Soviet as any of them. In 1977 he wrote about Cuba's massive power in Africa as a Soviet threat. "To refuse to recognize that Cuba operates as an extension of Soviet power" was to be blind. In 1982 he expanded and generalized his views in "The Soviet Empire and the Third World." For years, he argued, the Soviets had cultivated the image of being friends to national liberation movements, but third-world countries were learning the reality. Soviet aid "is used to prop up exploitive dictatorships that seek to hold power in the face of widespread opposition by building a repressive police state patterned on the Soviet model." In 1982 he favored the Afghan rebels against Soviet power, as did Reagan. He regarded the American troops in Grenada as a "rescue mission," as did Reagan. He did not explicitly back the Nicaraguan "contras," but he did excoriate the Sandinistas as Marxist-Leninist, as did Reagan.[9]

But putting Bayard Rustin in the neo-conservative camp would be a mistake. He was certainly as anti-Communist and anti-Soviet as any of them, but he was also a social democrat all his life. He scorned Reagan's domestic proposals. "Insensitivity and lack of compassion are increasingly becoming the hallmarks of the Reagan Administration's domestic program," he wrote in 1981.[10] He favored national health insurance, major expenditures for public housing, federal aid to education and massive job creation and training programs, and of course racial integration. He was a "cold war liberal," and pretty far liberal. A "cold war social democrat" would be a better term.

As if to contradict Freedom House's views on possible openings in a totalitarian regime, in 1980 and 1981 there was a crack in Eastern Europe's solidity. This was Solidarity, the Polish labor union led by Lech Wałesa, a worker at the shipyard in Gdansk. In keeping with its policy of supporting free (that is, not government-controlled) labor unions in Eastern Europe, the AFL-CIO wanted to help Solidarity. But Edward Muskie, secretary of state, as well as Wałesa himself were worried that too open support from the West might lead to a crackdown from the relatively open Polish government, or even from the Soviet Union. Leaders of the AFL-CIO might have been admitted to Poland as individuals, but the leaders would only go as representatives of American labor, and this the Polish government would not allow. Tom Kahn, Rustin's old friend and co-worker, was now the foreign policy adviser to Lane Kirkland, who had succeeded George Meany as head of the AFL-CIO. It was natural that Kirkland, acting through Kahn, would think of Rustin as a possible source of contact. Through some back-channel communications and through the brief presence in the United States of Mirek Domintzyk, head of the Kielce (an industrial city south of Warsaw) regional Solidarity, a letter of invitation came to Bayard Rustin at the A. Philip Randolph Institute to lecture in Poland and visit Kielce. Such a visit was a way for the AFL-CIO to visit Solidarity, but not quite the AFL-CIO and not quite the national Solidarity.

An associate of Rustin's at the APRI, Adrian Karatnycky, spoke

Polish and had previously been involved with some tentative contacts between American labor and Solidarity. He arranged the itinerary, and he, Rustin, and another close associate, Charles Bloomstein, arrived in Warsaw on April 20, 1981. Rustin had been in Poland two years previously as "also a member" of the U.S. Holocaust Commission, but this time he was the main show. Rustin, a tall, elegant African American, well dressed and sometimes sporting a walking stick, made quite an impression on the streets of Warsaw. The three were received warmly, and over the next few days, they met with leaders of a number of regional branches and with important dissidents, some of whom later were prominent in the government of a free Poland. They talked with publishers of an outspoken newspaper, with Catholic laypeople, but not with Wałesa, whom they assumed they had come to see. About the fourth night, at something like 11:30, Mirek Domintzyk appeared in Adrian Karatnycky's room. "Come, follow me!" he said. They went to the Hotel Solec, which was where Wałesa stayed when he was in Warsaw. There they went to Wałesa's room, where the future premier of a free Poland was relaxing, lounging back in a chair with his shoes off.

"You have ten minutes to tell me why I should see this man," said Wałesa.

Karatnycky explained who Bayard Rustin was, what he had done, and that he came from the AFL-CIO. Wałesa had never heard of Rustin, but when Karatnycky showed him a book of Rustin's essays, which Wałesa could not read, and pictures of Rustin with well-known people, Wałesa realized that this might be an important person. When Wałesa saw a picture of Rustin with Martin Luther King, an icon even in Communist Poland, Wałesa agreed to see him. Once again, Rustin's bona fides was proved through association with the civil rights movement and with King, now dead for a dozen years.

Rustin, Wałesa, and Karatnycky spent a long lunch together the next day. Rustin had expected to find a trade union. Instead, he found a mass popular movement, reminiscent of the mass movement he had experience with in the United States. Wałesa and he talked about the philosophy and practice of nonviolent protest, which seemed to both men to have relevance to Solidarity and Poland. Then they talked about practical matters. Wałesa knew that too direct contact was dangerous. He appreciated Lane Kirkland's expressions of support but suggested that individual unions in the United States might better establish relationships with particular regional branches of Solidarity. Then the lunch was over.

Rustin resumed a schedule of speaking, including interviews on Polish radio, and then returned home after spending ten days in Poland. The American labor movement had found a way, somewhat hidden from the governments of Poland and the Soviet Union, to funnel some support to Solidarity, and this support continued even after the imposition of martial law in December 1981.[11]

Bayard also traveled as an election observer as a member of delegations from Freedom House. Regimes in many countries encouraged international observers for their elections as a way of certifying the legitimacy of, say, a return from military to civilian rule. His most controversial stint as an election observer was probably when he was part of a nine-member mission from Freedom House that went to Zimbabwe-Rhodesia in April 1979. The internal politics of Zimbabwe-Rhodesia were complicated and shifting, with a four-sided civil war raging, but an election was held in April 1979. Whites were guaranteed 20 percent of the seats in the new parliament, which were won by Ian Smith's party, and Bishop Abel Muzorewa won a majority of the rest. The Freedom House delegation, co-chaired by former New Jersey senator Clifford Case and Bayard Rustin, testified before a House Subcommittee on Africa that there was intimidation on all sides, that all sides were about equally guilty, and that "the people have spoken." Rustin said the same thing on the McNeil-Lehrer news program. People who knew Africa better than Case or Rustin, specifically George Houser and the American Committee on Africa, were outraged. They felt Muzorewa was backed by the West out of cold war considerations and had been elected only because of repression, threats, and terror. Another critic, William Lucy of the Coalition of Black Trade Unionists, wrote to Bayard in April 1979, "The ultra-right wing forces here and abroad could not have had a better spokesman. . . . The damnable Rhodesian election ensures minority white entrenchment . . . under a black puppeteer hand-picked by Ian Smith." These critics felt that Robert Mugabe, whom the West had misrepresented as a Communist terrorist, would probably win a fair election.[12]

Muzorewa was not able to stop the war, and in another election in February 1980, Mugabe did indeed win overwhelmingly. Rustin was also part of a Freedom House delegation observing this second election, and in a report that he and Leonard Sussman prepared, they wrote that "Robert Mugabe's victory in Rhodesia is being called the first democratically-elected Marxist government in Africa. It is not!" The will of the people "was expressed in a pervasive climate of fear." Rustin and Sussman were worried, they wrote, by the possibility of "Zambia turning to the Soviets for military and other aid, Cuban troops occupying Angola." To George Houser and others on the left, Rustin seemed to be a participant in regarding Africa as simply a field for competition with the Soviets. Bayard "was playing the cold war game," said Houser. But as Bayard had feared, Mugabe set up a one-party dictatorship.[13]

On South Africa itself, Rustin, of course, found what he called "the cruel system of apartheid" hateful. He scorned what the Reagan administration termed "constructive engagement." He traveled to South Africa in 1983, at the invitation of Chief Gatsha Buthelezi, king of the Zulu area, and again in 1986, under the auspices of the International Rescue Committee, which had refugee camps in Lesotho and Swaziland, two nominally independent countries entirely surrounded by South Africa. Here his conclusions were appropriately tentative. He argued that "ending apartheid" was not an adequate goal. Of course apartheid should end, but as Idi Amin had shown in Uganda, something even worse might be established. It was important that apartheid be ended by means that would ensure a democratic postapartheid South Africa. Rustin was not enthralled by any of the potential leaders. Buthelezi, wrote Rustin, felt he was born to rule and therefore could not brook the kind of opposition that democracy necessarily included. Nelson Mandela, he feared in 1987, was simply too old and too ill, even if he were let out of prison. A decade later, this judgment looks ridiculous, but it was not entirely unreasonable in 1987. Oliver Tambo, perhaps, had possibilities.

Bayard was less bothered than might be expected by the number of Communists in the African National Congress's leadership. He knew that anyone against apartheid was called a Communist by the government, so that "Communist" in apartheid South Africa did not necessarily mean Soviet-dominated.

Rustin was against blanket American divestment in South Africa and favored the "Sullivan principles." The principles were drawn up in 1977 by the Reverend Leon H. Sullivan, black Baptist minister from Philadelphia. They stated that American firms should have equal pay for equal work by black and white workers, as well as training and career tracks to allow advancement in the firms for black South Africans equal to the possibilities for whites. Rustin hoped Americans would support those forces in South Africa working for nonviolent change, particularly the black trade unions. Two years before his death, he started "Project South Africa" as an activity of the Randolph Institute. Project South Africa had the goal of identifying organizations in South Africa that might be centers for democratic change and finding parallel organizations in the United States that could act as "sister" groups to South Africa. "Project South Africa" had identified some seventy groups in South Africa by the time Rustin died. All in all, his was a reasoned, moderate position.[14]

The problem with all his traveling around the world was that his knowledge was always what might be called journalistic. He was convinced of his own discernment, his omnicompetence. He was a good journalist. He met and talked with all sorts of people, official and unofficial, but one would not today consult Rustin's writing on South Africa to find out what was happening. In refugee camps in Thailand or Somalia, he could directly see the misery, and a journalistic knowledge was sufficient. But for deep understanding of the politics of Zimbabwe or South Africa or even of Barbados or Grenada, a few days' or a week's visit could not be enough. His essays on American race relations have a lasting value that his writing on Zimbabwe or El Salvador does not.

In the mid-1980s Bayard Rustin began speaking out on gay rights. In these years, Rustin became a little more open about his homosexuality. His style of dressing became a bit more flamboyant, often with clothes bought in thrift or secondhand shops. He wore more jewelry. He said many times that he had never denied his homosexuality. And yet there were signs he was not quite relaxed about the issue. His very flamboyance may have been, for him, an assertion, more than a calm self-acceptance. And in the mid-1970s, when Midge Decter of *Commentary* urged him to write an autobiography, he said he couldn't. "There's that homosexual thing," he said. In his "Reminiscences," a series of interviews for the Columbia University Oral History Project made just before his death, "that homosexual thing" is conspicuously absent.

In the 1980s, gay activists were asserting that "civil rights" was a phrase not only for ethnic groups or women but for all sorts of minorities, including those with a different "sexual orientation" than the majority. Rustin, who earlier had regarded homosexuality as a weakness or sin, now adopted that view. He made some eloquent speeches in support of gay rights. At the University of Pennsylvania in 1986 he compared the Stonewall Rebellion of 1969, when gays resisted the police at a nightclub in Greenwich Village, to Rosa Parks sitting in a bus in Montgomery, Alabama. But Walter Naegle said that these speeches were an occasional response to requests from others. Rustin was not really active in the gay rights cause beyond a few speeches and interviews.

On the other hand, he was active in the cause of Haitian refugees, who had a particular claim on Bayard Rustin. They were black, they were in the United States fleeing both cruel repression and poverty in their homeland, and they were being treated inhumanely in refugee camps. Rustin began writing about them in 1979, with a piece called "Black Refugees from Haiti: Victims of Discrimination." In December 1981, Freedom House, the A. Philip Randolph Institute, and the New York Friends Group jointly sponsored a conference on the refugees. From 1982 on, Rustin was a member of the "National Emergency Committee for Haitian Refugees," which combined Catholic clergymen with representatives of Freedom House. He visited refugee camps in Puerto Rico in 1982.[15]

Rustin, Walter Naegle, and Bruce McColm from Freedom House went to Haiti in late July 1987. This was after the fall of the dictators Duvalier, father and son, but before the possibility of democracy under Father Jean-Bertrand Aristide. Haiti was in considerable turmoil, and the Freedom House delegation wanted to assess the possibilities.

When Rustin and Naegle returned from Haiti on July 23, they seemed to have picked up some sort of intestinal bug, as they had before in tropical countries. Doctors prescribed a course of medication, and Naegle quickly recovered. Bayard seemed, if anything, to get worse, sometimes vomiting, often lying in bed, curled up, well into the day. He went to several doctors, who could not find his problem but said he should consider an exploratory operation if things got worse. Things did get worse, and in mid-August he had the operation at Lenox Hill Hospital. The surgery revealed that his appendix had actually burst some days before. There was peritonitis, which the surgeons cleaned up, and Bayard seemed to be recovering. On Sunday, August 23, Walter visited with him at the hospital. He seemed to be alert, articulate, but somewhat confused. He was convinced he was in London. Naegle attributed the confusion to reaction to medication, because he had had similar reactions during his hospitalization after his heart attack. Late that evening, the hospital called Walter to say he'd better come back, because Rustin seemed more confused and was asking for him. Naegle, already in bed, got dressed and took a cab to the hospital. When he got to Lenox Hill, the staff would not let him out of the lobby. Naegle called his sister, a professor of nursing at New York University, who he thought might have some influence. She arrived, but still the staff would not allow them to see Rustin. A couple of hours later, just after midnight, they were told that Bayard Rustin had died of cardiac arrest.[16] He was seventy-five years old.

Bayard Rustin's obituary was on the front page of the *New York Times* with a picture and was continued for nearly a full page inside. It went through his life from boyhood to the 1970s, emphasizing his importance to King and his central role in the 1963 march. The article ignored his last ten years, except to say that he was a strong supporter of Israel. There was not a word about Indochinese refugees or African politics. The *Times* said he had become more "conservative" but did not make clear what that word meant. It quoted James Farmer saying that "Bayard has no credibility in the Black community. Bayard's commitment is to labor, not to the Black man," but did not mention that Farmer was now a supporter of that separatism and Black Power that Rustin rejected. The obituary was followed by an editorial, "How Bayard Rustin Led." "Other civil rights leaders wielded power," concluded the editorial, "Bayard Rustin wielded influence. America is better for his having done so."

The front-page story in the *Amsterdam News* quoted the same statement from James Farmer and added that in Rustin's later years he was often considered an "unequivocal apologist for Israel, an unreconstructed Cold Warrior," and too close to organized labor, but the *Amsterdam News* covered his life more fully and accurately than the *Times*. It included a full page of pictures and, unlike the *Times*, did notice his work for the International Rescue Committee for Indochinese refugees, his election monitoring for Freedom House, and his leadership of Social Democrats, U.S.A. The *Amsterdam News* particularly praised his defense of Muhammad Ali's conversion to Islam and of Ali's refusal on religious grounds to be drafted. There was no mention of the newspaper's disagreements with Rustin over community control but rather a full page of quotations praising him. As if to underscore James Farmer's criticisms, the praise came from white Americans: Lane Kirkland, Senator Daniel Patrick Moynihan, Governor Mario Cuomo. There was also an editorial that did not end with vague phrases about power and influence but more accurately captured Rustin's values by quoting him on the down-to-earth needs of the black and white poor: "We have got to provide meaningful work at decent wages for every employable citizen. We must guarantee an adequate income for those unable to work. We must build millions of low-income housing units, tear down the slums, and rebuild our cities. We need to build schools, hospitals, mass transit systems." And the newspaper ended the editorial with the single-word sentence "Amen."[17]

A few days after his death Bayard's close friends, about seventy-five to a hundred of them, gathered at LuEsther Mertz's house at the UN Plaza to talk and cry together. Mertz was the mother of Joyce Mertz, Robert Gilmore's second wife, who had died in 1973. LuEsther carried on supporting Rustin's work after Joyce's death. "It was not quite sitting shiva," recalled Walter Naegle—not Jewish—of the gathering, "but it was something like that."

On October 1, there was a memorial service at the Community Church on Thirty-fifth Street in Manhattan. There were tributes from Norman Hill, Vernon Jordan, Lane Kirkland, Phiroshaw Camay of the South African black trade unions, Rabbi Marc Tanenbaum, Charles Bloomstein, Liv Ullman, John Lewis, Dewitt Rustin Luff, for the Rustin family, and Thomas Kilgore. Two themes were sounded again and again through the service. One was Rustin's intellectual contributions to the civil rights movement. Vernon Jordan called him "Chairman of the Ideas Committee" and declared him an "intellectual bank where we all had unlimited accounts." The second theme was Rustin's infinite capacity for compassion, whether it was for a homeless person on New York streets, a refugee in Thailand who found no way to be resettled, or Haitian refugees in Brooklyn. Perhaps there was also a third theme: his optimism. He was always sure that by fighting for progress, the mountain of social injustice could be reduced.

Of course there was music. The chorus first sang Bach's "Jesus, Joy of Man's Desiring," then later in the service the spiritual "Seeking for the City." The service closed with a tape of Bayard giving a slow and emotional "Nobody Knows the Trouble I've Seen." People left the church to Bayard's voice singing an up-tempo, joyous "Swing Low Sweet Chariot."[18]

16

Sui Generis

When Bayard Rustin spoke at Bowdoin College in October 1978, he was interviewed by a reporter for the *Portland (Maine) Press Herald*. The interview was to take place in a large, impressively high-ceilinged lounge at the college, with a large brick fireplace at one end, room for seating some two hundred people, and a grand piano in one corner. At times, when the room was empty, faculty or students might sit down at the piano and just play for a little while. That was happening when the reporter arrived. A tall, gray-haired man was playing Bach. No one else was in the room, so the reporter gingerly approached the piano player and said he was looking for Bayard Rustin.

"I am he," said the piano player.[1]

Whatever expectations the reporter might have had for a great civil rights leader, they were not of a man gently playing from the Anna Magdalena Bach notebooks. And that was characteristic for Bayard Rustin. He did not confirm anyone's expectations. Although he was a member of many groups, he did not simply fit the picture. He was his own person, a unique figure.

For example, he thought more highly of baroque music than Negro spirituals, and he had little interest in jazz. He had an art and antique collection as eclectic as his life. There was a large fourteenth-century Madonna in his living room, worth at the time of his death ten or twenty times what he had paid for it in the sixties. There was a collection of African sculpture, acquired not particularly to discover his African roots but simply because he liked the pieces. He had more than two hundred walking sticks, some with carved ivory heads and at least one with a sword inside. He was once arrested for carrying that one. A policeman noticed it, became suspicious, and arrested him for carrying a concealed weapon. He was in jail several hours before making bail, and later the charges were dropped.

Since he was as or even more interested in European than in African American music, since a great many—not all—of his close friends were white, since he did not live in Harlem and was only occasionally part of the black scene, it may be natural to ask whether he wanted to be white. The question itself betrays the stereotypes in the mind of the questioner. What is it to be white or black in the United States? Is it one or even a group of predetermined characteristics or ways of talking or thinking? Is a person, because of skin color, not permitted to like Bach better than Bessie? Not allowed to consider Shakespeare part of his or her heritage? Bayard had neither doubts nor problems about being black. In speaking of black folks he said and thought "we," not "they." Yet he was Bayard Rustin, not anybody's, black or white, stereotype of what that meant.

He was a figure of major importance in American life but quite lacking in self-importance. He maintained a certain spontaneity, childishness, roguishness, or what even might be called grown-up silliness all his life. He would sometimes grin at his white friends and say that what he wanted on his tombstone was "This Nigger Had Fun." And he certainly did![2]

Once, in 1986, Bayard, Charlie Bloomstein, and Walter Naegle visited Robert Gilmore at his country home in Millerton, New York. It was a difficult visit, since Gilmore had Alzheimer's, and it was painful to see their old friend in decline. As a relief from gloom, in the evening, the three friends plus the woman who was Gilmore's chief caregiver went out for a drink in a cocktail lounge nearby. There was a piano playing in the background. For no particular reason, Charlie and Bayard began softly singing a silly mock military march.

> Lloyd George knew my fa-a-a-ather
> Father knew Lloyd George
> Lloyd George knew . . .

Naegle was afraid of a scene as the singing got louder and more noticeable, but soon the piano player joined in. For a final chorus, Bayard sprang up and marched in place holding a sharp military salute. Instead of objecting, people in the lounge loved it, and when Bayard sat down, they laughingly applauded. This was characteristic of Bayard all his life: a serious central purpose to the day, but at the same time a certain, one might say youthful, exuberance.

He might be silly on occasion, but at base, Rustin was a rational man. Usually this led to sensible solutions, but sometimes it was a limitation. In 1983, Coretta Scott King organized a march commemorating the 1963 march and her husband's great speech. Rustin opposed it. In 1963, he said, there was a clear black agenda. In 1983, he insisted over and over again, there was no longer a black agenda—there was a poor people's agenda.

There was a black agenda, however, that Rustin did not really appreciate. Of course, he knew that racism still existed and needed to be fought, but the way of fighting it, he thought, was by eliminating the kind of poverty that encouraged racism's expression. But racism was more than just the understandable, if regrettable, fears of the white poor. Rustin consistently underestimated the staying power of the nonrational, purely racial prejudice. He also underestimated the need for people who had been told for generations that they were, as a group, inherently inferior to assert group pride, also the nonrational. He favored incorporating black history into American history, but he did not understand the need many black students had for a black studies curriculum or what he called "feel good" courses. Once in the 1970s, A. J. Muste's youngest son, then an English professor at Ohio State, wanted to talk to Bayard about how to set up a black studies program. Rustin simply dismissed the subject. He would not even discuss it, and this was with the youngest son of his old mentor.[3] He himself had no need for a "feel good" course, no need to assert racial self-confidence. He had been brought up by a family who appreciated his brilliance; he had been successful in school, an integrated high school. He had plenty of self-confidence, individual and racial, and could not fully empathize with people who felt the need for psychological self-affirmation.

Although he is often accused of abandoning his principles, Bayard Rustin was a person of consistent attitudes. He was quoted in that *New York Times* obituary as saying he had changed his position but insisting that it was always in response to changes in the objective situation. He did abandon international pacifism. Earlier in his life he put peace as a first requisite, then democracy. Later in his life he said that democracy and its preservation came first. He became far less religious. Through all his life, however, certain values and conceptions were constant: (1) There must be change in the direction of greater social justice. (2) Change within countries must come through nonviolent means. (3) A crucial part of racial injustice was economic injustice. (4) The goal was integration, not racial separation or what has since come to be called "identity politics." (5) The goal of political action was attainable progress. Things had to move, in fact, for the people he often referred to as "the masses of Negro people" (and he occasionally used the term "lumpen"). Sometimes this might mean action in the streets, defying laws (though always willing to suffer the legal consequences). Sometimes it might mean an entirely legal demonstration or march. Sometimes it might mean working within the political system, with Congress, the Department of Justice, or the president. The goal was to make a difference now, in this world, for the people now on earth.

People who accuse Rustin of abandoning radicalism do not realize that for him radicalism was instrumental, not a stance. For what he called "no-win" people, any victory had to be disregarded and a new radical stance developed. Rustin wanted to accomplish something, not strike an intellectual pose. He joined the Young Communist League because it opposed war and racial discrimination. When they abandoned these goals, he abandoned the Young Communists. When pacifism seemed futile and the civil rights movement seemed hopeful, he concentrated on civil rights. If the Democratic Party adopted the goals he had been fighting for, he enthusiastically supported the Democrats, but when they lost interest in the goals, he lost interest in the party. When the civil rights movement aided its enemies by adopting suicidal policies, empty slogans, and posturing, he did not follow. Rustin might be accused of being uncritical of the labor movement, but he was always working within it for change, and change in the most recalcitrant parts of the movement, not supporting labor in everything labor did. One can find considerable consistency between the young man in the Ashland, Kentucky, prison and the grand old man in Bangkok.

Looking at the attainments of the civil rights movement during the dozen years after 1954, one can justly stand amazed that so much was accomplished and that so much of that progress was against the American grain. The progress was against deeply rooted racial institutions and attitudes, and the progress was made largely through this most un-American mechanism of NVDA. Looking at the years after about 1966, one is tempted to say, "If only . . ." If only the March on Washington coalition could have held together. If only integration had been more real and less token. If only the Johnson presidency had not been destroyed by the Vietnam War. If only NVDA could have been successfully modified to suit northern realities. If only loud black voices for nationalism and separatism had been rejected more quickly by the black community before they galvanized white opposition. If only conservative politicians had not exploited racial fears.

And yet, despite all those things happening, there is slow progress, and on the basis that Bayard Rustin was predicting. Educational institutions are helping to create a growing black middle class, and economic growth is slowly producing realistic possibilities for better-educated black people. The civil rights years have not, as Bayard Rustin hoped, led to a reexamination of the basic structures of American society, but those years have allowed more African Americans than before to participate more fully in that society. Impatience, anger, and action for social change, however, are still called for.

Notes

Introduction

1. Eleanor Clark to Doris Grotewohl, May 3, 1944; Bayard Rustin (hereafter cited as "BR") to Grotewohl, May 5, 1944; Grotewohl to BR, May 24, 1944, all from Bayard Rustin Papers (hereafter cited as "BRP"). Hereafter, if no other collection is cited, reference is to these papers. The original collection is in the Library of Congress, Washington, D.C. They are published on microfilm: University Publications of America, *The Papers of Bayard Rustin*, 1988.

   For dates of conviction and entering Ashland: Sentence Notice to Inmate, Department of Justice, Penal and Correctional Institution, U.S. Northeastern Penitentiary, Lewisburg, Pa., August 4, 1945, in Bureau of Prisons records, National Archives, Washington, D.C.

2. *Newsday*, February 15, 1988.

1 Preparation, Personal and Political

1. Information about Archie Hopkins and Bayard's mother's promiscuousness from Dr. Robert Ascher, interview with author, September 16, 1996. The source of the name "Bayard" was that "my aunt was studying French when I was born and was very impressed with Chevalier Bayard who was a pacifist knight." BR to Mrs. Bayard W. Almond Jr., May 27, 1969.

2. For use of "mama," see BR to Bessie LeBon, Jamaica, N.Y., September 14, 1950, FOR Papers, SCPC, DG 13, ser. D, boxes 51 and 52.

3. Information about Bayard Rustin's childhood necessarily comes mostly from his own memories in interviews at various times. For much, there is no other source. Memory being a selective and creative process, it becomes difficult to get through memory to another level of reality. There is also the factor that, as Rustin's friends and opponents say, he was a bit of a bullshitter. But on the other hand, the memories are what inform later attitudes and actions, so that maybe they become the reality. Rather than beginning each sentence

with "According to Rustin," or "Apparently," or other such words, I here say it once, to count, except where otherwise specified, for the childhood years generally. All the memories seem a little too organized, a little too prescient. Accounts of his early childhood come primarily from "The Reminiscences of Bayard Rustin," Columbia Oral History Project, Columbia University, 1986–1987 (hereafter cited as "'Reminiscences,' COHP"), and an interview called "Pacifism," with Andrew Lightman, 1985, BRF. In an interview with Nicholas Lemann, n.d. (but toward the end of BR's life), he says it was his grandmother's grandmother who was bought from slavery; BRF.

4. Description of the house in intake interview, Bureau of Prisons, March 29, 1944, National Archives, Washington, D.C.

5. "Reminiscences," COHP, 6.

6. Ibid., 1–2. The 1910 census gives the population as 11,767, of which 1,868 were Negro.

7. She was not a charter member, though, of the West Chester Branch of the NAACP. Charter members are listed in the branch files of the NAACP, in the Library of Congress, Washington, D.C.

8. For example, see Beale Morgan to BR, May 2, 1969, and BR's reply, May 21.

9. An intake interview of the Bureau of Prisons, March 29, 1944, noted that "his education opportunities have been exceptional for one who was attached to a family group with no greater financial resources than [his] parents."

10. Alex Haley, *The Autobiography of Malcolm X* (1964; New York: Grove Press, 1966), 36.

11. *Philadelphia Inquirer*, August 26, 1987. Claiming that it was an attempt to deny being American, Martin Mayer, "The Lone Wolf of Civil Rights," *Saturday Evening Post*, July 11, 1964, 78.

12. The information about his emerging awareness of his homosexuality is from an interview with *Open Hands: Journal of the Reconciling Congregation Program* (Spring 1987): 3–7, a magazine active in the gay rights movement. By that time he had not only become open about his homosexuality but was pressing the issue of gay rights as a continuation of his fight against prejudice of any kind. We are dealing, thus, with memories of half a century earlier, about a highly emotional issue, in a different context. He makes the process sound smooth and conflict-free. It is hard to believe that it was, and as later events indicate, there was more emotional turmoil than appears in this interview. There is also a problem in terminology. In the 1987 interview, he used the term *gay*, which was anachronistic for the 1930s.

The report from his time in prison is H. M. Janney, Chief Medical Officer, "Neuropsychiatric Progress Report," dated October 25, 1944. This is from the Bureau of Prisons. There is abundant evidence both then and later that he was ambivalent and conflicted about his own homosexuality.

13. The yearbook of West Chester High, in the BRF.

14. An FBI report dated December 24, 1943, gives his address from 1934 to 1937 as Burleigh Hall. Cheyney State wrote Walter Naegle in 1997 that it would release Bayard Rustin's transcript only under court order. This probably means that there was something potentially criminal, perhaps connected with his homosexuality, involved in his leaving the college. When Naegle finally got the material from Cheyney State, the reasons for dismissal were given as "social irregularities" and "morally weak." Also see August Meier Papers, Schomburg Library, New York, notes of Jonathan Gottlieb typescript. n.p., n.d.; p. 12 says that he was dismissed for his "lackadaisical behavior and to rumors of an affair between Rustin and [Milton] Brown."

15. The irregular attendance at Wilberforce: Gladys L. Powell, Registrar, to R. M. Larkin, Warden's Assistant, Federal Correctional Institute, Ashland, Ky., March 18, 1944. Whether he left Wilberforce because of the inadequate intellectual challenge, a strike against bad food, refusal to take ROTC, or some homosexual incident is unclear. Time and completing courses at Cheyney, W. M. Menchab, Dean of Instruction, Cheyney Training School for Teachers, to Warden's Assistant, Federal Corrections Institution, Ashland, Ky., March 13, 1944. Both Bureau of Prisons files.

16. For Rustin's musical activities, *Cheyney Record*, November 24, 1934, November 1935, December 1935.

17. For his peace summer, see *Cheyney Record*, November 20, 1937. Clippings are in BRF.

18. BR to Davis Platt, September 1, 1944, says he has a very limited use for higher education. BR to Platt, March 16, 1945, talks about reading at Cheyney State of James, Santayana, Royce. All in BRF. BR's description of "Sugar Hill" is typescript of an interview with *Open Hands*, February 2, 1987, 5.

19. The FBI report giving his WPA employment is dated January 10, 1944, BRF. It is confirmed by R. E. White of the Federal Works Agency to Warden's Assistant, Federal Correctional Institution, Ashland, Ky., March 15, 1944, Bureau of Prisons files.

20. The incident is described in detail in Martin B. Duberman, *Paul Robeson* (New York: Knopf, 1988), 341–345. The *Baltimore Afro-American*, April 30, 1949, ran a front-page story quoting Walter White, Mary McLeod Bethune, Charles Huston, and others but not mentioning Rustin, who, in discussing the incident many years later with Duberman, probably gave himself a more prominent role than he actually played.

    Any civil rights activity was always denounced as Communist by opponents. Black spokespeople and newspapers were at pains to make clear that Robeson did not speak for the race, which he did not.

21. BR interview with *Open Hands*, February 2, 1987. The interview as published is shorter than the typescript transcript in the BR papers. The passage about singing with Josh White and others is that typescript, p. 7. Alain Locke is p. 14. The words *gay* and *straight* are anachronisms here because Rustin gave the interview after the words came into use. This phase of his life is also in the "Reminiscences," COHP, 27–28.

22. The phrase "When Harlem Was in Vogue" is from a book of that title by David Levering Lewis (New York: Knopf, 1981). Charles Bloomstein, interview with author, December 29, 1994.

23. The transcript is from the office of the registrar. A letter from CCNY to the Bureau of Prisons, dated March 13, 1944, also reports him as enrolled, in the School of Education, only for the academic year 1940–1941. The quotation on the Communist Party being American is from *Young Communist Review* (July 1938): 33, though in the same issue there are articles praising Stalin and Soviet society. In 1940 the *Young Communist Review* changed its name to the *Weekly Review*, thus dropping "Communist" from its identification. I have also looked at *Clarity*, which described itself as the "theoretical organ" of the YCL. Bayard Rustin's name does not appear in that, either. *Clarity*, vols. 1–2 (Westport, Conn.: Greenwood Reprint Corp., 1970).

24. Comments about Communists and Socialists from Jonathan Gottlieb typescript on the basis of August Meier's notes of interviews with BR, August 19, 1978, Meier Papers.

25. Working on Powell's campaign from BR interview with Andrew Lightman.

For the campaign itself, and factionalism within the movement, see Charles V. Hamilton, *Adam Clayton Powell, Jr: The Political Biography of an American Dilemma* (New York: Atheneum, 1991), 96–99.

26. Emphasis on peace and the Oxford Oath from many flyers of the YCL in the CCNY Archives. The strike against war is a flyer for the strike April 20, 1939. Rustin talked about this period in his life in "Reminiscences," COHP, 28–39.

27. On the ASU election, see the flyer dated October 1, 1937.

28. On the rally against the purge trials, see an undated 1938 flyer by the "American Committee for the Defense of Leon Trotsky." The most prominent member of the committee was John Dewey.

29. BR Interview with Andrew Lightman.

30. The story of the 1941 march has been told so many times that I tell it here only as it concerned Bayard Rustin. The standard older work is Herbert Garfinkel, *When Negroes March: The March on Washington Movement in the Organizational Politics for FEPC* (Glencoe, Ill.: Free Press 1959), particularly chap. 2. The quotations from the Youth Division is 67, Randolph 68. A detailed account of Randolph's meeting with the president is in Jervis Anderson, *A. Philip Randolph: A Biographical Portrait* (New York: Harcourt Brace Jovanovich, 1972), 256–258. The text of the order was written by a young White House lawyer named Joseph Rauh, who would be important many years later in the civil rights movement. See also *Baltimore Afro-American,* June 21, June 28, July 5, 1941. "Reminiscences," COHP, 38–48. *Amsterdam (N.Y.) Star News*, July 5, 1941. The paper did not even mention Rustin's rejection. Roy Wilkins in *Crisis* 48 (August 1941): 247.

2   Nonviolent Direct Action

1. Carleton Mabee, *Black Freedom: The Nonviolent Abolitionists from 1830 through the Civil War* (New York: Macmillan, 1970), claims in his introduction that he will show how the abolitionists used a similar strategy as the civil rights movement of the 1960s. His evidence, however, proves the reverse. Rustin points out the differences in his interview "Pacifism" with Andrew Lightman, 1985, Bayard Rustin Fund. South Africa had some small tradition, too, for Mohandas Gandhi had begun his nonviolent protests in that country.

2. On the contrast between the Indian and American circumstances, BR interview with Andrew Lightman.

3. BR on understanding the point of view of the opponent, Ibid.

4. Richard Gregg, *The Power of Non-Violence* (Philadelphia: J. B. Lippincott, 1934); the quotation is 57. Gregg was always pretty far from the mainstream. In 1956 he predicted that "after the U.S. has used up all of its natural stored resources, it will revert to a village economy living on its annual income of solar energy. This is my guess, anyhow." *Liberation* 1, no. 8 (November 1956): 10. Krishnalal Shridharani, *War without Violence: A Study of Gandhi's Method and Its Accomplishments* (New York: Harcourt, Brace, 1939). Charles Chatfield, *For Peace and Justice: Pacifism in America, 1914–1941* (Knoxville: University of Tennessee Press, 1971).

5. Jo Ann Ooiman Robinson, *Abraham Went Out: A Biography of A.J. Muste* (Philadelphia: Temple University Press, 1981). Nat Hentoff, *Peace Agitator: The Story of A.J. Muste* (New York: Macmillan, 1963).

6. Both the Harlem ashram and Ahimsa farm are described in Chatfield, *For*

Peace and Justice, 215–216. See also J. Holmes Smith, "Our New Ashram," *Fellowship* 7, no. 1 (January 1941): 2. That Rustin was a nonresident member is from the interview with Andrew Lightman.

7. James Farmer, interview with author, March 18, 1996. The phrase seems inappropriate under the circumstances, but the choice of words was James Farmer's.

8. James L. Farmer, "The Race Logic of Pacifism," *Fellowship* 7, no. 2 (February 1942): 7–8. By 1945, Farmer was suggesting an organization of returning veterans to oppose, by nonviolent means, Jim Crow in transportation, public accommodations, and housing. See his "The Coming Revolt against Jim Crow," *Fellowship* 9, no. 5 (May 1945): 99–100.

9. United States Department of Justice, Bureau of Prisons, *Federal Prisons* (Washington, D.C.: 1944), 7. During the war years, every issue of the FOR's journal, *Fellowship*, had articles about COs and CO laws. Almost every month saw an article by A. J. Muste, as well as regular articles by Richard Gregg and Muriel Lester, who would later accompany Bayard Rustin to India. For the years of the blitz, there were regular pieces from Vera Brittain on England.

10. About six thousand objectors served time in prison, three-quarters of them Jehovah's Witnesses, whereas some twelve thousand served in CPS camps, some twenty-five thousand in noncombatant roles in the military. Mulford Q. Sibley and Philip E. Jacobs, *Conscription of Conscience: The American State and Conscientious Objectors* (Ithaca, N.Y.: Cornell University Press, 1952), 83–85. These figures are from the Selective Service System; Sibley and Jacobs think they are too low. The aspect of pacifism most relevant to the FOR and Bayard Rustin is in Cynthia Eller, *Conscientious Objectors and the Second World War: Moral and Religious Arguments in Support of Pacifism* (New York: Praeger, 1991). See also Susan Dion, "Pacifism Treated as Subversion: The F.B.I. and the War Resisters League," *Peace and Change* 9, no. 1 (1983): 43–54. Gretchen Lemke-Santangelo, "The Radical Conscientious Objectors of World War II: Wartime Experience and Postwar Activism," *Radical History Review* 45 (1989): 5–29. Glen Zeitzer and Charles F. Howlett, "Political versus Religious Pacifism: The Peace Now Movement of 1943," *Historian* 48, no. 3 (1986): 373–393.

11. BR to Local Board No. 63, November 16, 1943. A. Philip Randolph (hereafter cited as "APR") to "Bayard," April 17, 1944.

12. Among other places where he said that, interview with Andrew Lightman. Of course, he made that statement after he was no longer a pacifist.

13. Report of Youth Field Worker—Bayard Rustin, September 30 to November 28, 1941, FOR Papers, SCPC.

14. BR to A. J. Muste, April 28, 1942, FOR Papers, SCPC.

15. This incident is recounted in Bayard Rustin, "Non-Violence vs. Jim Crow," *Fellowship* 8, no. 6 (July 1942): 120. He later said that these "lone" incidents were learning experiences and that nothing significant toward changing the situation could occur until a large mass of people were involved. From the interview with Andrew Lightman.

16. BR interview with Andrew Lightman.

17. BR, "Report of a Youth Secretary," September 12, 1942, FOR Papers, SCPC. J. Holmes Smith made the same point in "Non-Violent Direct Action," *Fellowship* 7, no. 12 (December 1941): 207.

18. *Fellowship: The Journal of the Fellowship of Reconciliation*, October 1942, as quoted in Bayard Rustin, *Down the Line: The Collected Writings of Bayard Rustin* (Chicago: Quadrangle Books, 1971), 11.

19. Program of the New York Institute on Race Relations and Non-Violent Solutions at the Grace Congregational Church, April 2, 3, 4, 1943, clipping collection, Bayard Rustin Fund. See also Lillian Smith, "The White Christian and His Conscience," *Fellowship* 11, no. 8 (August 1945): 137–138, which pulls no punches.

20. A. J. Muste to John Swomley, July 7, 1943, in which A. J. says how important the California people think BR is. John Nevin Sayre Papers, SCPC, ser. A, box 14. Minutes of the Executive Committee, Northern California FOR, September 1, 1943, from which the quotation on BR's skills has been taken. Jean McKay to BR, September 4, 1943. Obviously to FOR, NVDA on the domestic scene was simply one aspect of pacifism. There is a detailed account of the San Francisco workshop in the BRP.

21. The episode at Stoner's is described in several places, among others James Tracy, *Direct Action: Radical Pacifism from the Union Eight to the Chicago Seven* (Chicago: University of Chicago Press, 1996), 32; James Farmer, *Lay Bare the Heart* (New York: Arbor House, 1985), 113–114; and August Meier and Elliott Rudwick, *CORE: A Study in the Civil Rights Movement* (Urbana: University of Illinois Press, 1975), 13–14.

22. Flyer announcing the race relations institute and Lincoln Temple Congregational Church, July 30, July 31, and August 1, 1943, with Rustin and Randolph on the same panel. *Syracuse Post Standard*, February 7, 1943. Memo on the need for more trade union leadership is an undated memo, in the 1943 file. There is no signature, but it is written in Rustin's logical style and is consistent with his approach. The memo about a joint demonstration favoring the abolition of the poll tax is by John Swomley of FOR, April 3, 1944, in the FOR Papers, SCPC.

23. George M. Houser, *No One Can Stop the Rain* (New York: Pilgrim Press, 1989), 7. Tracy, *Direct Action*, 3. George Houser, interview with author, October 10, 1996.

24. John Dixon to BR, September 4, 1943, and December 6, 1943. Mrs. Frank McCarthy to BR, November 5, 1943. Marie D. Nelson, memo, "Statement Regarding Protest Strike against Racial Segregation in the Federal Correction Institution at Danbury, Conn." November 17, 1943.

3 *Prison*

1. The description of Ashland is in part from a pamphlet, Bureau of Prisons, "Daily Life: The Federal Correctional Institution, Ashland, Kentucky." The pamphlet was printed in 1951. No earlier ones are extant, because paper was conserved during the war, but the institution had not changed drastically since Rustin was incarcerated.

2. The remark about the "limey" accent is in an FBI report dated December 24, 1943, obtained by BR under the Freedom of Information Act, in BRF.

3. Even in the notorious San Quentin prison, there was a strike led by COs, after which the dining room was desegregated. Caleb Foote to A. J. Muste, April 20, 1945, FOR Papers, SCPC.

4. The incident in the dining hall is described in George M. Houser, *Erasing the Color Line* (New York: Fellowship Publications, 1945), 48. The little book, more a pamphlet, has a foreword by A. Philip Randolph endorsing nonviolent action.

5. William H. Measaw to Associate Warden, November 14, 1944. E. J. Weale to

Associate Warden, November 14, 1944. Bureau of Prisons files, National Archives, Washington, D.C.

6. Handwritten letters from BR to Dr. Hagerman, July 15, July 17, 1944, to Dr. Janney, the prison medical officer, July 18, 1944. Bureau of Prisons files. Muste's is "Memo on Visit to Ashland, Kentucky, Federal Correctional Institution, July 27, 1944," FOR Papers, SCPC.

7. BR to Kessel Johnson, March 15, 1945. Bureau of Prisons files.

8. BR's letters to Davis Platt are full of discussions of books. Letters of March 2 and 16 and April 9, 1945, are good examples. Davis Platt very kindly gave me permission to see them.

9. Plans for desegregating cell block, paper left in BR's cell at the time of his release. Bureau of Prisons files. The visit of mother and grandmother is from F. J. Fitzpatrick to Warden of Lewisburg Federal Penitentiary, November 11, 1945. R. P. Hagerman to the Director, Bureau of Prisons, November 15, 1944, saying, "This man has been given opportunity, to an extent which other inmates would seldom dream of." Bureau of Prisons files.

10. R. P. Hagerman to Director of Prisons, November 10, 1944; J. L. Watson to the Captain, November 11, 1944. Julia Rustin to BR, April 20, 1945. All in Bureau of Prisons files. There is no indication that Bayard attended the funeral, but there is some evidence that he made another visit home in early April 1945. See BR to Davis Platt, April 9, 1945, BRF.

11. Davis Platt is given permission to bring the mandolin in G. H. Wray to Visiting Room Officer, June 20, 1944. Memo "Special Progress Report" on Bayard Rustin, September 15, 1944. R. P. Hagerman to Director, Bureau of Prisons, October 9, 1944. "He would be in danger, should he be released into the inmate population. . . . Strong and bitter inmate feeling against him is apparent." Hearing summary with word-for-word excerpts is in Bureau of Prisons files, September 22, 1944. The phrase "psychopathic personality, homosexuality" is in Hagerman to James V. Bennett, November 15, 1944. All in Bureau of Prisons files. H. M. Janney, "Neuropsychiatric Progress Report, October 25, 1944," Bureau of Prisons files. A. J. Muste to BR, October 22, 1944.

12. In BR to Davis Platt, October 2, 1944, he wrote, "Many are the wiles of the devil and few the children of men who can escape them." In long, tortured letters to Davis Platt, April 5, April 20, 1945, he speaks of his desire to struggle against his homosexuality, to be the kind of man he wants to be so as to be effective in his social goals, of the possibilities of a life with a woman, also of the difficulty of "making progress" in the monosexual world of prison. "Is celibacy the answer?" he wondered. Platt letters, BRF. BR to Muste, October 26, 1944. Bureau of Prisons files. Why this letter remained in the bureau is unclear. Did Rustin not mail it?

13. Bennett to Hagerman, June 15, 1945. Hagerman to Bennett, June 22, 1945. Both Bureau of Prisons files. The reference to Springfield means the medical prison at Springfield, Mo. The prison system considered homosexuality to be a medical defect.

14. Confined to the library is from Rustin's "Reminiscences," COHP, 72. His memory does not coincide exactly with the record at Lewisburg. He says that his time at Lewisburg was all spent confined to the library. He says nothing about assignment to the Farm Colony, but he was recalling from forty years later. "Conduct Record" of Bayard Rustin, n.d. but the last entry is March 5, 1946, U.S. Northeastern Penitentiary, Lewisburg, Pa., says his work in the prison farm was satisfactory. James V. Bennett to the Honorable Brian

McMahon, United States Senate, April 10, 1946. Someone, perhaps Muste, must have complained to Senator McMahon, because Bennett's letter is in answer to questions from McMahon. Both Bureau of Prisons files.

15. BR to James V. Bennett (the date of writing is somewhat obscured, but the date of receipt is stamped March 26, 1946).

16. His transfer to the Farm Colony; "Release Progress Report, June 21, 1946." All Bureau of Prisons files. Farms and factories at Lewisburg from a pamphlet, "United States Penitentiary, Lewisburg, Pa.," Leavenworth, Kans., 1939, 9–11. Dates of release from BR's release card, Bureau of Prisons files.

4 *After Prison, to Prison*

1. The building being "taken over by the movement" and the mood are from William Sutherland, interview with author, March 28, 1997. Sutherland talked about Bayard at parties, as did Ralph DiGia, interview with author, January 3, 1997.

2. Memo, George Houser, [no addressee], June 19, 1944. George M. Houser, *Erasing the Color Line* (New York: Fellowship Publications, 1945), which gives examples of the kind of thing he had in mind, including the demonstrations in various prisons.

3. On arguing that Jesus had sometimes provoked conflict, BR and Houser to Reuben A. Tanquist, December 8, 1947.

4. On NAACP quiet support, "Reminiscences," COHP, 300. On Thurgood Marshall telling Rustin he would supply lawyers, see BR interview, on tape, not transcribed, tape dated 1970, not more precisely, in MSRC.

5. Trying to get white southerners and northern liberals, George Houser to Nelle Norton, May 14, 1947.

6. On McKissick joining, BR 1970 interview, tape, not transcribed, in MSRC. Confirmed by McKissick, interview with Robert White, October 16, 1968, MSRC.

7. This account is a combination of George M. Houser and Bayard Rustin, "Journey of Reconciliation," typescript, n.d., FOR Papers, SCPC; typescript by George Houser, "A Personal Retrospective on the Journey of Reconciliation," n.d. but refers to the journey as forty-five years ago, given to me by George Houser; George Houser, interview with author, October 10, 1996; and "Reminiscences," COHP, 288–303. James Peck remembered not one Negro teacher but "a delegation of local Negroes." *Liberation* 6, nos. 4–5 (Summer 1961): 19. Junius Scales, a prominent member of the Communist Party, convicted in 1958 under the Smith Act, recalled that the entire Jones family had to leave town for a while, and that he (Scales) and a non-Communist friend organized a round-the-clock watch on his house for two days. Scales left the party in 1957. Junius Irving Scales and Richard Nickson, *Cause at Heart: A Former Communist Remembers* (Athens: University of Georgia Press, 1987), 278–279. Conrad J. Lynn, *There Is a Fountain: The Autobiography of a Civil Rights Lawyer* (Westport, Conn.: L. Hill, 1979), 112, says that young Communists were on the roof with rifles. This seems highly unlikely to me, since Jones was a pacifist and would hardly have allowed armed men on his roof. No account by other participants mentions rifles. BR, in an interview with Dudley Clarendon, August 16, 1983, recalls that they were all terrified, and he said that the house was protected by members of the University of North Carolina football team, whose captain was a member of Jones's congregation. BRF.

8. James Farmer, *Lay Bare the Heart* (New York: Arbor House, 1985), 196.

9. Account of the summer 1947 events, a mimeographed pamphlet called "Interracial Workshops," n.d. On ammonia and chemical warfare, BR's speech to Grand Valley State College, March 25, 1984. Both in BRP.

10. George Houser ran another workshop two years later, but Rustin was not involved. See Houser, "Project Brotherhood," *Fellowship* 16, no. 2 (February 1950): 13–17. This workshop, too, was inspiring for the participants but had little effect on race relations in Washington, D.C.

11. President's Committee on Civil Rights, *To Secure These Rights* (Washington, D.C.: GPO, 1947), 62–69. President's special message on civil rights, reprinted from *Public Papers of the Presidents of the United States: Harry S Truman* (Washington, D.C.: GPO, 1961–66), vol. 6 (1948): 62–69.

12. Colmer's speech in Congress, *Congressional Record*, 80th Cong., 2d sess., April 8, 1948, 4270.

13. David McCullough, *Truman* (New York: Simon and Schuster, 1992), 587–589. Alonzo Hamby, *A Man of the People: A Life of Harry S. Truman* (New York: Oxford University Press, 1995), 433–435. See also Donald McCoy and Richard Reutten, *Quest and Response: Minority Rights and the Truman Administration* (Lawrence: University Press of Kansas), particularly chaps. 5–6.

14. The *casus bilii* was a propsed civil rights plank in the platform that simply repeated Truman's civil rights proposals to Congress. Truman actually opposed the plank, but the larger issue was the trend. The leader of the rebel group was Mayor Hubert H. Humphrey of Minneapolis. Bayard Rustin was a firm supporter of Humphrey for all of the latter's political career.

15. Roger Baldwin to APR, May 23, 1945, indicates that APR is already thinking of the campaign against military segregation. BR to APR, November 11, 1947; APR to Harry S Truman, December 10, 1947; Houser to APR, February 14, 1948, with enclosures. "Statement Counseling Non-registration to Be Made by A. Philip Randolph When Asked by Negro and White Youths of Draft Age If They Should Register and Submit to Induction under the 1948 Draft Act," n.d.; "Fellowship Group Backs Randolph on Army Stand," *New York Age*, March 4, 1948; George Houser to APR, August 18, 1948; press release by Grant Reynolds and APR, October 11, 1948; "Reminiscences," COPH, 83–84; Jervis Anderson, *A. Philip Randolph: A Biographical Portrait* (New York: Harcourt Brace Jovanovich, 1972), 274–282. The *Amsterdam News* in a frontpage editorial rejected Randolph's (and Rustin's) call for civil disobedience but praised the final outcome. See *Amsterdam News*, July 24, 1948, and August 21, 1948. No mention was made of the news conference about which Rustin felt so guilty.

16. For an account of the trial, see *Durham (N.C.) Morning Herald*, March 18, 1948. The case was not taken further because money ran out and some key evidence, the bus tickets to prove the accused were in interstate transportation and thus under federal jurisdiction, mysteriously disappeared.

17. Jill Wallis, *Mother of World Peace: The Life of Muriel Lester* (Middlesex, England: Enfield Lock, 1993). Lester's autobiographies, *It Occurs to Me* (New York: Harper and Brothers, 1937) and *It So Happened* (New York: Harper and Brothers, 1947).

18. Rustin's account of the trip from interview "Pacifism," with Andrew Lightman, 1985, BRF.

19. "Recent Comments on Bayard Rustin," Muriel Lester, Alshabad, India, December 26, 1948. Typescript, John Nevin Sayre Papers, SCPC.

20. A. J. Muste to Muriel Lester, January 4, 1949. Sayre Papers.
21. John Nevin Sayre to Ray Newton of AFSC, January 13, 1949. Sayre Papers.
22. BR to John Nevin Sayre, A. J. Muste, Ray Newton, Percy Bartlett, n.d. but it says, "I am writing this memo on the eve of my going to serve a 30 day sentence in North Carolina." Sayre Papers.
23. My account is taken from his typescript. The *Post* articles are August 22–26, 1949.
24. Among many letters to relatives of inmates, see BR to Mrs. Carrie Slater, Durham, N.C., April 15, 1949, asking her to send her husband, Sylvester, his pipe, which he left in the dresser drawer. Talks about the importance of contacts with "family and friends." About letters being returned unopened, BR to Buddy Dixon, Durham, N.C., April 22, 1949. Arthur I. Morris of *Pittsburgh Courier* to BR, April 26, 1949. Rustin also got *Look* and the *Chicago Defender*. *Time* magazine declined to send a free subscription.
25. On BR's contribution to the campaign to end the chain gang, see Herbert Marshall of Political Science Department, University of North Carolina, to BR, July 6, 1949. Lee M. Brooks, Department of Sociology, University of North Carolina, to BR, September 29, 1949, in which Brooks says that "all the real leaders in Raleigh are determined that the present convict system under the Highway Department must be discarded." Sam Ragan of *Raleigh News and Observer* to BR, December 20, 1949, which indicates that there was already a reform campaign. All FOR Papers, SCPC.
26. Andrew Young, interview with author, May 28, 1997. Andrew Young, *An Easy Burden: The Civil Rights Movement and the Transformation of America* (New York: HarperCollins, 1996), chaps. 5–7.
27. Houser to BR, August 3, 1951; Houser to "Dear Friend," August 3, 1951; Memo, BR and George Houser to Cicero Committee of the Chicago Council Against Racial and Religious Discrimination, n.d. Bernard Brown, Assistant Field Secretary of the NAACP to BR, August 15, 1951, thanking him for his presence. "The story of your life, alone, gives new inspiration for us to carry on this great fight." Dick Bennett, of FOR, telegram to BR, September 20, 1951, saying that FOR is considering having him stay on in Chicago. *Baltimore Afro-American*, July 21, 1951, 1 and 2. The story can be followed in the *New York Times*, July 13 through 17 and, among others, July 20, 24, 28. Clark's move to Norwalk, August 11. There were some signs of things to come, however. Town officials were indicted and then acquitted of not performing their duties under state law. They were then convicted in federal court of denying the Clarks their civil rights. See *New York Times* (hereafter cited as "*NYT*"), May 13, 1952.
28. *NYT*, June 4, 1952. Karnovsky convicted. Truman praising the decision, Adlai Stevenson's actions in the crisis, and himself for having the federal case brought is *NYT*, October 12, 1952. The fact that Truman made his speech in Harlem indicates that the Democratic Party was taking the black vote seriously, at least the national Democratic Party and in some places.
29. A. J.'s skepticism, William Sutherland, interview with author, March 28, 1952. On first contacts between FOR and South Africa and setting up the American Committee on Africa, George Houser, interview with author, October 10, 1996.
30. BR, "African Revolution," *Fellowship* 11, no. 10 (November 1952): 1–6.
31. For BR's itinerary, BR to Arthur Brown, May 22, 1952. The *Education Sun* of New York University's School of Education, October 8, 1952; *Chicago Sun-Times*, November 21, 1952; *CIO News*, November 28, 1952; *Janesville (Wis.) Daily Gazette*, December 1, 1952.

5 *Crash*

1. On the general climate for homosexuals in the post–World War II years: John D'Emilio, "Gay Politics and Community in San Francisco since World War II," in *Hidden from History: Reclaiming the Gay and Lesbian Past*, ed. Martin Duberman, Martha Vicinus, and George Chauncey Jr. (New York: Meridian, 1989), 446–471. For the American Psychiatric Association and also American psychoanalysts, see *NYT*, December 12, 1998.
2. David McReynolds, interview with the author, September 30, 1996.
3. Rustin claiming it was trumped up, "Reminiscences," COHP, 98. John Swomley to BR in prison, January 27, 1953. BR to Swomley, March 8, 1953, from prison. Both John Swomley Papers, SCPC. BR to John Nevin Sayre, Feb. 27, 1953, John Nevin Sayre Papers, SCPC.
4. Statement adopted by the executive committee of the Fellowship of Reconciliation on January 28, 1953, FOR Papers, SCPC.
5. John Muste, telephone interview with author, August 7, 1996.
6. Dr. Robert Ascher, interview with author, September 16, 1996. Rustin, before his death, had come to Dr. Ascher, released him from all restraints of doctor-patient confidentiality, and told him to talk to any interested scholar.
7. The controversies within the WRL are detailed in two memos from Roy Finch, one undated, "Confidential Memo to the Executive Committee and National Advisory Council," and another that was just a few days later, dated August 25, 1953, "Memo to the Executive Council and National Advisory Council." Both WRL Papers, SCPC.

6 *Must Converge*

1. Joseph Beam, "Veteran Activist Still Fights for Blacks and Gays," *Philadelphia Gay News* 10, no. 17 (March 7–13, 1986). Clipping without page numbers in BRP.
2. The literature on this subject is vast, but sufficient for this sentence is Richard M. E. Sterner et al., *The Negro's Share: A Study of Income, Consumption, Housing, and Public Assistance* (New York: Harper and Brothers, 1943).
3. Statement praising Truman's civil rights record for the Kentucky Commission on Human Rights, dated September 13, 1972.
4. *Montgomery Advertiser*, December 5, 1955.
5. BR dates Smith's telegram as "a few days after the boycott began," in interview with T. H. Baker, June 17, 1969, Lyndon B. Johnson (hereafter cited as "LBJ") Library, Austin, Tex. Lillian Smith to Martin Luther King (hereafter cited as "MLK"), March 10, 1956. Margaret Rose Gladney, *How Am I to Be Heard: The Letters of Lillian Smith* (Chapel Hill: University of North Carolina Press, 1993), 194.
6. This account is from James Farmer, interview with author, March 18, 1996, and is similar to how he recalls the events in *Lay Bare the Heart* (New York: Arbor House, 1985), 186–187. It differs somewhat from Rustin's "Reminiscences," COHP, and accounts in Taylor Branch, *Parting the Waters: America in the King Years* (New York: Simon and Schuster, 1988), 177, and David Garrow, *Bearing the Cross: Martin Luther King and the Southern Christian Leadership Conference* (New York: Random House, 1986), 66–69.
7. MLK not yet a pacifist: BR interview, "Pacifism," with Andrew Lightman, 1985, Bayard Rustin Fund.
8. This account of Rustin's reasons for leaving Montgomery is from James

Farmer, interview with author, March 18, 1996. Not all sources agree that Rustin was in Montgomery in December 1955, but this is certainly his own and Farmer's memory. An unidentified clipping in the BR clipping file, dated by the archives as January 1956, identifies him already as "a close associate of Martin Luther King, in Montgomery, Alabama," which would mean the account in his "Montgomery Diary" in *Liberation* of April 1956 was his second stay there. Rustin also dates his first visit to Montgomery as December 1955 in an interview with August Meier and Elliott Rudwick, May 29, 1974. August Meier Papers, Schomburg Library, New York. On the *Manchester Guardian* and *Le Figaro*, see BR to MLK, March 8, 1956, in Clayborne Carson, ed., *The Papers of Martin Luther King Jr.* (Berkeley: University of California Press, 1992–1994), 3:164.

9. Glen Smiley, interview with Katherine Shannon, September 12, 1967, MSRC. Smiley said he arrived February 15, 1956, replacing Rustin. If this date is correct, it is another indication that Rustin had already been there.

10. BR, "Report on Montgomery, Alabama," issued and distributed by the War Resisters League, 5 Beekman Place, New York, March 21, 1956. On setting up the workshop, BR to Caroll G. Bowen of Oxford University Press, February 21, 1956.

11. John Swomley to Wilson Riles, February 21, 1956, expressing the doubts of various FOR people. Remarks that BR has asked the AFSC to release their college secretary, Bob Gillmore, to work with Bayard and "be in contact with white people for him." Robert Gillmore and his wife, Joyce Mertz, became the major financial support for BR during the 1960s. Obviously they knew each other already, but this is the earliest reference I have seen in the written record. John M. Swomley to Charles Walker, n.d. but probably about February 22: "We must not be involved with Bayard." Both John Swomley Papers, SCPC.

12. "Reminiscences," COHP, 136–138. The "Reminiscences" are in 1987, but he says about the same thing in an interview now at MSRC, given in 1970 with an unidentified interviewer. Most scholars put his days in Montgomery as February 21–29, 1957. This, however, was his second involvement in the bus boycott and with King. Further evidence of this is that the incident with Worthy and the gun is referred to as being on his second visit in BR's interview with Andrew Lightman.

13. BR to Ralph [DiGia?] and Arthur [Brown?] from Montgomery, February 25, 1956, WRL Papers, SCPC. The "dingy hotel" is from the 1970 interview with BR, MSRC, cited in n. 12 above. This tape also indicates that this was his second trip. The purpose of the trip being, originally, to set up a workshop is BR to Carroll G. Bowen of Oxford University Press, February 21, 1956, explaining why he could not think about writing a memoir at this time. It is interesting that some people thought he was already well known enough to write a memoir.

14. *Montgomery Advertiser*, March 7, 1956.

15. John Swomley to Smiley, February 29, 1956. There are two letters with this date. Swomley writes that the meeting was called by James Farmer, who is working for a labor union now, by Bob Gillmore of the AFSC, whom Bayard wanted to be his co-worker in the South, and by A. Philip Randolph. Smiley to Swomley, [dated by the archives March 2, 1956, which is about right]. The letter is handwritten, so the punctuation is sometimes a bit hard to make out. Swomley Papers, SPCP.

16. BR, "Montgomery Diary," *Liberation* 1, no. 3 (April 1956): 7–10. The *Mont-*

gomery Advertiser, February 21, 1956, does talk about the crowds of Negroes but indicates that the indicted men had to be brought in by deputies. They came willingly, but the newspaper does not mention anyone walking into the police station and surrendering.

17. That the speech was written by BR, Glenn Smiley to John Swomley, February 29, 1956, from Montgomery. Swomley Papers, SCPC. Quotation is from *NYT*, February 24, 1956.

18. The picture of Parks and King is *Baltimore Afro-American*, December 17, 1955. By the end of the month they got King's name right.

19. Ralph Helstein, President, United Packinghouse Workers of America (hereafter cited as "UPWA"), to MLK, April 2, 1956. Acknowledgment by King, April 12, 1956, UPWA Papers, SHSW.

20. BR, "Notes of a Conference. How Outsiders Can Strengthen the Montgomery Nonviolent Protest," n.d. and no addressee but probably February 1956, written to either the FOR or WRL. The author is not specifically identified, but it could only be BR.

Baker's character from author's telephone conversation with Joanne Grant, May 1998, author of *Ella Baker: Freedom Bound* (New York: John Wiley and Sons, 1998); the video "Fundi," New Day Films, 1981; and Robert Moses, interview with author, December 22, 1997, and Rachelle Horowitz, telephone interview with author, February 3, 1998. On founding of "In Friendship": Stanley Levison, interview with James Mosby, February 14, 1970, MSRC. See also Ella J. Baker to MLK, February 24, 1956, in Carson, *Papers of Martin Luther King Jr.*, 3:139.

21. David J. Garrow in *The F.B.I. and Martin Luther King* (New York: Penguin, 1981) concludes that Levison may well have been a Communist at one time but by 1955 had certainly severed any ties. One thing is certain: Levison never did anything except aid King and the movement.

22. On Rustin and Muste's working relationship, David McReynolds, interview with author, October 11, 1996.

23. MLK, "Our Struggle," *Liberation* 1, no. 3 (April 1956), or Carson, *Papers of Martin Luther King Jr*, 3:236–241. The Faulkner article is "A Letter to the North," *Life*, March 5, 1956, 51–52. The *Baltimore Afro-American* headline is March 3, 1956. Most of the front page is devoted to articles relating to the boycott.

24. Account of the office from Rachelle Horowitz, interview with author, October 8, 1996.

25. Accounts of the rally: *Baltimore Afro-American*, June 2, 1956; a page-one story with picture of Lucy (now Foster) and Mrs. Roosevelt. *NYT*, February 24, p. 8. Rustin's account of Powell is "Reminiscences," COHP, 120–122. Rustin in 1987 said it was Josh White, but the *New York Times*, the day after the rally, says Harry Belafonte sang. Most of the money to MIA, and also making connections to unions: interview with Stanley Levison, February 14, 1970, MSRC.

---

7 *From the "Spirit of Montgomery" to the SCLC's First Campaign*

1. MLK to BR, September 20, 1956, BRP.

2. BR, "Fear in the Delta," in *Down the Line* (Chicago: Triangle, 1971), 62–87. Part of this appeared as "Terror in the Delta," in *Liberation* 1, no. 9 (October 1956): 17–19.

3. This is a conversation as recalled thirty years later, so the exact words are not

certain. Rustin tells approximately the same story, with the words just a bit different, in an interview on June 17, 1969, LBJ Library, Austin, Tex. Rustin claimed that the SCLC was his idea. Joseph Lowery dismisses that claim and says the SCLC was formed by southern ministers. There is no reason that the conversation that Rustin recalled and Lowery's claims cannot both be true. That the idea had previously been discussed by Baker, Levison, and Rustin, in Levison's house, is "Interview with Ella Baker," September 4, 1974, by Eugene Walker, Southern Oral History Project, Southern Historical Collection, University of North Carolina, 10–11. Forming some sort of larger organization than MIA was not, at the time, a huge decision. It was an obvious next step, and not at all certain to succeed.

4. BR, "Working Papers" for the Southern Negro Leaders Conference on Transportation and Non-Violent Integration, Atlanta, January 10–11, 1957. They are not signed, but Ella Baker confirmed that they were written by Rustin in "Interview with Ella Baker," Southern Oral History Project, 37.

5. The maintenance of segregation on the buses, *Montgomery Advertiser*, December 6, 1956, 1. Lillian Smith's participation, *Montgomery Advertiser*, December 6, 1956, 2–A. Workshop itself described in *Montgomery Advertiser*, December 7, 1956, 6–C.

6. Glenn Smiley's account and regret in interview with Glenn Smiley, September 12, 1967, MSRC.

7. Participation of the union representatives is detailed in the "Report on the Southern Leaders Conference on Transportation and Non-Violent Integration," by Russell R. Lasley, n.d. but clearly soon after the conference, perhaps January 14, 1957. Back in Chicago, the UPWA decided on vigorous suppport for King's organization. See memo with the same title "by Lasley and C[harles] Hayes," director of the Chicago local. Both Lasley and Hayes were African American. UPWA Papers, SHSW.

8. This account of the two initial meetings of SCLC is from a pamphlet, *The SCLC Story*, ed. Ed Clayton (Atlanta: SCLC, 1963), 13–14, which also identifies the Working Papers as by BR, and from Joseph Lowery, interview with author, May 27, 1997.

9. The "jury trial amendment" ended up with a complicated compromise that gave judges the discretion to require jury trials. See *Congressional Quarterly Almanac*, 1957, 553.

10. Feldman had met Horowitz in Psychology 101 at Brooklyn College, was another of the Rustin acolytes, would be important in the New York City teachers' strike in 1968, and would be elected president of the American Federation of Teachers in 1997. From Sandra Feldman, interview with author, May 21, 1997.

11. A typescript of the speech is in BRP, microfilm 4:1019–1028. Judging from quotations in the *Baltimore Afro-American*, May 25, 1957, it is the speech he actually delivered.

12. BR to MLK, May 10, 1957. Press releases from Prayer Pilgrimage office May 8 and undated but May 1957.

13. Andrew Young, interview with author, June 28, 1997.

14. *NYT*, May 18, 1957; *Life*, June 3, 1957, 14–15; *Time*, August 12, 1957, 13.

15. The plans are laid out in a fund-raising letter from M. L. King. See one example, MLK to H. E. Tate, Lexington, Ky., February 20, 1958. MLK Papers, Boston University (hereafter cited as "BU"): 71A:9a.

16. David Garrow, *Bearing the Cross: Martin Luther King and the Southern Christian Leadership Conference* (New York: Random House, 1986), 103, men-

tions Medgar Evers, in Jackson, Mississippi, as opposing the "Crusade for Citizenship" rally.

17. The list of churches and ministers is in the BRP, microfilm 5:673–674. Rustin's draft of the telegram to Rogers is 5:709. The ambitious follow-up is outlined 5:698–704. Rustin's editing, in Rustin's hand, of King's speech is 5:680–684. The detailed nature of Rustin's involvement in the crusade can be seen in BR to MLK, November 18, 1957, with which he encloses a draft of a letter to be sent to those on the advisory committee (MLK Papers, BU). *Newsweek*, February 24, 1958, 32, as cited in Garrow, *Bearing the Cross*, 104, on small results of Crusade for Citizenship.

18. Chester Bowles to MLK, January 28, 1957, urging King to go to India; BR to MLK, February 19, 1957, reports that Harris Wofford begs King to come to India, also encloses a list of people who want to see him in London, and that Hallam Tennyson, Lord Alfred's grandson, wants to interview him on BBC. Sutherland to BR, January 24, 1957; BR to Sutherland, February 6, 1957; Sutherland to BR, February 12, 1957; MLK to BR, February 23, 1957, enclosing travel schedule. MLK Papers, BU. On Sutherland's wife, Maya Angelou, *The Heart of a Woman* (1981; New York: Bantam, 1982), 268. Sutherland, interview with author, March 28, 1997. The trip was financed, to a large extent, by the Christopher Reynolds Foundation. See BR to MLK, October 28, 1957, and Stephen S. Cary, of the foundation, to BR, February 1, 1957, both in the MLK Papers, BU. Probably no one gave Rustin the ax. Both he and King realized that their association should not be too obviously close.

19. BR, "To the Finland Station," *Liberation* 11, no. 4 (June 1958): 9–10. Paul Byrne, *The Campaign for Nuclear Disarmament* (London: Croom Helm, 1988), 42–45. Richard Taylor and Colin Pritchard, *The Protest Makers* (London: Pergamon, 1980). David Marquand, "England, the Bomb, the Marchers," *Commentary* 29 (May 1960): 380–386. Peregrine Worsthorne, "Britain and the Bomb," *Reporter* 21 (July 23, 1959): 22–23.

8 *Marching, Marching*

1. The drama of Little Rock is well described in Harry Ashmore, *Hearts and Minds* (New York: McGraw-Hill, 1982), 251–282. One of the "Little Rock nine," Ernest Green, later became a close associate of Bayard Rustin's in the A. Philip Randolph Institute.

2. On BR's views of the Little Rock crisis: Ralph DiGia, interview with author, January 3, 1997. Susan Pines, "Remembering Bayard Rustin," *Nonviolent Activist: The Magazine of the War Resisters League* 4 (December 1987): 9. *Liberation* 2, no. 8 (November 1957): 4–12.

3. David Garrow, *Bearing the Cross: Martin Luther King and the Southern Christian Leadership Conference* (New York: Random House, 1986), 104.

4. On Levison and *Stride toward Freedom*, ibid., 105. Levison had significant input. It is not clear from the sources now available whether or not Rustin did. Randolph form letter asking for support, dated September 19, 1958.

5. The Retail, Wholesale and Department Store Workers Union comprised most of the black retail workers in Harlem. That office simply had more room than Randolph's offices, a few doors away.

6. Reuther's range of support for liberal causes can be seen in Kevin Boyle, *The UAW and the Heyday of American Liberalism, 1945–1968* (Ithaca, N.Y.: Cornell University Press, 1995), and Nelson Lichtenstein, *The Most Dangerous Man in Detroit: Walter Reuther and the Fate of American Labor* (New

York: Basic Books, 1995). For Horace Sheffield, see particularly 375–377. For the shifting nature of race relations in the automobile plants, see Kevin Boyle, "The Kiss: Racial and Gender Conflict in a 1950s Automobile Factory," *Journal of American History* 84, no. 2 (September 1997): 496–524.

7. This information is all from undated material in the BRP about the Youth March.
8. The story of the stabbing is from *NYT*, Sunday, September 21, 1958, 1 and 40.
9. Statement of APR, September 23, 1958.
10. The statement to the president and the specifics on the delegation are from BRP. The events of the march are from the *Baltimore Afro-American*, November 1, 1958, 1 and 8.
11. E. Frederic Morrow, *Black Man in the White House: A Diary of the Eisenhower Years by the Administrative Officer for Special Projects, the White House, 1955–1961* (New York: Coward-McCann, 1963), 233.
12. This version of the text is from *Congressional Record*, 86th Cong., 1st sess., May 20, 1959, 8696–8697.
13. *Washington Star*, April 19, 1959. See also Morrow, *Black Man in the White House*.
14. *Baltimore Afro-American*, April 25, 1959, 1.

9 Serving Two Masters

1. The chronology is from WRL executive committee meetings, in the WRL Papers, SCPC.
2. Sheet in the BRP headed "Text of Cablegram to Bayard Rustin, 11/14/59 prepared by A.J. Muste and Stan Levison." Tom to Bayard in Accra, November 11, 1959.
3. The account of the march is from A. J. Muste, "Africa against the Bomb," *Liberation* 4, no. 10 (January 1960): 4–7; "Reminiscences," COHP, 341–343; William Sutherland, interview with author, March 28, 1997.
4. BR to Maude Ballou (King's secretary), March 4, 1960, May 4, 1960; Ballou to BR, June 24, 1960; BR to King, June 7, 1960; BR to King, June 16, 1960; BR to Harvey Pressman, June 30, 1960; BR to King, July 5, 1960. All from MLK Papers, BU. The total amount of money raised, eighty-five thousand dollars, is from the *Baltimore Afro-American*, October 22, 1960, 9. Rustin also organized the financing of an advertisement in the *New York Times* defending King that became the basis for the Supreme Court case *New York Times Co. v. Sullivan* (1964). This case protected the right of citizens to criticize public officials, even if some of the criticism was incorrect.
5. The new name and purpose: *Baltimore Afro-American*, May 14, 1960. Robert Moses, interview with author, December 22, 1997.
6. Robert Moses, interview with author, December 22, 1997. Moses in that interview said that Bayard said he should go to Atlanta and that Ella Baker sent him to Amzie Moore. Rachelle Horowitz in a letter to me of November 9, 1998, says it was BR who sent Moses to Moore. The event is briefly described in the *Baltimore Afro-American*, May 28, 1960.
7. Maya Angelou, *The Heart of a Woman* (1981; New York: Bantam, 1982), 58–68. Maya Angelou was proud enough of "Cabaret for Freedom" also to mention it in her entry for "Who's Who in America." I have looked in vain for notices of the cabaret in other sources. That it was Sunday matinee, Rachelle Horowitz to author, November 11, 1998.
8. Notice of a news conference to be held in Randolph's office, June 10, 1960;

the memo is dated June 8. The announcement of the program is from *NYT*, June 10, 1960, 18, and the *Baltimore Afro-American*, June 18, 1960, 2, 18. Memo in the BRP, n.d., "Statement of Aims and Methods of March on Conventions." The same aims are in BR to MLK, June 15, 1960, which also included a demand that both parties oppose colonialism, East and West, and oppose apartheid. These international aims were not included in the final list of demands. Rustin's position in the organization is detailed in "Memorandum on a Meeting with Reverend Kilgore, June 27, 1960." That memorandum also indicates that Tom Kahn would work with Rustin. Rustin's salary would be paid by the King Defense Committee, which indicates that committee had a surplus after King was acquitted.

9. *New York Courier*, July 9, 1960.
10. FBI report, September 11, 1963. At that point, King was considering whether or not Rustin might be brought back into SCLC.
11. The Kilgore Committee and Rustin quote are from BR interview, June 17, 1969, LBJ Library, Austin, Tex., and Taylor Branch, interview with BR, September 24, 1984, in BRF.
12. "Reminiscences," COHP, 266–267. Rustin says in this interview that Powell threatened to accuse King of having a homosexual relationship with Rustin, which was not true. The interviewer leads Rustin into thinking it was 1964 rather than 1960. That BR was deeply depressed, Rachelle Horowitz in a letter to the author, November 9, 1998. That he had told MLK, August Meier, conversation with author, November 24, 1998. Rustin may have misinterpreted MLK's earlier attitude, or Rustin may have invented it. Martin Mayer, "The Lone Wolf of Civil Rights," *Saturday Evening Post*, June 11, 1964, 78. WRL executive committee meeting, September 10, 1960, "Statement on Rustin's resignation as secretary to Martin Luther King" [capitalization as in original]. Nat Hentoff, "Adam Clayton Powell: What Price Principle," *Village Voice*, July 14, 1960. If Rustin felt any bitterness at King's not rejecting his resignation, he does not show it. The Hentoff article criticizes King, and Rustin, in his note of transmittal, separates himself from this criticism. Jo Ann Ooiman Robinson, *Abraham Went Out: A Biography of A. J. Muste* (Philadelphia: Temple University Press, 1981), 122. Robinson also gets the date wrong, giving it as 1962. She quotes Muste as being critical of King. Garrow, in *Bearing the Cross*, 139–140, says Rustin was bitter.
13. Ella Baker to BR and Stanley Levison, July 16, 1958.
14. King continuing to consult with BR, interview with BR, June 17, 1969, LBJ Library. That there was a similar "Research Committee" in California: Andrew Young, interview with author, May 5, 1997.
15. Rustin talking to King about jail and the militants (both Rustin and the *Baltimore Afro-American* used that term) from a BR interview with Taylor Branch, September 24, 1984. It is not clear when this conversation took place. BRF.
16. Rustin in Atlanta with future SNCC leaders, John Lewis, with Michael D'Orso, *Walking with the Wind: A Memoir of the Movement* (New York: Simon and Schuster, 1988), 90.
17. The "Temporary Student Nonviolent Coordinating Committee," which had its main office at the SCLC office in Atlanta, to Dear Friend, September 30, 1960, giving plans for the October meeting. SNCC Papers, microfilm (Sanford, N.C.: Microfilming Corp. of America, 1981).
18. That he was an invited speaker at the General Conference, Marion Barry to Walter Reuther, August 25, 1960, which includes the schedule. Walter Reuther

Papers, Archives of Labor and Urban Affairs, Walter P. Reuther Library, Wayne State University, Detroit (hereafter cited as Reuther Library). His disinvitation, interview with Julian Bond, January 22, 1968, MSRC. In the SNCC Papers, a list of speakers has many names crossed out with substitutes. Rustin's is crossed out with no substitute. SNCC Papers, microfilm, reel 1, 169–170. Cleveland Sellers, with Robert Terrell, *The River of No Return* (Jackson: University Press of Mississippi, 1990), 42–43, says Rustin's name was withdrawn at the behest of the United Packinghouse Workers of America. Julian Bond, in an interview with the author, October 7, 1996, thought it was the UAW. The reasoning of the Packinghouse Workers is not clear, since they had a strong Communist background themselves, and by this time Rustin was anti-Communist. Also, Robert Moses, interview with author, December 22, 1997, confirms the reason for Stembridge's resignation, but Moses did not know the source of the objection. Jane Stembridge, in a telephone conversation with the author, March 3, 1998, thought that maybe Bond was correct, with the UAW acting through the SCLC. Both the Packinghouse Workers and the UAW worked with Rustin before and after 1960, so both explanations for the withdrawn invitation have plausibility problems. Neither the papers of the UPWA at the State Historical Society of Wisconsin nor the UAW records at the Reuther archives in Detroit have any record of the event. James Forman in *The Making of Black Revolutionaries* (1972; New York: Macmillan, 1985), 219, wrote that it was the AFL-CIO. Ella Baker to APR, June 5, 1961, A. Philip Randolph Papers, Library of Congress, Washington, D.C., is somewhat unclear but seems to support that conclusion. I have found no record in the George Meany Archives, Silver Springs, Md., but that explanation is certainly more plausible than the alternatives. Glenn Smiley was invited but had other obligations. Richard Gregg was a speaker. Marion Barry to Richard Gregg, September 6, 1960; Barry to Smiley, September 8, 1960, both in SNCC Papers, microfilm. The *Baltimore Afro-American*, October 15, 1960, 7, identified King as president of the Southern Christian Leadership Conference, "under which the student committee functions." Within a couple of years, Rustin was again being invited to SNCC national meetings: William Mahoney of SNCC to Tom Kahn, October 22, 1963, Student Activists Collection, Reuther Center, Detroit.

19. *Liberation* 4, no. 9 (October 1960): 3. There was no unanimity among black celebrities. Jackie Robinson supported Nixon, whereas Powell excoriated the Republican candidate.
20. "Reminiscences," COHP, 354
21. Courtland Cox, interview with author, October 26, 1998.
22. On the founding of the World Peace Brigade, see Barbara Deming, "International Peace Brigade," *Nation* 194, no. 7 (April 7, 1962): 303–306. Bradford Lyttle, "Brummana Conference for a World Peace Brigade," Final Report, n.d. [January 1962?], A. J. Muste Papers, SCPC. "Reluctant acceptance" of conditions in "Notes of a Preparatory Meeting October 12, 1961." Muste Papers, SCPC. Also, William Sutherland, telephone interview with author, July 16, 1997.
23. Much of the story of the World Peace Brigade and Bayard Rustin's role is from William Sutherland, telephone interview with author, July 16, 1997. Rustin's activities are further detailed in a long letter to A. J., from Dar es Salaam, n.d. but clearly March 1962. Muste Papers, SCPC, aided by records of the executive committee meetings of the War Resisters League, SCPC. The Nyerere quotation is from his *Freedom and Unity (Uhuru no Umoja)* (London: Ox-

ford University Press, 1967), 59. See also Andrew Roberts, *A History of Zambia* (New York: Africana Publishing Co., 1979), 218–221. A. Philip Randolph kept track of events in Africa. "Maida" [Springer, of AFL-CIO] to APR on stationery of Kenya Federation of Labour [*sic*], March 8, 1962, Randolph Papers.

BR in "Reminiscences," COHP, 340, indicates that some half a million people were gathered at the Northern Rhodesian border, but he claims too much. Sutherland said in the July 16 interview with the author that the march never took place because the British agreed to the election. For contemporary confirmation: Anton Nelson, Usa River, Taganyika, to Editor *World Peace Brigade Reports*, September 7, 1962. Nelson was a friend of Bill Sutherland's and had raised money for the World Peace Brigade. He writes, "No march was ever organized, nor begun nor carried out." About the center for nonviolent training, he writes, "I stayed at his [Bill Sutherland's] digs for a week early in April, and there was no center, no personnel except him, and he was getting a job with the Taganyikan government. . . . The AFA project was an expensive experiment or failure." Muste Papers, SCPC.

24. Notes of a "London Working Committee of the World Peace Brigade for Nonviolent Action: meeting April 10, 1962," indicates that Rustin and Sutherland were in Dar es Salaam, trying to set up the "centre." Muste to Ray Kinney, Garden Grove, Calif., September 17, 1962. A fund-raising letter with a rather desperate tone, for the center. Muste Papers, SCPC. Minutes of the World Peace Brigade, London, January 9, 1963, Rustin and A. J. were there. Indicates that the Dar es Salaam center project is not going well, and some feeling that it should be given up. Muste Papers, SCPC. By April 27, 1966, Ralph DiGia wrote Robert Gilmore asking if the World Peace Brigade could return at least some of the fifteen hundred dollars that the War Resisters League had loaned it, since the brigade "seems to have apparently ceased functioning." DiGia to Gilmore, April 27, 1966, Muste Papers, SCPC.

10 *Convergence*

1. Ralph DiGia, interview with author, January 3, 1997. BR interview with Dudley Clarendon of *NYT*, n.d. [1983?], BRF.
2. Undated notice of "Staff Functions, Locations and Phone Extensions," in BRP (reel 8, frame 523); Rachelle Horowitz, interview with author, October 8, 1996.
3. *NYT*, August 4, 1963, 70. Editorial on August 7, 32. Rustin and Tom Kahn drew up the original plans. See Jervis Anderson, *A. Philip Randolph: A Biographical Portrait* (New York: Harcourt Brace Jovanovich, 1973), 324.
4. That Rustin and Kahn prepared the memo, Rachelle Horowitz to author, November 9, 1998. Dorothy Miller (SNCC) to APR, March 25, 1963; APR to Roy Wilkins, March 25, 1963; APR telegrams to Martin Luther King and to Dorothy Height and to Rosa Gregg (NCNW), all March 26, 1963. James Farmer to APR, April 1, 1963; Whitney Young to APR, April 2, 1963; Horace Julian Bond to APR, April 1, 1963. A. J. Muste to APR, April 5, 1963; APR to Muste, April 13, 1963. Muste Papers, SCPC. "A. Philip Randolph Calls for March on Washington," *Liberation* 7, no. 1 (April 1963): 12.
5. Minutes of a meeting of the Negro American Labor Council, 217 West 125th Street, New York, April 23, 1963.
6. Andrew Young, *An Easy Burden: The Civil Rights Movement and the Transformation of America* (New York: HarperCollins, 1996), 251.

7. Andrew Young, interview with author, February 28, 1997.
8. Jones to Levison, May 13, 1963. MLK to Levison from Chicago, June 6, 1963. Conference call with MLK, Levison, Clarence Jones, Ralph Abernathy, Andrew Young, June 9, 1963. Levison to MLK at Sheraton, Atlanta, June 12, 1963. David Garrow, ed., *The FBI Martin Luther King File*, pt. 2, The King-Levison File (Frederick, Md.: University Publications of America, 1987) (hereafter cited as "Garrow, *FBI File*").
9. Rustin, in an interview with Taylor Branch in 1983, recalled that Wilkins had telephoned him to warn of his opposition. Taylor Branch, *Parting the Waters* (New York: Simon and Schuster, 1988), 846.
10. There are many accounts of this meeting and Wilkins's imperious designation of "you stay, you go." My sources are John Lewis, interview with author, May 20, 1997; Norman Hill, interview with James Mosby, March 12, 1970, MSRC, which talks about preliminary thinking of Hill, Rustin, and Farmer. James Farmer, interview with author, March 18, 1996. Farmer said that Randolph was not officially a member of the "Big Six" but Height was, so Randolph had to ask permission to attend, which was of course given. There is a good description of the meeting in Branch, *Parting the Waters*, 847. For an account ignoring internal differences, see *NYT*, July 3, 1963.
11. Economic demands were included in Manual #1, not in Manual #2. Opposition to including the specific economic demands, John D. Arnold, Nassau Chapter, Universalist Fellowship for Social Justice, to Cleveland Robinson, August 4, 1963, reply by BR, August 8, 1963, saying they have been eliminated.
12. That phrase is from Manual #1, n.d.; it is repeated in later publicity.
13. "Reminiscences," COHP, 385. At the march, a small group of American Nazis, surrounded by police and national guard troops, were kept off to one side, grousing, according to the *Daily Telegraph* (London), August 29, 1963.
14. For UAW support specifically, see Walter Reuther to [Wm.?] Massey, August 22, 1963, and Bill Oliver to Reuther, August 24, 1963, the latter indicating that about forty-five hundred UAW members will attend the march. Both are in the Walter Reuther Papers, Archives of Labor and Urban Affairs, Reuther Library. There are also numerous other memos indicating a major effort by the union.
15. Careful accounts were kept throughout the months before and after the march. I here summarize a nearly final account: Cleveland Robinson to APR, November 2, 1964.
16. David McReynolds, review of Jervis Anderson's *Bayard Rustin: Troubles I've Seen* in *Nonviolent Activist: The Magazine of the War Resisters League* 14 (November–December 1997): 20, which accuses him of being too close to organized labor, and Herbert Hill, telephone interview with author, November 15, 1997, saying that "Shachtman was the key."
17. Meany's position was interpreted by the *New York Times*, probably correctly, as meaning that Meany considered the march an "unwise legislative tactic." See *NYT*, August 14, 1963. Reuther and Randolph openly criticized the decision by the AFL-CIO executive committee. Donald Slaiman, interview with author, January 11, 1997.
18. John Lewis, with Michael D'Orso, *Walking with the Wind: A Memoir of the Movement* (New York: Simon and Schuster, 1998), 215.
19. It is not clear who wrote what, between Tom Kahn and Bayard, but their thinking was virtually interchangeable anyway, so it may not be important. About the parking of buses, Rachelle Horowitz, interview with author, October 8, 1996.

20. BR Memo to staff, August 6, 1963.
21. Courtland Cox, interview with author, October 26, 1998.
22. Anna Arnold Hedgeman to APR, August 16, 1963. Typescript, "Proposed Program—Lincoln Memorial," n.d. There is no indication of authorship on the memo. Why Dorothy Height was not included is not clear.
23. Dorn to March on Washington, August 26, 1963; Olin Johnston to APR, telegram, August 22, 1963. Arthur Krock, July 13, 1963, clipping unidentified, but he was syndicated.
24. I take the text of Randolph's defense of Rustin from the *New York Times*, August 16, 1963. That the reply was drafted by Kahn and Rustin is "Memorandum," Tom Kahn and Bayard Rustin to A. Philip Randolph, August 16, 1963.
25. List, n.d., on March on Washington stationery, of participating organizations. There are also letters of support from scores of organizations, most undated but probably early August 1963.
26. BR, "To Whom It May Concern," August 20, 1963, saying that no more buses were available for charter.
27. A few examples of letters detailing people coming to the march: Charles Oldham of St. Louis to "Norm" [Hill], August 2, 1963. Central Branch of NAACP to March on Washington, August 13, 1963. Courtland Cox to marchers, n.d., giving fares from various points in the South to Washington, D.C. Benedict H. Hanson of Episcopalian Community Service to March on Washington, August 13, 1963. Constance Timberlake of Kansas City, Missouri, Committee on the March on Washington to BR, August 13, 1963. Memos from Rachelle Horowitz to BR every few days, including August 12, 15, 19, 22. Her last tally was sixty-seven thousand people.
28. That the objections originally came from Robert Kennedy, Courtland Cox, interview with author, October 26, 1998. That BR, Horowitz, and Kahn thought the speech was excellent, Horowitz to author, November 9, 1998.
29. John Lewis, interview with author, May 20, 1997, in which Lewis indicated that it was Randolph who pressed for the necessity of change and that in the room under the Lincoln Memorial it was others, not Rustin, particularly Tom Kahn, who were concerned with the particulars of the wording. Rustin, of course, also supported revision of the remarks. MSRC interview with Norman Hill, March 12, 1970, recalling that Rustin chaired the meeting. Lewis's own memories of the revising and controversy are in John Lewis, with Michael D'Orso, *Walking with the Wind: A Memoir of the Movement* (New York: Simon and Schuster, 1988), 219. That Farmer was in prison in Plaquemine, Louisiana, interview with Farmer, October 1969 [no specific date], in LBJ Library, Austin, Tex.
30. BR interview with Dudley Clarendon of *NYT*, n.d. [1983?], BRF. Ed Brown, conversation with author, March 22, 1999.
31. The march has been well described elsewhere, so I repeat only what is necessary to understand Bayard's role and a little about the mood. The standard account is Thomas Gentile, *March on Washington: August 28, 1963* (Washington, D.C.: New Day Publications, 1983). See, for instance, Branch, *Parting the Waters*, 877–883, and Garrow, *Bearing the Cross*, 281–285. A good description is in Robert Weisbrot, *Freedom Bound* (New York: Penguin, 1991), 83–85. Peter Goldman, *Death and Life of Malcolm X* (New York: Harper and Row, 1973), 107, reports that Bayard Rustin by chance met a disconsolate Malcolm X at the march and jokingly offered to let him speak, which Malcolm declined. The incident is plausible but has no citation in the Goldman book.

32. "Reminiscences," COHP, 229. BR interview with Dudley Clarent of *NYT*, August 16, 1983, BRF.
33. Maya Angelou, *All God's Children Need Traveling Shoes* (1986; New York: Vintage, 1991), 123–125.
34. Alan Gartner, interview with author, September 18, 1996. Anne Moody, *Coming of Age in Mississippi* (1968; New York: Dell, 1976), 307.
35. BR to "Dear Friends," September 2, 1963, inviting them to party. BR to Joyce Runham Brown, September 9, 1963.
36. Memo, BR to ten chairmen of the march, September 3, September 5, 1963, working on the plan. Undated memo but clearly before September 16, saying that it is unworkable.
37. BR to local committees and contacts of the MOW. News release about the Foley Square meeting, dated September 17, 1963. Form letter, BR to "Dear Friends," soliciting for the WRL.
38. BR, "The Meaning of the March on Washington," *Liberation* 8, no. 7 (October 1963): 11–13.

11 *Transitioning*

1. Records submitted to the ILGWU housing committee indicate that his income in 1981 was about $51,000 and by 1986 had grown to $119,000. Records furnished by the BRF. Charles Bloomstein had invested wisely on Rustin's behalf.
2. Peter Drucker, *Max Shachtman and His Left: A Socialist's Odyssey through the American Century* (Atlantic Highlands, N.J.: Humanities Press, 1994). Sandra Feldman, interview with author, May 20, 1997; Rachelle Horowitz, interview with author, February 3, 1998.
3. James Farmer, interview with author, March 18, 1996; Norman Hill, interview with author, October 9, 1995; Alan Gartner, interview with author, September 18, 1996. James Peck, interview with James Mosby, February 19, 1970, MSRC. Roy Bennett telephone call to Stanley Levison, September 3, 1963, Garrow, *FBI File*. August Meier and Elliott Rudwick, *CORE, A Study in the Civil Rights Movement, 1942–1986* (Urbana: University of Illinois Press, 1975), 324. CORE National Convention in *NYT*, July 4, 1964. Hill's resignation, *NYT*, September 4, 1964.
4. The story of Farmer heading a literacy campaign within the Office of Economic Opportunity is told in Farmer's autobiography, *Lay Bare the Heart* (New York: Arbor House, 1985), 300–304. This was December 1965 and the first weeks of 1966. BR to [Harry Wachtel?], January 2, 1966. BR to Harry Wachtel, January 4, 1966. When BR heard that Floyd McKissick was to be the new national director, "R. replied with an obscenity." The specific obscenity is not identified in the FBI transcript. All are from FBI, New York Office, wiretaps, BRF (all BR phone taps are in BRF).
5. Clarence Jones to A. Philip Randolph and MLK, September 11, 1963, FBI phone tap on BR. Later in the call, MLK speculates about the idea of having BR head the New York office of the SCLC.
6. Rachelle Horowitz, interview with author, February 3, 1998. Andrew Young, *An Easy Burden: The Civil Rights Movement and the Transformation of America* (New York: HarperCollins, 1996), 281.
7. The flap about the visit to the Soviet embassy is well described in Nat Hentoff, "The Paper Bolshevik," *Village Voice*, February 13, 1964, 5. On possibilities with the SCLC, BR interview with Taylor Branch, September 24, 1984, BRF.

Roy Bennet [but the FBI is uncertain] to Levison, February 29, 1964. Clarence Jones to Levison, March 2, 1964; Levison to Jones, March 11, 1964; Jones to Levison, March 13, 1964; Jones to Levison, March 14, 1964; and Levison to Jones, March 14, 1964, all in Garrow, *FBI File.* BR to [blank], January 19, 1964, says the NAACP has offered him a job, but he "feels it's an effort to control him," and he turned it down. FBI phone taps on BR.

8. The story of the MFDP is told in many places, among them John Dittmer, *Local People: The Struggle for Civil Rights in Mississippi* (Urbana: University of Illinois Press, 1994); Kay Mills, *This Little Light of Mine: The Life of Fannie Lou Hamer* (New York: Dutton, 1993); Howard Zinn, *SNCC: The New Abolitionists* (Boston: Beacon Press. 1964); Clayborne Carson, *In Struggle: SNCC and the Black Awakening of the 1960s* (Cambridge: Harvard University Press, 1981). For Lowenstein in particular, see William Chafe, *Never Stop Running: Allard Lowenstein and the Struggle to Save American Liberalism* (New York: Basic Books, 1993).

9. Rachelle Horowitz to Tom Kahn, December 16, [1963], from Jackson, Mississippi, Archives of Labor and Urban Affairs, Walter Reuther Library, Wayne State University, Detroit. Antiwhite sentiment also mentioned in a "conversation" with Tom Kahn, January 14, 1964, August Meier Papers, Schomburg Library, New York.

10. BR to unidentified, December 3, 1963, FBI, New York Office, wiretap. It is not certain that this was a conversation with Horowitz, but in any case, it is an expression of Bayard's sentiments at the time. His reference was to the Industrial Workers of the World (IWW).

11. Rachelle Horowitz, interview with author, October 8, 1996.

12. BR press release, "The Meaning of the Boycott," February 3, 1964. "Curriculum Guide for Freedom Schools." Draft of a letter from A. Philip Randolph to "Dear Brother," that is, union members, asking for support of the boycott as part of the labor struggle. Instructions to Picket Captains. Levison to Ann Jones says that the American Jewish Congress is supporting the boycott. Garrow, *FBI File*, January 26, 1964.

13. Debate with Donovan and boycott eve rally, *NYT*, February 3, 1964. Other cities picked up the idea of a boycott. See *NYT*, January 26, 1964.

14. BR sleeping at the church, *NYT*, February 4, 1964, *New York Herald Tribune*, February 4, 1964.

15. Sandra Feldman, interview with the author, May 20, 1997. Memo by BR[?], n.d. but before February 3, 1964, saying that teachers who call the United Federation of Teachers office should be assured that the UFT will defend them.

16. The FBI taps on Rustin's phone report many conversations about how difficult Galamison is, that he should not be allowed to go off half-cocked, that he was "bad news," and call him a "negro extremist." For example, BR to [name blanked out], February 10, 1964; BR to Cleveland Robinson, February 12, 1964; BR to [blanked out], March 16, 1964, all FBI, New York office, wiretaps. August Meier interview with Rustin and Normal Hill, February 28 and 29, 1964, Meier Papers.

17. For second boycott, see *NYT*, February 23, 1964; for opposition to it, *NYT*, March 3, 1964. NAACP opposes second boycott is "Statement of Frederick D. Jones, Education Chairman, New York State Conference of NAACP Branches, February 17, 1964." For March on Albany, see *NYT*, March 3, March 11, 1964. In fact, the City-Wide Committee broke up in recrimination, and the effort at further action fell apart. For Galamison's angry statement, *NYT*, May 19, 1964.

18. Rachelle Horowitz, interview with author, February 3, 1998; Robert Moses, interview with author, December 22, 1997. Edwin King, interview with William Chafe, March 10, 1988, COHP.

19. The controversy about the National Lawyers Guild is from notes of an interview by August Meier with BR, June 17, 1964. Meier Papers. See the Chafe interview with Edwin King, cited in previous note.

20. I was there and remember the evening, but this account is a shortened version of "Notes on the News," by John Cole, editor of the *Brunswick Record*, May 14, 1964. For the stall-in, which turned out to be a fiasco, *NYT*, April 24, 1964; ABC News, April 22, 1964, at the Museum of TV and Radio, New York. For BR's words: FBI, New York office report, March 16, 1964; Norman Hill to BR, April 8, 1964, FBI, New York office, wiretaps. BR did participate in picketing inside the World's Fair, essentially in support of James Farmer's efforts, and was arrested.

21. For Rustin participating in the training, see Doug McAdam, *Freedom Summer* (New York: Oxford University Press, 1988), 67, and John Lewis, with Michael D'Orso, *Walking with the Wind: A Memoir of the Movement* (New York: Simon and Schuster, 1998), 249. "Under control," BR to MLK, June 8, 1964; to Robert Moses, June 16, 1964, all from FBI, New York office, wiretaps.

22. "Hot Summer," talk to FOR National Council, April 1964.

23. Details of this dramatic incident in *NYT*, September 22, 1964. Report of inflammatory literature: BR to New York office of FBI, September 15, 1964, New York office, phone taps. That the tap was placed on his office telephone, November 15, 1963, FBI memorandum dated August 18, 1964, "Justification for Continuation of Technical or Microphone Surveillance." FBI reports, BRF. It was removed January 27, 1966. Walter Naegle to author, December 8, 1998.

24. FBI, New York office, wiretap, July 26, 1964.

25. BR, "Hot Summer: Gathering Racial Crisis in America," *Fellowship* 9, no. 4 (July) 1964): 5–10, which was a printed version of his April address. Unidentified article, BR, "The Harlem Riot and Nonviolence," n.d. but obviously 1964, soon after the riots, in BRP. M. S. Handler, "Negro Factions Are Considering a United Front," *NYT*, July 24, 1964. For the conference with Wagner, *NYT*, July 28, 1964. Front-page articles on the riots are *NYT*, July 20 and 27. Hill and BR against the SCLC moving north is BR interview, June 17, 1969, LBJ Library, Austin, Tex. Phone call with Wachtel is August 3, 1965, FBI, New York office, wiretaps.

26. James Farmer, interview with author, March 18, 1996. Farmer, *Lay Bare the Heart*, 299–300. *NYT*, July 30, 31, August 3, 1964.

27. Rachelle Horowitz, interview with author, October 8, 1996. Author's conversation, not really an interview, with Martha Norman, who was part of the MFDP effort in Mississippi in 1964 and had assumed a rejection and new party; April 4, 1998. BR to Mrs. S. Jones, June 13, 1967, in which he claims he was involved in the formation of the MFDP, campaigned for it before the 1964 convention, and went to Atlantic City as a lobbyist for it. He also said he helped raise money so that the loyal Mississippi delegates could go to the 1968 convention in Chicago.

28. LBJ, conversation with Carl Sanders, governor of Georgia, LBJ tapes, LBJ Library.

29. FBI report, August 15, 1964, summarized report of telephone calls but not a transcription, says that Rustin was advising King to try to convince LBJ. BR telephone call to MLK predicting that LBJ will simply talk the time away,

August 18, 1964. BR to Cleveland Robinson, LBJ will just talk the time away, FBI phone taps, August 18, 1964. BR to Rachelle Horowitz, August 24, 1964, saying that the meeting between MLK and LBJ had gone just as they predicted. All FBI wiretaps.

30. The quotation and the reasoning are from Robert Moses, interview with author, December 22, 1997.

31. Joseph Rauh, interview with Katherine Shannon, August 28, 1967, MSRC.

32. For the black press, see, for example, *Baltimore Afro-American*, September 5, 1964.

33. Walter Mondale, interview with author, December 17, 1917.

34. King and Rustin persuading Moses, from interview with BR, June 17, 1969, LBJ Library. This is from an interview with Edwin King by William Chafe, March 10, 1988, COHP. Edwin King remembers Hamer not being there. Bob Moses remembers that she was present. It is possible that they were mixing up different meetings—there were so many. Rustin had previously agreed with Rauh's position, that Johnson should agree to seat both delegations. BR to Rauh, August 18, 1964, FBI, New York office, wiretaps.

35. The meeting at the church is from Myron Kolatch, "Waiting for '68," *New Leader*, September 14, 1964, 6–8. A less contemporaneous account, but by one who was there, is James Forman, *The Making of Black Revolutionaries* (1972; New York: Macmillian, 1985), 392–393. John Dittmer, *Local People: The Struggle for Civil Rights in Mississippi* (Urbana: University of Illinois Press, 1994), 298, does not include him as present. Taylor Branch, *Pillar of Fire: America in the King Years, 1963–65* (New York: Simon and Schuster, 1998), 469–473, follows Forman's account. King quotation from Ed Brown (who was there), conversation with the author, March 23, 1999.

36. BR quotation from interview with BR, June 17, 1969, LBJ Library. The Hamer statement is in "Eyes on the Prize," PBS video, episode 5, "Mississippi, Is This America?" The Gray quote is in "Will the Circle Be Unbroken?" broadcast #19, "Freedom Summer," by the Southern Regional Council, 1997.

37. Interview with BR, June 17, 1969, LBJ Library.

38. Moses thinking back on it, Robert Moses, interview with author, December 22, 1997. Lewis, *Walking with the Wind*, 282.

39. For BR's continuing involvement, see BR to Theresa Pozzo of the MFDP, September 29, 1964; BR to S. Jones, June 13, 1967. James Foreman in *The Making of Black Revolutionaries* speaks of the "liberal-labor syndrome," "liberal-labor bigwigs," and "liberal-labor jackals"; especially see 386–407.

12 *From Protest to Politics*

1. BR to A. J., November 7, 1964, FBI, New York office, wiretaps.

2. Lots of FBI, New York office, wiretaps of BR making arrangements in November 1964. For example, November 3, 1964, arranging a reception with Ralph Bunche; November 7, 1964, and November 16, 1964, about arrangements in Britain. Freda Nuell of Christian Action [United Kingdom] to BR, November 26, 1964, and December 6, 1964.

3. Arrangements, FBI report, October 20, 1964, November 10, 1964, lots of calls that month about details. FBI reports and FBI, New York office, wiretaps. About the speech: BR to A. J., November 7, 1964, November 29, 1964, FBI, New York office, wiretaps. Taylor Branch in *Pillar of Fire*, 543, says that Rustin came back from cruising the local nightlife to confront the scandal. BR, in "Reminiscences," COHP, 469–470, says he was sleeping in his room. Either

is plausible. BR to [blanked out], December 16, 1964, tells of the incident and specified the prostitutes were coming out of E. D. King's room. FBI report, December 17, 1964, confirms the report, pointing out that the prostitutes were white.

4. BR, "From Protest to Politics," *Commentary* 39 (February 1965): 25–31. His ideas were given further circulation when they were summed up in an editorial by James Reston, "Washington: The Push to the Left," *NYT*, May 26, 1965.

5. BR to Tom Kahn, February 21, 1965. BR to [blank], February 22, 1965, both FBI, New York office, wiretaps.

6. A transcript of the debate is in *Freedom Review* 24 (February 1993): 73–77.

7. As of 1997, the memo was unavailable because it was in that portion of the Meany Papers that had not yet been organized, at the George Meany Center, Washington, D.C.

8. Meany had criticized segregation in unions at the NAACP Legal Defense and Educational Fund dinner in 1957. *Baltimore Afro-American*, May 25, 1957.

9. The story of the founding of the A. Philip Randolph Institute is from Don Slaiman, interview with author, January 11, 1997.

10. Announcement, *NYT*, March 12, 1965. Prospectus of the APRI Educational Fund, A. Philip Randolph Papers, Library of Congress, Washington, D.C. Budgets of the APRI from the Walter Reuther Papers, Archives of Labor and Urban Affairs, Reuther Library. Story of his proposing five thousand dollars from Walter Naegle, interview with author, June 8, 1995. His salary from the APRI Educational Fund eventually reached seventy thousand dollars. This plus speaking and writing fees gave him an income of a bit more than one hundred thousand dollars in 1986. Naegle to author, December 6. 1998.

11. BR to George Meany, December 6, 1965.

12. Stephanie Harrington, "It's Hard to Break a Habit in New York," *Village Voice*, January 8, 1967. BR to Jack Blumstein, July 30, 1968.

13. BR interview with Dudley Clarendon of *NYT*, n.d. [1983?], BRF.

14. The founding of the JAP from Ernest Green, interview with author, May 20, 1997, and Donald Slaiman, interview with author, January 11, 1997. Thomas R. Brooks et al., *Black Builders: A Jobs Program That Works*, pamphlet (New York: League for Industrial Democracy, n.d. [1971?]). The Buildings Trades Council meeting at which Green and Rustin were present is from the interview with Donald Slaiman. He could not place the date precisely, but it is probably the one described in *NYT*, August 30, 1964.

15. Rustin quoted *NYT*, November 13, 1965. New York Supreme Court ruling, *NYT*, August 25, 1964. Failures of Negro applicants to pass first exam, *NYT*, February 14. Rustin's retelling of the story, "Questions and Answers, 'Right to Work' Roundtable," California Negro Leadership Conference, San Francisco, February 18, 1967.

16. F. Ray Marshall and Vernon M. Briggs, *The Negro and Apprenticeship* (Baltimore: Johns Hopkins University Press, 1967), especially 72–83.

17. For instance, see BR's and Norman Hill's testimony, "Affirmative Action in an Economy of Scarcity," to the House of Representatives Special Subcommittee on Education, James Q. O'Hara, Chairman, September 17, 1974, in BRP at 17:802–817.

18. Andrew Young, interview with author, May 28, 1997.

19. Katzenbach to BR, March 9, 1968. Conference call, March 9, 1968, both FBI, New York office, wiretaps. In later calls, A. J. Muste was also included, show-

ing that Rustin had not entirely abandoned his old pacifist associates and that A. J. now recognized the centrality of the civil rights movement in NVDA.

20. BR to Wachtel, March 15, 1965, FBI, New York office, wiretaps. BR and Tom Kahn, "Johnson So Far: Civil Rights," *Commentary* 39 (June 1965): 44. Bayard repeated his enthusiasm for Johnson several times in BR interview for the LBJ Library, Austin, Tex., June 17 and June 30, 1969.

21. MLK to BR, FBI, New York office, wiretap, March 19, 1965.

22. John Lewis, with Michael D'Orso, *Walking with the Wind: A Memoir of the Movement* (New York: Simon and Schuster, 1998), 345.

23. BR to Wilkins, August 14, 1965; MLK to BR August 14, 1965, both from FBI report, August 16, 1965.

24. Transcription of a speech by BR given October 19, 1965, at the Nineteenth Annual Conference of the National Association of Intergroup Relations Officials, Chicago. The last paragraph is from U.S. Senate, *Hearings of the Subcommittee of Executive Reorganization of the Committee on Government Operations*, 89th Cong., 2d sess., December 6, 1966, 1855 (hereafter cited as "*Hearings*, Ribicoff Committee").

25. That young Negroes see that violence produces results, see *NYT*, April 24, 1966, Rustin's address to Chicago teachers. The "damn you" from commencement address given at the University of the Virgin Islands, June 1969, from Margo H. Tyler, Public Information Officer, University of the Virgin Islands, to BR, June 23, 1969. BR, "The Watts 'Manifesto' and the McCone Report," *Commentary* 41 (March 1966): 29–35.

26. David Garrow, *Bearing the Cross: Martin Luther King and the Southern Christian Leadership Conference* (New York: Random House, 1986), 455. August Meier, notes of an interview with BR, February 1, 1966, in which Rustin said he urged King not to go to Chicago but instead to travel from city to city urging blacks to vote, because the exercise of political power is the "primary factor in their getting freedom." August Meier Papers, Schomburg Library, New York. Norman Hill to BR, July 16, 1965 in which BR advises against King's going into the North "unless he is invited by two civil rights groups who are prepared to fight if the shit hits the fan." Norman Hill to BR, July 19, 1965, FBI, New York office, wiretaps. U[nidentified] female to BR, November 11, 1965, Rustin says that King "is not capable of organizing the North." FBI, New York office, wiretaps.

27. Joseph Lowery, interview with author, May 27, 1997. Interview with Bayard Rustin, June 30, 1969, from the LBJ Library. The details can be followed in Garrow, *Bearing the Cross*, 431–475, and James R. Ralph, *Northern Protest: Martin Luther King and the Civil Rights Movement in Chicago* (New York: Oxford University Press, 1993).

28. The phrase did not make it into the final version.

29. The Freedom Budget was already being talked about by November 1965. See Woodrow Ginsburg of Industrial Union Department [of AFL-CIO] to BR, December 3, 1965.

30. FBI reports (not transcript, although conversation is sometimes verbatim), June 14, June 21, 1966.

31. In 1964, William F. Buckley had already seen ominous signs in the civil rights movement. See his "Leftward March," *National Review* 16 (January 14, 1964): 11–13.

32. Melman to Spock, November 1, 1966; BR to Irving Howe, November 10, 1966; Norman Thomas to BR, August 31, 1966; Keyserling to Thomas, December

21, 1966. Norman Thomas to Leon Keyserling, December 14, 1966. Keyserling to Thomas, December 21, 1966.

33. *Hearings,* Ribicoff Committee (sudocs: Y4. G 74–16, Ur1/4/pt. 9), 1854, 1861. *NYT,* October 27, 1966. The "frustration stupidity" from the "Visual Encyclopedia of the 20th C." Also BR, "Black Power and Coalition Politics," *Commentary* 42 (September 1966): 35–40.

34. United States Senate, Subcommittee on Employment, Manpower, and Poverty of the Committee on Labor and Public Welfare, *Hearings,* 90th Cong., 1st sess., May 8 and 9, 1967, 1774 (sudocs Y4. L 11/2, P86/4/pt. 6).

35. Hyman Bookbinder to BR, March 28, 1967; BR to Bookbinder, April 6, 1967. By 1973, BR had qualified praise for the Great Society at least in contrast to Richard Nixon's policy. See BR, "What About the Great Society?" APRI news release, March 8, 1973. See also BR, "The Lessons of the Long Hot Summer," *Commentary* 44 (October 1967): 39–45, and the letters in reaction to it. Access to Humphrey, FBI report, February 16, 1965. Rustin did not know it, but these personal contacts would probably have proved fruitless as well. Johnson had rejected Willard Wirtz's plea for a jobs program at the very outset of the War on Poverty. Irwin Unger, *The Best of Intentions* (New York: Doubleday, 1996), 82–83.

13 *Increasing Isolation*

1. Ralph DiGia, interview with author, January 3, 1997. DiGia cannot remember precisely when this conversation took place, but it was after 1966 and before the election of 1968.

2. David Garrow, *Bearing the Cross: Martin Luther King and the Southern Christian Leadership Conference* (New York: Random House, 1986), 437–440 and passim.

3. For Rustin's anger that the SCLC called for a unilateral pullout, see FBI report, April 26, 1966.

4. A. J. to BR, April 8, 1965, FBI, New York office, wiretaps.

5. News release, April 16, 1965, by Norman Thomas, A. J. Muste, Bayard Rustin, Robert Gilmore, H. Stuart Hughes, Ed Clark, Roger Locard, Emily Parker Simon, Alfred Hassler, Charles Bloomstein, Harold Taylor, BRP. For debates on this issue within the Fellowship of Reconciliation, the War Resisters League, and the American Friends Service Committee, see Guenter Lewy, *Peace and Revolution: The Moral Crisis of American Pacifism* (Grand Rapids, Mich.: William B. Erdman Publishing Co., 1988), pt. 2. Elements in all three organizations rejected a policy of exclusion, and some supported the National Liberation Front.

6. Staughton Lynd to BR, April 19, 1965. See also Gardner Cox, Mrs. Anne Farnsworth, Martin Peretz to Norman Thomas, A. J. Muste, Bayard Rustin et al., April 27, 1965.

7. That Rustin signed the "Declaration," John Lewis, with Michael D'Orso, *Walking with the Wind: A Memoir of the Movement* (New York: Simon and Schuster, 1998), 355. The text is reproduced in Marvin Gettlement et al., eds., *Vietnam and America* (New York: Grove Press, 1985), 301. The quotations are from a phone call from a "UDF" (by which the FBI meant "unidentified female") to BR, November 11, 1965. He makes much the same point in a conversation with a "UDM" the same day. Both from FBI, New York office, wiretaps.

8. *NYT,* November 28, 1965. It was a page-one story with a picture, continued

on the inside of the paper. Phone call, Wachtel to BR, November 28, 1965, FBI, New York office, wiretaps.

9. James Finn, *Protest: Pacifism and Politics, Some Passionate Views on War and Nonviolence* (New York: Random House, 1967), 328–41. In 1965, even Robert McNamara was urging "withdrawal with honor." Robert Dallek, *Flawed Giant: Lyndon Johnson and His Times* (New York: Oxford University Press, 1998), 343.

10. Julian Bond, interview with author, January 22, 1968, MSRC.

11. On resigning as executive secretary of the WRL: BR to A. J., January 28, 1965. BR to Edward P. Gottleib, January 28, 1965. Roy [Finch] to BR, February 9, 1965. Ralph DiGia to BR, March 3, 1965. David McReynolds, interview with author, October 11, 1996. McReynolds could not date the party exactly, just "late 60s or early 70s." "Remembering Bayard Rustin: An Interview with Ralph DiGia and Igal Roodenko," *Nonviolent Activist: The Magazine of the War Resisters League* 4 (December 1987): 6–9.

12. BR, "Vietnam: Where I Stand," *Amsterdam News*, May 10, 1967. BR, "Dr. King's Painful Dilemma," *Amsterdam News*, March 3, 1967.

13. Staughton Lynd, "Coalition Politics or Nonviolent Revolution?" *Liberation* 9 (June/July 1965): 18.

14. Interview with James Farmer, University of Texas Oral History Project, July 20, 1971, tape 2, p. 9.

15. Bob Moses, calling himself by his middle name, Robert Parris, spoke at one of the first antiwar rallies in Berkeley, May 21–22, on how the civil rights movement could relate to the antiwar movement. Robert Parris speech in James Petras et al., eds., *We Accuse* (Berkeley: Diablo Press, 1965), 148–153. Robert Moses, interview with author, December 22, 1997, in which Moses said he always assumed that Rustin was acting "for domestic reasons."

16. Draft statement, Levison to BR, January 17, 1967, King-Levison wiretaps. BR, "The Trouble with Adam," *Amsterdam News*, March 3, 1967. Press release of the united leadership, APRI press release dated January 23, 1967. Norton to Horowitz, n.d. [March 1967?].

17. For contemporaneous accounts, see Tom Hayden, *Rebellion in Newark: Official Violence and the Ghetto Response* (New York: Vintage, 1967), and Robert E. Conot, *Rivers of Blood, Years of Darkness* (New York: Bantam, 1967). United States, Kerner Commission, *Report of the National Advisory Commission on Civil Disorders* (New York: Bantam, 1968), the quotations on employment are on 414–415. Lyndon Johnson was furious that the report did not give him more credit for what had already been accomplished, and he thought its spending goals "unrealistic." Dallek, *Flawed Giant*, 516. Also, interview with Harry McPherson, October 28, 1970, LBJ Library, Austin, Tex., 19–21. BR's enthusiasm in "Well, Now They Know," *Amsterdam News*, March 23, 1968. His more detailed view: BR, *The Report of the National Advisory Commission on Civil Disorders: An Analysis* (New York: A. Philip Randolph Institute, n.d. [1968?]).

18. "Questions and Answers, 'Right to Work' Roundtable," California Leadership Conference, San Francisco, February 18, 1967. Mimeographed transcript, BRP. On preparing the pamphlet, BR to Clarence Mitchell, March 17, 1967; BR to "Roy" [Wilkins], March 17, 1967, Robert Carter, General Counsel of the NAACP, to BR, March 21, 1967. BR to Carter, March 24, 1967. BR to "Whitney" [Young], March 22, 1967. BR to Cesar Chavez, November 18, 1967. Chavez to BR, December 13, 1967. BR to Chavez, December 20, 1967. Chavez to BR, January 23, 1968.

19. BR to MLK, January 29, 1968. The copy in BRP is obviously a draft, because it has penciled corrections.

20. BR answering questions on many subjects at the executive board of the International Union of Electrical Radio and Machine Workers, March 26, 1968. Marian Logan, wife of Arthur Logan, friend and personal physician of Rustin, was assistant secretary of the board of SCLC. She made the same points to King in a memo on March 8. See Marian Logan to MLK, March 8, 1968, in BRF, but not in microfilmed papers.

21. The description of the White House meeting and service are in Harry McPherson, inteview with T. H. Baker, October 28, 1970, LBJ Library.

22. "Ruffians" feeling guilty is interview with BR, June 17, 1969, LBJ Library.

23. Description of the rally from complete coverage in a CBS News "Special Report," April 8, 1968, at the Museum of TV and Radio, New York.

24. One of many sources speaking of administrative confusion, conversation between Marian Logan and Stanley Levison, June 6, 1968, King-Levison phone taps.

25. This sequence of events is from interview with BR, June 30, 1969, LBJ Library.

26. Joint news conference with Abernathy and Rustin, *NYT*, May 25, 1968. BR, "The Nineteenth of June Mobilization," *Amsterdam News*, May 23, 1968. Confusion and misery in "Resurrection City," among many other news stories, *NYT*, Sunday, May 26, 1968. Mud and rain, many stories but see particularly *Baltimore Afro-American*, May 18 and June 1, 1968.

27. Mobilization to Support the Poor People's Campaign, press release, June 3, 1968.

28. Ralph Abernathy, *And the Walls Came Tumbling Down* (New York: Harper and Row, 1989), 522.

29. Hosea Williams, from *Time*, June 14, 1968, 32. The sequence of events from interview with BR, June 17, 1969, LBJ Library. The "genius and kook" remark from BR interview with Taylor Branch, September 24, 1984, BRF. Hosea Williams on "billies" from Tom Kahn, "Why the Poor People's Campaign Failed," *Commentary* 46 (September 1968): 53.

30. Williams statement: *Baltimore Afro-American*, April 27, 1968. The fourteen points are in the BRP microfilm edition at 684. BR's press release of withdrawal, n.d. [June 7, 1968]. *NYT*, June 8, 1968, on Rustin's resignation. Abernathy reassuring Reuther, Reuther to UAW Officers, Board Members and Regional Directors, June 11, 1968, Walter Reuther Papers, Archives of Labor and Urban Affairs, Reuther Library, 517:21. Arthur Logan, telegram to Ralph Abernathy, June 6, 1968. Copy of Urban League telegram [to Abernathy?], n.d. [June 7, 1968?], saying that Rustin's being coordinator "was condition on which Urban League agreed to participate." They did end up participating anyway.

31. BR, press release, n.d. [June 6, 1998?]. On the "Mobilization," *NYT*, June 20, 1968, 1, 30. Accounts of the day, *Baltimore Afro-American*, June 22, 1968.

32. Marian Logan to Stanley Levison, June 6, 1968, King-Levison phone taps. FBI report, "Southern Christian Leadership Conference," July 24, 1968, reporting on a conversation between Stanley Levison and BR, July 21, 1968. Not presented as a transcript, but seems to be at points.

33. Eleanor Holmes Norton, interview with author, May 19, 1997.

34. Audiotape (not transcribed) interview with BR, October 29, 1985, UFT Papers, Wagner Archives, New York University. Interviewer not identified.

35. Jonathan Kozol's *Death at an Early Age* (Boston: Houghton Mifflin, 1967) had major national impact.
36. New York Civil Liberties Union, *The Burden of Blame*, November 1968. Sandra Feldman, *The Burden of Blame-Placing*, n.d. [1968] (both are pamphlets). Nat Hentoff, "Ocean Hill–Brownsville and the Future of Community Control," *Civil Liberties*, no. 250 (February 1969): 1–5. Several letters in December 1968 between the UFT and the New York Civil Liberties Union, for instance, Herbert Latner of the UFT to Sheldon Ackley, Chairman of the New York Civil Liberties Union, December 14, 1968. *Crisis* 60 (June 1969): 362, the NAACP opposing the UFT and favoring community control. Negro American Labor Council to "Dear Member," September 21, 1968, favoring community control. Cleveland Robinson is listed as president. The founder was A. Philip Randolph, who favored the UFT. Kenneth Clark opposed the UFT; see Rebecca C. Simonson (she was one of the founders of the UFT) to David S. Seeley of the Metropolitan Applied Research Center (Clark's organization), January 13, 1969. Maurice J. Goldbloom, "The New York School Crisis," a *Commentary Report*, 1969, pro-UFT and opposed to McCoy. Press release from National Urban League, n.d. [September 1968?] and of the New York Association of Black School Supervisors and Administrators, September 17, [1968?], both opposing the UFT and supporting decentralization. All from UFT Papers. Benjamin R. Epstein, National Director of Anti-Defamation League, to "Bayard," September 19, 1968, supporting the APRI advertisement of that day and opposing local control.
37. Typescript, "Community Control," apparently not published, in BRP. Dated March 14, with no year, but internal evidence implies 1968.
38. Cornell student to BR, n.d.; Edward Urquhart to BR, September 18, 1969; John Hunter to BR, September 25, 1968; Susan Orestes to BR, September 13, 1968; Robert A. Gilbert to BR, September 30, 1968. Paragraphs and punctuation as in originals.
39. "Chaos in Our Schools," editorial, February 10, 1968. "Stick by Your Guns" (the first sentence was "Stick *to* your guns" [emphasis mine]), editorial, October 19, 1968. Floyd McKissick, for example, February 17, 1968; Roy Wilkins, for example, March 18, 1968. BR, "Light, Not Heat, Needed in Dispute," October 5, 1968. All *Amsterdam News*. BR to Robert Curvin, October 9, 1968. Norton to BR, October 18, 1968.
40. B. Louis to APR, September 19, 1968. In December 1968, a poem to Albert Shanker supposedly by a fifteen-year-old Negro student was read over WBAI-FM: "Hey, Jew boy, with that yarmulka on your head / you pale-faced Jew boy—I wish you were dead." *NYT*, January 16, 1969.
41. The "Poynter Circular" is 6:246 in BRP. It is also in Bayside Interracial and Interfaith Council to UFT, November 22, 1968, in the UFT Papers. Reply from Sandra Feldman, January 23, 1969, saying that the UFT had not distributed the circular but had given it to the ADL. She points out that Poynter had received high praise in the "SCOPE" bulletin, an organization headed by Galamison. Typescript, n.d., no author, "The Left of Center Press and Ocean Hill–Brownsville" quotes among others Marvin Hoffman, Sol Stearn, and I. F. Stone saying that the UFT exaggerated the extent of anti-Semitism. Folder 58, UFT Papers. In my talks with Sandra Feldman and Rachelle Horowitz, they both say there was a great deal of antiwhite feeling but not much specifically anti-Jewish. The issue is explored in greater depth in Jonathan Kaufman, *Broken Alliance: The Turbulent Times between Blacks and Jews*

in America (New York: Scribner, 1988). For a longer-term history, Murray Friedman, *What Went Wrong? The Creation and Collapse of the Black-Jewish Alliance* (New York: Free Press, 1995).

Thomas R. Brooks, "Tragedy at Ocean Hill," *Looking Forward*, publication of the LID, from *Dissent* 16 (January–February 1969): 28–40. Jewish Labor Committee, *News* (January 1969): 1, called community control of schools a "cruel hoax." Tom Kahn to "Dear Friend," [September 1968?], on the stationery of the "Ad Hoc Committee to Defend the Right to Teach," which lists Kahn and Michael Harrington as co-chairmen. All UFT Papers.

42. Rachelle Horowitz to author, November 9, 1998.
43. *Amsterdam News*, October 5, 1998.
44. The complex story can most easily be followed in Diane Ravitch, *The Great School Wars: A History of the New York Public Schools* (New York: Basic Books, 1974), particularly 312–378. BR praised this work in an APRI news release, May 2, 1974. Other important overviews are David Rogers, *110 Livingston Street: Politics and Bureaucracy in the New York City Schools* (New York: Random House, 1968). David Rogers and Norman H. Chung attempted an assessment of how "decentralization" worked in *110 Livingston Street Revisited: Decentralization in Action* (New York: New York University Press, 1983). See also Jerald Podair, "'White' Values, 'Black' Values: The Ocean Hill–Brownsville Controversy and New York City Culture, 1965–75," *Radical History Review* 59 (Spring 1994): 39–64. See also Podair's dissertation, "Like Strangers: Blacks, Whites, and New York City's Ocean Hill–Brownsville Crisis, 1945–1980" (Princeton University, 1997), and Daniel Hiram Perlstein, "The 1968 New York City School Crisis: Teacher Politics, Racial Politics, and the Decline of Liberalism" (Ph.D. diss., Stanford University, 1995). Elaine Woo, "Blow Up the Schools!" *Los Angeles Times Magazine*, December 1, 1996, 17–23, 50–54. Tamar Jacoby, *Someone Else's House: America's Unfinished Struggle for Integration* (New York: Free Press, 1998), pt. 1, treats all militants as self-serving phonies. In my view, some were and some were not.

The idea of employing "paraprofessionals," all minority, many from welfare rolls, was an idea pioneered by Frank Riesman and implemented by Albert Shanker and the UFT. See Arthur Pearl and Frank Riesman, *New Careers for the Poor: The Non-professional in Human Services* (New York: Free Press, 1965). Another version was published the following year by the APRI Educational Fund as *A Basic Strategy against Poverty*.

45. Rebecca C. Simonson to David S. Seeley, January 13, 1969, UFT Papers. For the reaction in the 1990s, see *NYT*, June 12, 1996, reporting a 5 percent turnout for local school board elections. *NYT*, December 18, 1996, with a page-one headline, "Albany in Schools Accord to Give Chancellor Power and Weaken Local Boards." A page-nine article the same day was headed "Crew [chancellor of New York City schools] to Use New Power Quickly in 27 Districts." A summary article in *NYT*, December 22, 1996, has the subhead "Decades Later, New York Moves to Undo a Legacy Crippling Its Schools."
46. See, among other places, BR, "'Black Power' and Coalition Politics," *Commentary* 44 (September 1966): 35–40. He thought of having the SCLC expel CORE and SNCC from recognized civil rights groups. See BR and Harry Wachtel: FBI, New York office wiretap, October 17, 1966.
47. Thomas R. Brooks, "A Strategist without a Movement," *NYT Magazine*, February 16, 1969, 14–15, 104–107. He is identified as a board member of the LID in Thomas R. Brooks et al., *Black Builders: A Job Program That Works*, pamphlet (New York: League for Industrial Democracy, 1970).

14 *The 1970s*

1. For example, *AFL-CIO News,* May 26, 1973, where the APRI organized a conference on the theme "The Union Card and the Ballot Box."
2. Syndication mentioned in BR to Lorraine W. Addelston, President of the Junior High Principals Association, March 6, 1969, responding to an inquiry about BR's views on black anti-Semitism.
3. BR, "Conflict or Coalition? The Civil Rights Struggle and the Trade Union Movement Today" (address at the Constitutional Convention of the American Federation of Labor and the Congress of Industrial Organizations), October 3, 1969. I have used this speech both because Donald Slaiman recalled its impact to me in an interview and because it sums up many points Rustin made many times elsewhere. Donald Slaiman, interview with author, January 11, 1997. As late as 1974 he argued with Kevin Philips's analysis that white working people were shifting to the Republicans in reaction to racial issues. See "Blacks, Labor, and the Democrats," APRI news release, October 17, 1974. On union racism, in addition to the words quoted, BR wrote to David [McReynolds?] February 13, 1970, "I have never denied the existence of racism. No doubt many workers are racists and would consciously or unconsciously like to see blacks remain at the bottom." But unions, Rustin insisted, have helped blacks because of their common economic interests. He did not mention many cases in which black and white workers perceived their interests as opposed to each other.
4. BR to Reuther, January 11, 1968, Walter Reuther Papers, Archives of Labor and Urban Affairs, Reuther Library.
5. BR to Louisa Alga, January 8, 1969.
6. Rachelle Horowitz to Patricia Roberts Harris, November 15, 1971, an example of many similar letters explaining that he had had a heart attack but was recovering well. That it occurred at the Gilmore farm, Jervis Anderson, *Bayard Rustin: Troubles I've Seen* (New York: Harper Collins, 1997), 334. Dr. Arthur Logan on heart attack victims: Rachelle Horowitz, interview with author, May 19, 1997.
7. Ernest Green, interview with author, May 20, 1997.
8. BR's statement of 15 percent, *NYT,* May 19, 1975. Other 1975 statistics in this paragraph, Office of Program Evaluation, Employment and Training Administration, U.S. Department of Labor, *Apprenticeship Outreach Programs: A Summary Review* (Washington, D.C.: Department of Labor, 1976).
9. BR, "The New Labor Secretary: A Sign from Carter," APRI news release, January 4, 1977.
10. Figures on accomplishments of the RTP from "Proposal to Operate Targeted Outreach Programs under the U.S. Department of Labor National Targeted Outreach Program," solicitation number ONP-62-1, n.d. [1982?]. In such a grant application, the RTP would put its results in the most positive light. With the figures so far available, I find it difficult to estimate costs, but I would guess that expenses were on the order of one thousand dollars per placement. Cihan Bilginsoy, of the University of Utah Economics Department, "Apprenticeship Training in the U.S. Construction Industry" (unpublished MS in my possession), shows that by the time the program ended, about 20 percent of apprentices in the building trades were "minority," which in this study includes Asian, black, Hispanic, and Native American. Rustin in 1979 said that "black youngsters now fill nearly 20% of all new apprenticeship slots" in selected trades. BR, "A Sneak Attack on Black Construction Workers," APRI news release, June 14, 1979.

11. These devices are described in Herbert Hill, *Labor Union Control of Job Training: A Critical Analysis of Apprenticeship Outreach Programs and the Hometown Plans* (Washington, D.C.: Institute for Urban Affairs, Howard University, 1974), 30–34.

12. Martin Gopan, "The Job Scene: An Open Letter to Bayard Rustin," *Bay State Banner*, November 21, 1968. "Black Monday" described in *NYT*, September 22, 1969.

13. Hill, *Labor Union Control*, 40, 65.

14. BR to Dorothy Knoke, February 9, 1968. Hill's speech in *NYT*, July 5, 1973. "Roy" to "Bayard," July 17, 1973.

15. Testimony of Rustin and Norman Hill, "Affirmative Action in an Economy of Scarcity." Testimony actually delivered by Norman Hill to the House of Representatives Special Subcommittee on Education, James G. O'Hara, Chairman, September 17, 1974. Typescript in BRP, 17:802–817. Herbert Hill, white, and Norman Hill, black, are unrelated.

16. For one of many possible examples, see *AFL-CIO News*, March 17, 1973, 5.

17. Ernest Green, interview with author, May 20, 1997; Don Slaiman, interview with author, January 11, 1997.

18. Statistics on the RTP are from the General Accounting Office Reports: *Questionable Need for Some Department of Labor Training Programs* (Washington, D.C.: General Accounting Office, 1978). Unemployment figures for the building trades are p. 5. *Federal Efforts to Increase Minority Opportunities in Skilled Construction Craft Unions Have Had Little Success* (Washington, D.C.: General Accounting Office, 1979). Figures for minority membership in building trades unions, p. 5. These figures do not differentiate between apprentices and full union membership. *Award and Administration of Contracts to Recruitment and Training Program, Inc., during Fiscal Years 1978–81* (Washington, D.C.: General Accounting Office, 1982). Figures on appropriations for the RTP are p. 8.

19. Nathan Glazer, *Affirmative Discrimination: Ethnic Inequality and Public Policy* (New York: Basic Books, 1975). Glazer has again changed his mind. See "Nathan Glazer Changes His Mind, Again," *NYT Magazine*, June 28, 1998, 23–25. Thomas Byrne Edsall, with Mary D. Edsall, *Chain Reaction: The Impact of Race, Rights, and Taxes on American Politics* (New York: Norton, 1991); see particularly chap. 7, "Race, Rights and Party Choice," 137–154. Gerald M. Pomper et al., *The Election of 1980, Reports and Interpretations* (Chatham, N.J.: Chatham House Publishers, 1981), 71, showed that the votes of union households for Jimmy Carter dropped by 12 percent between 1976 and 1980. Carter received the smallest percentage of labor union support of any recent Democratic candidate.

20. Jonathan Kaufman, *Broken Alliance: The Turbulent Times between Blacks and Jews in America* (New York: Scribner, 1988), for example, 117–118.

21. BR, "The Premise of the Stereotype," *Amsterdam News*, April 8, 1967.

22. Ethel Minor, "Third World Round Up: The Palestinian Problem: Test Your Knowledge," *SNCC Newsletter* (June–July 1967): 4–5. See Clayborne Carson, *In Struggle: SNCC and the Black Awakening of the 1960s* (Cambridge: Harvard University Press, 1981), 268, for the increasingly outspoken anti-Israel and anti-Jewish statements of some SNCC members. BR to Dr. M. T. Mehdi of the Action Committee on American-Arab Relations, September 13, 1967.

23. *ADL Bulletin*, pamphlet (New York: Anti-Defamation League, 1968).

24. *NYT*, Sunday, June 28, 1970. Leaving out the sentence, Charles Bloomstein, interview with author, January 2, 1997. "You've got to sign," Julian Bond, interview with author, October 7, 1996.

25. Roodenko article from an unidentified clipping in the WRL Papers, SCPC. Undated but refers to the ad of June 28, with no year, so the clipping is probably 1970. "Ann" Davidon to "Bayard," October 26, 1973.

26. For example, BR, "The PLO: Freedom Fighters or Terrorists?" *Miami Times*, December 19, 1974. "Fringe Thinkers," *NYT*, August 21, 1972.

27. *NYT*, November 23, 1975. That Bayard intended BASIC to last: Charles Bloomstein, interview with author, January 2, 1997. See also BR, "Black-Jewish Relations," *New Leader* 62 (September 1979): 5–7.

28. BR to President of the United States, December 12, 1978. Defending the memorial as not for Jews alone, BR letter to the editor, *NYT*, May 18, 1984.

29. "An Interview with Bayard Rustin," *Open Hands* 2 (Spring 1987): 4.

30. *NYT*, August 16, 1979. BR, "Andrew Young, the PLO, and Black-Jewish Relations," *New Leader* 62 (September 1979), separately reprinted article.

31. BR, "To Blacks: Condemn P.L.O. Terrorism," *NYT*, August 30, 1979. Kaufman, *Broken Alliance*, 254, but Kaufman gives no source for what is given as a direct quotation from Jackson.

32. BR, "Blacks and Jews Still Need Each Other," *Newsday*, October 7, 1979, "Ideas" section, 1–2. In the summer of 1998, Julian Bond, now head of the NAACP, said it was time for Jews and blacks to unite again—but it was such a different time that it was hard to picture how that might happen.

15 *Grand Old Man—and a New Civil Right*

1. *NYT*, May 2, 1977.

2. The 1976 visit from Rustin's schedule notebooks, BRF. The 1979 trip, *NYT*, October 16, 19, 1979.

3. BR, "The Israeli Incursion into Lebanon: A Personal Report and Reflections on My Trip to Israel and Lebanon. August 15–23, 1982," pamphlet (New York: APRI, n.d. [1982]). BR, "The Truth about Lebanon," APRI news release, September 16, 1982. BR, "The Vibrancy of Israel's Democracy," APRI news release, September 30, 1982.

4. *NYT*, October 27, 1984.

5. Aaron Levenstein, *Escape to Freedom: The Story of the International Rescue Committee* (Westport, Conn.: Greenwood, 1983).

6. This summary of the views of Freedom House is from Leonard Sussman and Adrian Karatnycky of Freedom House, interviews with author, September 17, 1998, and Carl Gershman, chairman of the National Endowment for Democracy, interview with author, October 26, 1998.

7. Robert DeVecchi, interview with author, October 28, 1998. *Washington Post*, July 20, 1979.

8. Memo from Leo Sternberg to Members of the Southeast Asia Commission, January 26, 1978. IRC Itinerary, n.d. [January 1978?]. "The International Rescue Committee's Chronology of the Citizens Commission on Indochinese Refugees: 1978," n.d. [April 1978?]. Leo Cherne, "A Personal Memoir," typescript, n.d. [1978] (about Bayard singing and rushing back to Miami.) Rabbi Marc Tanenbaum at Memorial Service for Bayard Rustin, October 1, 1987, recalling the incident at Nong Khai, video in author's possession and BRF. Robert DeVecchi, just retired as president of the IRC, interview with author, October 28, 1978. "Black Americans Urge Admission of the Indochinese Refugees," advertisement in the *NYT*, March 19, 1978. The "March for Survival" from BR's travel schedule, BRF, and *NYT*, February 7, 1980. U.S. House of Representatives, *Oversight Hearings before the Subcommittee on*

Immigration, Refugees, and International Law of the Committee on the Judiciary, September 16, 17, 23, 1981 (Sudocs Y4. J89/1:97/23), 182–189.

9. BR, "Cuban Intervention: A Threat to Africa's Integrity," APRI news release, December 22, 1977. BR, "The Soviet Empire and the Third World," APRI news release, July 15, 1982. BR, "Human Rights and Political Advancement" (speech to a conference, "Democratic Challenge in Latin America," Lisbon, Portugal, July 28–30, 1984).

10. Also, for example, "Social Insecurity," a guest column by BR in Albert Shanker's "Where We Stand," *NYT*, August 4, 1981.

11. Adrian Karatnycky, interview with author, September 17, 1989. BR, Charles Bloomstein, Adrian Karatnycky, "Visit to Poland April 20 to April 30, 1981," typescript. BR, Charles Bloomstein, Adrian Karatnycky. "A. Philip Randolph Educational Fund Report to President Lane Kirkland on—Poland and the American Labor Movement," typescript. BR, "Report on Poland," typescript. This last is a personal account with detailed quotations from Solidarity members and Rustin's thoughts. Copies of all three typescripts given to me by Charles Bloomstein. BR, "For Basic Rights: Similarities Noted in Struggle of Polish Labor, U.S. Blacks," *AFL-CIO News*, May 16, 1981. Whether any of this support originated with the U.S. government is impossible at this time to tell.

12. Lucy to BR, April 25, 1979. See BR, "The War against Zimbabwe," *Commentary* 68 (July 1979): 25–32, in which Rustin responds to his critics.

13. George Houser, interview with author, October 10, 1996. George Houser, *No One Can Stop the Rain* (New York: Pilgrim Press, 1989), 326–344. BR and Leonard Sussman, "Zimbabwe Deserves American Attention," typescript, n.d. but clearly 1980. "Rustin Changes Line," *Southern Africa* 12 (July/August 1979): 21. U.S. House of Representatives, *Hearings before the Subcommittee on Africa and on International Organizations of the Committee on Foreign Affairs*, (Sudocs Y4.76/1:R34/2/979) April 2, May 14, 16, 21, 1979, 111–125.

14. There are long passages in "Reminiscences," COHP, about South Africa, and these are virtually contemporaneous with his trip in 1986. See particularly 389–458. He sums up that 1983 trip in BR, *South Africa: Is Peaceful Change Possible?*, pamphlet (New York: New York Friends Group, 1984). On "Project South Africa," Carl Gershman and David Peterson, interview with author, October 27, 1998, and material supplied by David Peterson.

15. BR, "Black Refugees from Haiti: Victims of Discrimination," APRI news release, August 9, 1979. BR, "The Haitian Dilemma," APRI news release, October 29, 1981, in which Rustin argues that the Reagan administration had made things worse.

16. Walter Naegle, interview with author, September 16, 1998.

17. *NYT*, August 25, 1987; *Amsterdam News*, August 29, 1987. Two other major black newspapers, the *Baltimore Afro-American* and the *Chicago Defender*, did not mention Bayard Rustin's death.

18. Video: "Memorial Service for Bayard Rustin, October 1, 1987," BRF.

16 Sui Generis

1. *Portland (Maine) Press Herald*, October 7, 1978.

2. He did not have a tombstone. He was cremated and his ashes buried at Robert Gilmore's home in upstate New York.

3. See, for example, "The Myth of Black Studies," typescript in BRP, apparently a draft of part of what became "The Myth of the Black Revolt," *Ebony* 66, no. 10 (August 1969): 96–104. The part on black studies is 101. See also *U.S. News and World Report* 66, no. 8 (May 12, 1969): 8, in which Rustin is quoted saying that colleges should "stop capitulating to the stupid demands of Negro students."

Index

About the Author

Daniel Levine is the Thomas Bracket Reed Professor of History and Political Science at Bowdoin College. He received his A.B. from Antioch College and his Ph.D. from Northwestern University. He has held Woodrow Wilson, Social Science Research Council, Fulbright, and Guggenheim fellowships. He is author of *Varieties of Reform Thought* (1965), *Jane Addams and the Liberal Tradition* (1972), *Poverty and Society* (1988), and numerous articles. He lives in Brunswick, Maine, with his wife, Susan. They have two children and three grandchildren.